THE FATHERS
OF THE CHURCH

A NEW TRANSLATION

VOLUME 113

THE FATHERS
OF THE CHURCH

A NEW TRANSLATION

EDITORIAL BOARD

BARSANUPHIUS AND JOHN

LETTERS
VOLUME 1

Translated by

JOHN CHRYSSAVGIS

THE CATHOLIC UNIVERSITY OF AMERICA PRESS
Washington, D.C.

Copyright © 2006
THE CATHOLIC UNIVERSITY OF AMERICA PRESS
All rights reserved
Printed in the United States of America

The paper used in this publication meets the minimum requirements of the
American National Standards for Information Science—Permanence of Paper
for Printed Library Materials, ANSI z39.48–1984.

LIBRARY OF CONGRESS CATALOGING-IN-PUBLICATION DATA
Barsanuphius, Saint, 6th cent.
[Biblos psychophelestate periechousa apokriseis. English]
Letters / Barsanuphius and John ; translated by John Chryssavgis.
p. cm. — (The fathers of the church ; v. 113)
Includes bibliographical references and index.
ISBN-13: 978-0-8132-0113-9 (cloth : alk. paper)
ISBN-10: 0-8132-0113-6 (cloth : alk. paper)   1. Spiritual life—Orthodox
Eastern Church.   2. Asceticism—Orthodox Eastern Church.   3. Monastic and
religious life.   I. John, the Prophet, Saint.   II. Chryssavgis, John.
III. Title.   IV. Series.

BR60.F3B2513 2006
[BR65.B273]
270 s—dc22
[270

2006006979

CONTENTS

ACKNOWLEDGMENTS

The first draft of this translation was prepared during a sabbatical at the Center of Theological Inquiry in Princeton, New Jersey. It was a delight to bask in that environment for the spring semester of 2002.

I am indebted to the brotherhood of The Holy Transfiguration Monastery in Brookline, Massachusetts. The insightful counsel and gracious support of the elder and monks in that community, deriving from personal experience of the monastic life and skilled reading of the monastic texts, proved invaluable.

I am also grateful to the Rt. Rev. Bishop Sava of Troas for entrusting me with his draft translation of the [first 190] *Letters,* the treasured fruit of his doctoral studies at the University of Oxford.

Ms. Melissa Lynch generously offered her time and assistance in the careful compilation of the scriptural index.

Finally, the entire publication has benefited enormously from the editorial skills and invaluable suggestions of Dr. Carole Burnett, staff editor at The CUA Press.

Any portions of this translation that also appear in my previous volume, *Letters from the Desert,* are used by permission of St. Vladimir's Seminary Press, Crestwood, New York 10707, www.svspress.com.

ABBREVIATIONS

GCS   Die griechischen christlichen Schriftsteller der ersten
        drei Jahrhunderte. Leipzig.

PG   Patrologia Graeca, ed. J.-P. Migne. Paris.

PL   Patrologia Latina, ed. J.-P. Migne. Paris.

PO   Patrologia Orientalis. Paris.

ROC   *Revue de l'orient chrétien*. Paris.

SC   *Sources chrétiennes*. Paris.

SELECT BIBLIOGRAPHY

Texts and Translations

Barsanuphe et Jean de Gaza: Correspondance. Edited with notes and index by F. Neyt and P. de Angelis-Noah. French translation by L. Regnault. *SC* 426–27 and 450–51. Paris, 1997–2001.

Barsanuphius. *Doctrina.* PG 86: 891–902. [Teaching on Origen, Evagrius, and Didymus]

Barsanuphius and John: Questions and Responses. In *Philokalia.* 3 vols. Thessalonika: Byzantion Editions, 1988–1989.

Barsanuphius and John: Questions and Responses. Greek Fathers of the Church. Thessalonika, 1988. [In Greek]

Barsanuphius and John: Discerning and Hesychastic Texts; Questions and Responses. 3 vols. Kareas, Athens: Holy Monastery of St. John the Forerunner, 1996–1997.

Chitty, D. J., ed. and trans. *Barsanuphius and John: Questions and Responses.* PO 31, 3 (Paris, 1966): 445–616. Also published by New Sarov Press, Blanco, TX, 1998. [Partial critical edition of the Greek text with English translation]

Dorotheus. *Questions and Responses.* PG 88: 1811–22. [Incorporated among his Instructions]

John Rufus. *Plerophoriae.* Edited by F. Nau. PO 8, 1 (Paris, 1912).

Lovato, M. F. T., and L. Mortari, eds. *Barsanufio e Giovanni di Gaza: Epistolario.* In *Collana di Testi Patristici* 93. Rome, 1991.

Mark the Deacon. *The Life of Porphyry, Bishop of Gaza.* Translated by G. F. Hill. Oxford, 1913.

————. *Vie de Porphyre, évêque de Gaza [par] Marc le Diacre.* Edited and translated by H. Gregoire and M.-A. Kugener. Paris, 1930.

Nikodemus of Mt. Athos. Βίβλος ψυχωφελεστάτη περιέχουσα ἀποκρίσεις διαφόροις ὑποθέσεσιν ἀνηκούσαις, συγγραφεῖσὰ μὲν παρὰ τῶν ὁσίων καὶ θεοφόρων πατέρων ἡμῶν Βαρσανουφίου καὶ Ἰωάννου, ἐπιμελῶς δὲ διοθωθεῖσα καὶ τῇ τῶν ὁσίων βιογραφίᾳ, καὶ πλατυτάτῳ πίνακι πλουτισθεῖσα παρὰ τοῦ ἐν μοναχοῖς ἐλαχίστου Νικοδήμου τοῦ ἁγιορείτου. Venice, 1816. [Also contains a substantial introduction by Nikodemus himself]

Pachomius Hieromonk. Opisanie roukopisei solovetskago monastyria nakhodiachlchikhsia v biblioteke Kazanskoi doukhovnoi Akademii I. Kazan, 1881.

Prepodobnykh ottzev Varsanoufiia Velikago I Ionna roukovodstvo k doukhovnoi zisni, v otvetakh na voprocheniia outchenikov. Perevod s gretcheskag. Moscow, 1883.

Regnault, L. *Maîtres spirituels au désert de Gaza: Barsanuphe, Jean et Dorothée.* Selected texts and introduction. Sable-sur-Sarthe: Abbaye de Solesmes, 1967.

Regnault, L., Ph. Lemaire, and B. Ottier, trans. *Barsanuphe et Jean de Gaza: Correspondance.* Sable-sur-Sarthe: Abbaye de Solesmes, 1971. [Complete French translation from the Greek and Georgian]

Rose, S., ed. *Saints Barsanuphius and John: Guidance toward Spiritual Life. Responses to the Questions of Disciples.* Platina, CA: St. Herman of Alaska Brotherhood, 1990. [Partial English translation from the Russian edition, *Rukuvodstvo k Duchovnoi Zhizni,* Moscow, 1855]

Schoinas, S., ed. *Vivlos Psychopelestate . . . Varsanoufiou kai Ioannou* [as above in the book by Nikodemus]. Volos, 1960. [In Greek; English translation of full title as follows: "Most edifying book, containing responses on various matters written by our holy and God-bearing Fathers Barsanuphius and John"]

Soterchos, P. M. *The Great Old Man Barsanuphius and his Disciple Saint John the Prophet.* Athens, 1988. [Selections from the two elders, in Greek]

Sozomen. *Historia ecclesiastica.* GCS 56. Edited by J. Bidez and G. C. Hanson. Berlin, 1960.

Barsanuphius and John: Secondary Sources

Angelis-Noah, Paula de. "La méditation de Barsanuphe sur la lettre *êta.*" *Byzantion* 53, fasc. 2 (1983): 494–506.

Binns, J. *Ascetics and Ambassadors of Christ: The Monasteries of Palestine 314–631,* Oxford: Clarendon Press, 1994.

Brown, P. *The Body and Society. Men, Women and Sexual Renunciation in Early Christianity.* New York: Columbia University Press, 1988.

Cameron, A. "On the date of John of Gaza." *Classical Quarterly,* n.s. 43 (1993): 348–51.

Chitty, D. *The Desert a City: An introduction to the study of Egyptian and Palestinian monasticism under the Christian Empire.* Oxford: Blackwell, 1966. Reprint, Crestwood, NY: St. Vladimir's Seminary Press, 1995.

———. "The Books of the Old Men." *Eastern Churches Review* 6 (1974): 15–21.

———. "Abba Isaiah." *The Journal of Theological Studies,* NS, 22 (1971): 47–72.

Chrestou, P. *Greek Patrology.* Thessalonika: Patriarchal Institute of Patristic Studies, 1976. [In Greek]

Chryssavgis, J. *Soul Mending: The Art of Spiritual Direction.* Brookline, MA: Holy Cross Press, 2000.

Festugière, A. J. *Les moines d'Orient.* Paris, 1961–. See especially vol. 4, 1965.

Garitte, G. "Le menée georgien de Dumbarton Oaks." *Le Muséon* 77 (1964): 29–64, esp. 43 and 55.

Hausherr, I. "Barsanuphe (saint)." *Dictionnaire de spiritualité.* Vol. 1. Paris, 1937.

————. *Direction spirituelle en Orient autrefois. Orientalia Christiana analecta* 144. Rome: Pontificium Institutum Orientalium Studiorum, 1955. See also the English translation: *Spiritual Direction in the Early Christian East.* Translated by Anthony P. Gythiel. Kalamazoo, MI: Cistercian Publications, 1990.

————. "Noms du Christ et voies d'oraison." *Orientalia Christiana analecta* 157. Rome: Pontificium Institutum Orientalium Studiorum, 1960.

Hevelone-Harper, J. L. *Disciples of the Desert: Monks, Laity, and Spiritual Authority in Sixth-Century Gaza.* Baltimore, MD: Johns Hopkins University Press, 2005.

Janin, R. "Barsanuphius." *Dictionnaire d'histoire et de géographie ecclésiastiques.* Vol. 6. Paris: Letouzey et Ané, 1912–.

Neyt, F. *Les lettres à Dorothée dans la correspondance de Barsanuphe et de Jean de Gaza.* Doctoral diss., University of Louvain, 1969.

————. "Citations 'Isaiennes' chez Barsanuphe et Jean de Gaza." *Le Muséon* 89 (1971): 65–92.

————. "Précisions sur le vocabulaire de Barsanuphe et Jean de Gaza." *Studia Patristica* 12 (Berlin, 1975): 247–53.

————. "Un type d'autorité charismatique." *Byzantion* 44, fasc. 2 (1974): 343–61. Also appeared in English as "A Form of Charismatic Authority," in *Eastern Churches Review* 6 (1974): 52–65.

————. "L'*Apsephiston* chez les Pères de Gaza." *Uberlieferung der geschichtlichen Untersuchungen.* Berlin: Akademie-Verlag, 1981.

Perrone, L. *La chiesa di Palestina e le controversie cristologiche: dal concilio di Efeso (431) al secondo concilio di Constantinopoli.* Brescia: Paideia, 1980.

————. Εἰς τὸν τῆς ʿΗσυχίας Λιμένα.' Le lettere a Giovanni di Beersheva nella corrispondenza di Barsanufio e Giovanni di Gaza." Pages 463–86 in *Memorial Dom Jean Gribomont (1920–1986).* Rome, 1988.

————. "Le lettere a Giovanni di Beersheve nella corrispondenza di Barsanufio e Giovanni di Gaza." *Studia Ephemeridis Augustinianum* 27. Rome, 1988.

————. "Dissenso dottrinale e propaganda visionaria: Le Pleroforie di Giovanni di Maiuma." *Augustinianum* 29 (1989): 451–95.

————. "Monasticism as a Factor of Religious Interaction in the Holy Land during the Byzantine Period." Pages 67–95 in A. Kofsky and G. G. Stroumsa, eds. *Sharing the Sacred: Religious Contacts and Conflicts in the Holy Land. First–Fifteenth Centuries CE.* Jerusalem: Yad Izhak Ben Zvi, 1998.

Rapp, C. "'For next to God, you are my salvation': Reflections on the Rise of the Holy Man in Late Antiquity." Pages 63–81 in J. Howard-Johnston and P. A. Hayward, eds. *Essays on the Contribution of Peter Brown.* Oxford: Oxford University Press, 1999.

————. "Monasticism, Prayer and Penance in Late Antiquity." *Bulletin of Saint Shenouda the Archimandrite Coptic Society* 6 (2000–2001): 83–93.

Regnault, L. "Dorothée de Gaza." *Dictionnaire de spiritualité.* Vol. 3. Paris, 1954.

_____. "Théologie de la vie monastique selon Barsanuphe et Dorothée." Pages 315–22 in *Théologie de la vie monastique: Études sur la tradition patristique.* Paris: Aubier, 1961.

_____. "Jean de Gaza." *Dictionnaire de spiritualité.* Vol. 8. Paris, 1974.

Vailhé, S. "Jean le Prophète et Séridos." *Echos d'Orient* 8 (1905): 154–60.

_____. "Les lettres spirituelles de Jean et de Barsanuphe." *Echos d'Orient* 7 (1904): 268–76.

_____. "Saint Barsanuphe." *Echos d'Orient* 8 (1905): 14–25.

Vamvakas, D. Τὸ ἐν παντὶ εὐχαριστεῖν τῶν ὁσίων καὶ θεοφόρων πατέρων ἡμῶν Βαρσανουφίου καὶ Ἰωάννου. Hagion Oros: Karyai, 1991. [In Greek]

Veselinovich, K. A. *Barsanuphius the Great, John the Prophet and Dorotheus the Abba.* Doctoral diss. Athens, 1941. [In Greek]

Voulgarakis, I. A. "Missionsangaben in den Briefen der Asketen Barsanuphius und Johannes." In A. Kallis, ed. *Philoxenia.* Munster, 1980.

General References

Abel, F.-M. "Gaza au VIᵉ siècle d'après le rhéteus Chorikios." *Revue biblique* 40 (1931): 5–31.

_____. *Histoire de la Palestine depuis la conquête d' Alexandre jusqu'à l'invasion arabe.* Paris: J. Gabalda, 1952. See esp. Part 3, 267–406.

Aharoni, Y. *The Land of the Bible.* Rev. ed. Philadelphia: Westminster Press, 1979.

Anderson, G. *Sage, Saint, and Sophist: Holy Men and their Associates in the Early Roman Empire.* London and New York: Routledge, 1994.

Avi-Yonah, M. *The Madaba Mosaic Map.* Jerusalem: Israel Exploration Society, 1954.

Bottini, G. C., L. Di Segni, and E. Alliata, eds. *Christian Archaeology in the Holy Land: New Discoveries. Essays in Honour of Virgilio C. Corbo.* Jerusalem: Franciscan Printing Press, 1990.

Brown, P. "The Rise and Function of the Holy Man in Late Antiquity." *Journal of Religious Studies* 61 (1971): 80–101. Reprinted as pages 391–439 in Martin, J., and B. Quint, eds. *Christentum und Antike Gesellschaft.* Darmstadt, 1990.

Brun, P.-M., ed. *La vie de saint Dosithée.* In *Orientalia Christiana* 26. Rome, 1932. Pages 85–124. Also published in *SC* 92. Edited by L. Regnault and J. de Préville. Paris, 1963.

Bury, J. B. *A History of the Later Empire from Arcadius to Irene (395 A.D.–800 A.D.).* London and New York: Macmillan and Co., 1889. Unaltered reprint, Amsterdam: Adolf M. Hakkert, 1966.

Canivet, P. "Dorothée de Gaza est-il un disciple d'Evagre?" *Revue des études grecques* 78 (1965): 336–46.

Chryssavgis, J. *In the Heart of the Desert: The Spirituality of the Desert Fathers and Mothers.* Bloomington, IN: World Wisdom Books, 2003.

Dan, Y. "On the ownership of the land of the village of Thavatha in the Byzantine period." *Scripta Classica Israelica* 5 (1979–1980): 258–62.

Garitte, G. "Chronique." *Revue d'histoire ecclésiastique* 60 (1965): 287–88.

Glucker, C. A. M. *The City of Gaza in the Roman and Byzantine Periods.* BAR International Series 325. Oxford: B.A.R., 1987.

Guillaumont, A. *Aux origines du monachisme chrétien.* Spiritualité orientale 30. Bégrolles-en-Mauges: Abbaye de Bellefontaine, 1979.

Guy, J.-C., ed. *Les Apophtegmes des Pères du désert.* Bégrolles-en-Mauges: Abbaye de Bellefontaine, 1966.

_____. *Les Apophtegmes des Pères,* I–IX. *SC* 387. Paris, 1993.

Hirschfeld, Y. *The Judean Desert Monasteries in the Byzantine Period.* New Haven: Yale University Press, 1992.

Jones, A. H. M. *The Cities of the Eastern Roman Provinces.* Revised by Michael Avi-Yonah. 2d ed. Oxford, 1971.

Miller, J. I. *The Spice Trade of the Roman Empire: 29 B.C. to A.D. 641.* Oxford, 1969.

Mortari, L. *Vita e detti dei Padri del Deserto.* Rome: Città Nuova, 1971.

Nau, F. "Histoire des solitaires égyptiennes." *ROC* (1907): 43–69, 171–89, and 393–413; (1908) 47–66 and 266–97; (1909) 357–79; (1912) 204–11 and 294–301; and (1913) 137–46. English translation in B. Ward. *The Wisdom of the Desert Fathers.* Oxford: SLG Press, 1975.

Regnault, L., ed. *Les sentences des Pères du désert. Nouveau recueil.* 2d ed. Sable-sur-Sarthe: Abbaye de Solesmes, 1977.

_____. "Les *Apophtegmes* des Pères en Palestine aux Ve et VIe siècles." *Irénikon* 54 (1981): 320–30. Later appeared as pages 73–83 in Regnault, L. *Les Pères du désert à travers leurs apophtegmes.* Sable-sur-Sarthe: Abbaye de Solesmes, 1987.

Roll, I. "The Roman Road System in Judea." In *The Jerusalem Cathedra.* Vol. 3. Edited by L. I. Levine. Jerusalem: Yad Izhak Ben-Zvi Institute; Detroit: Wayne State University Press, 1983.

Rubin, Z. "Christianity in Byzantine Palestine: missionary activity and religious coercion." In *The Jerusalem Cathedra.* Vol. 3. Edited by L. I. Levine. Jerusalem: Yad Izhak Ben-Zvi Institute; Detroit: Wayne State University Press, 1983.

Stemberger, G. *Juden und Christen im Heiligen Land: Palästina unter Konstantin und Theodosius.* Munich, 1987.

Vailhé, S. "Repertoire alphabetique des monastères de Palestine." *ROC* 4 (1899): 512–42; and 5 (1900): 19–48, 272–92.

_____. "Saint Dorothée et Saint Zosime." *Echos d'Orient* 4 (1901): 359–63.

_____. "Un mystique monophysite, le moine Isaïe." *Echos d'Orient* 9 (1906): 81–91.

Van Parys, M. "Abba Silvain et ses disciples." *Irénikon* 61 (1988): 315–30.

INTRODUCTION

INTRODUCTION

1. Palestinian Monasticism

The desert of Gaza proved a remarkable place of continuity and creativity for Christian monasticism toward the end of the fourth century. Its accessibility by sea and road, its proximity to Egypt and Syria as well as the Holy Land, but also its prominence in Hellenistic and Roman times, rendered it a singularly significant haven for monastic life from the fourth to the sixth centuries. Travelers journeyed from Palestine to Egypt to visit the elders of the Egyptian desert,[1] and as early as the mid-fourth century, some of the better known pilgrims to this region included Jerome, Rufinus, Palladius, Evagrius, and John Cassian.

Toward the end of the same century, a similar movement began in the opposite direction, from Egypt to Palestine, as monastics fled the renowned wilderness. The reasons for this monastic emigration were more than merely social or political; they included personal and religious factors, such as the earlier deaths of the two Macarii—of the Egyptian in 390, and of the Alexandrian in 393.

Palestine is divided into two distinct monastic regions: the first, centered around the Holy City, includes the territory around Jerusalem as far as the Dead Sea; the second lies in the southern region around Gaza. The Judean desert had a paradoxical twofold advantage, namely, its remoteness and accessibility. This region is characterized by a more erudite and international, almost elitist, dimension because of the presence of such figures as Melania the Elder, Rufinus, and Jerome. The dominant and formative monastic personalities of this region, however, emerge in the fifth and early sixth centuries: for example, Euthymius (376–473) and Sabas (439–532), whose biographical details are

---

1. *Letters* 30–31 recall a journey by John to Egypt.

recorded by their contemporary, Cyril of Scythopolis (fl. 524–558).[2]

Jerome is apparently unaware of the long pre-history of the region, unlike Eusebius, for instance, who narrates how, at the end of the second century, a bishop, Narcissus, fled to the wilderness near Jerusalem in order to avoid calumny. In addition, the anonymous and, at least according to some contemporary scholars, somewhat unreliable sixth-century *Life of Saint Chariton* relates the story of a confessor of the faith during the reign of Aurelian (ca. 275). In the desert immediately north of Jerusalem, Chariton the Confessor founded a monastery toward the end of the third century, which Euthymius found when he arrived there.[3]

In the southern parts of Palestine, Gaza enjoyed its own proper history of monasticism, the origins of which are recorded by Jerome and Epiphanius. Hilarion (ca. 292–ca. 372) lived for almost twenty of his earlier years in this region. Born in Thavatha, some five miles south of Gaza, he was schooled in Alexandria, where he met Antony the Great. On returning to his native region, he occupied a small cell near the port of Maiouma, receiving numerous visitors for spiritual counsel before spending the final years of his life on the island of Cyprus.

At some time between 380 and 400, Abba Silvanus, a Palestinian by birth and one of the renowned elders of the Egyptian desert, moved with his twelve disciples briefly to Sinai and, finally, to Palestine. In Scetis of Egypt, the Abba had lived with his disciples in the semi-eremitic monastic way, with scattered cells around his own dwelling and a central church for worship on Saturday and Sunday. The group adopted the same lifestyle when it settled near Gerara of Palestine. Silvanus died before 414 and was succeeded by Zaccharias, his foremost disciple. One of Silvanus's disciples, Zeno the Prophet, enjoyed considerable spiritual prestige in the first half of the fifth century, largely

---

2. Cf. R. Price, ed., *Lives of the Monks of Palestine* (Kalamazoo, MI: Cistercian Publications, 1990).

3. See Derwas Chitty, *The Desert a City* (Oxford: Blackwell, 1966; reprint, Crestwood, NY: St. Vladimir's Seminary Press, 1995), 14–15.

through his own disciple, Peter the Iberian, who became the prominent non-Chalcedonian bishop of Maiouma.

Another well-known monk and monastic author in this region was Abba Isaiah of Scetis. A later emigrant from Egypt, Isaiah had spent many years in a monastery but also in the desert of Scetis. He moved to Palestine, fleeing fame, between 431 and 451. He first settled near Eleutheropolis, moving finally to Beit Daltha near Gaza, some four miles from Thavatha, which was later to become familiar as the site of the monastery of Abba Seridos. There he stayed for several decades, serving for his contemporary ascetics and visitors as a living example of the old semi-eremitic Scetiote ascetic life, until his death in 489.[4]

There is, however, more to be told of these places. For Gaza and its environs would be indelibly marked by the presence of two remarkable elders in the next century, Barsanuphius and John, as well as by their *Letters* and their disciples, Abbot Seridos and especially Dorotheus.

2. *Barsanuphius and John*

We do not know exactly when—or, indeed, why—Barsanuphius, himself an Egyptian monk,[5] entered the hilly region of Thavatha (*Letter* 61) and chose to lead the enclosed life of a recluse in a cell near the village. From this position, he offered counsel to a number of ascetics who were gradually attracted around the Old Man as he developed a remarkable reputation for discernment and compassion. One of these monks, Abba Seridos, who also attended to Barsanuphius, was the abbot of a nearby monastic community, which was increasingly responsible for supporting the numerous monks who gathered around Barsanuphius.

The entire monastery in Thavatha assumed the form of a

---

4. More on Abba Isaiah in John Chryssavgis and P. R. Penkett, eds., *Abba Isaiah of Scetis: Ascetic Discourses* (Kalamazoo, MI: Cistercian Publications, 2002); and John Chryssavgis and P. R. Penkett, *In the Footsteps of the Lord* (Oxford: SLG Press, 2001).

5. Although the prefix in his name bears Syriac overtones. The language spoken in the monastery of Seridos was Greek, in spite of the presence of Egyptian monks, which accounts for the numerous copticisms throughout the correspondence.

loose community with many cells, where monks and hermits enjoyed varying degrees of enclosure. This monastery of Seridos
became the center of attraction for many monastics and visitors
during the sixth century, largely due to the presence in the region of the two Old Men, but partly also due to its far-reaching
activities, which included workshops (*Letters* 553–554), two guest-
houses (*Letters* 570, 595–596), a hospital (*Letters* 327 and 548),
and a large church (*Letter* 570). The monastery was built near
Gerara, in the southern part of Gaza, where Abraham and Isaac
had each stayed (cf. *Letter* 257).[6] In addition to these edifices,
Seridos constructed the cells of Barsanuphius and John. Seridos
was the only person permitted to communicate with Barsanuphius, acting as a mediator for those who wished to be counseled by
the elder. Since Seridos did not know Coptic, he recorded the
words of Barsanuphius in Greek.

Sometime between 525 and 527 another hermit, named John,
came from Beersheba to live beside Barsanuphius, who surrendered his own cell to him, while he himself moved to a new cell
that Seridos constructed for him nearby. Barsanuphius then became known as "the holy Old Man" or "the Great Old Man." John
came simply to be called "the Other Old Man" or "the Prophet."
The two shared the same way of life and supported one another's
ministry (*Letters* 224–225 and 571–572), with John assuming another monk, Dorotheus, as his mouthpiece.

While they shared the same God (*Letter* 20) and the same virtue (*Letter* 780), John responded primarily to matters of a prac-
tical nature and Barsanuphius to questions of a more spiritual
nature. Moreover, they supported one another's authority (*Letter* 305).

Sensational miracles and exceptional charismata are neither
the most striking nor the most appealing feature of these elders. While Peter Brown emphasizes the more "extraordinary"
characteristics of the Old Men,[7] Barsanuphius and John are in
fact far less "spectacular." They did not provide wisdom on request; nor did they attempt to solve all problems presented be-

6. See Gn 20.1 and 26.1, 6, 17.

7. See Peter Brown, *The Body and Society: Men, Women, and Sexual Renunciation
in Early Christianity* (New York: Columbia University Press, 1988), 213–40.

fore them. Their purpose was to inspire rather than to impress; their aim was to exhort rather than to excite.

In regard to dating the text itself, the correspondence contains certain historical details that prove helpful. For example, *Letters* 568–569 allude to the plague that spread through the Roman Empire in 542 and 543. *Letters* 600–607 deal with the controversy over Origenism, the first indications of which reached the monks of Palestine as early as 514 and the resolution of which took place in 553 with the fifth Ecumenical Council in Constantinople. *Letter* 821 refers to a decree by the Emperor Justinian relating to pagans and schismatics, which was issued in 528–29.

The monastery of Seridos still existed in the seventh century. Relics of the Great Old Man are believed to have been translated to southern Italy in the ninth century. A late twelfth-century text, entitled *Vita Barsanuphii*, was written by a certain priest in Oria, near Brindisi in southern Italy. Extracts of this appear in the *Acta Sanctorum*.[8] This *Life* contains certain hagiographical details, such as the translation of the relics of Barsanuphius to Italy in the tenth century. Local tradition claims that the relics are still preserved in the cathedral of that city. Barsanuphius is remembered on June 11 in the West and on February 6 in the East. The Eastern Church also commemorates Abbot Seridos on August 13 with Dorotheus of Gaza.

3. The Letters of the Old Men

The identity of the compiler or editor of the letters is not clear. Seridos could not possibly be the editor, since many letters deal with events surrounding his own death. Dorotheus, however, survived the two elders and his abbot, Seridos. Dorotheus would have had access not only to the manuscripts of the letters themselves, but would also have recalled the circumstances of the questions and the contents of any *lacunae*.[9] It has also been suggested that John of Beersheba, as Barsanuphius's closest friend, may be the editor of Barsanuphius's correspon-

---

8. Cf. Chitty, 140, and the introduction to the French edition in *SC* 426 (Paris, 1997), 31–32.

9. Cf. his *Teaching* 1, found in *SC* 92, 288, and PG 88.1697.

dence; however, while John is the recipient of around fifty letters, all of them from Barsanuphius, Dorotheus is the recipient of almost one hundred letters from both of the Old Men. It would be reasonable to conclude that Dorotheus was more acquainted with the two elders and with their letters addressed to the numerous visitors.

In all, there are—depending on the division adopted for some of the longer documents—approximately eight hundred and fifty letters, dictated by both of our elders, in response to a variety of issues presented by a diverse group of questioners. Almost four hundred of these letters (mostly the longer ones) belong to Barsanuphius, while almost four hundred and fifty letters (mostly the shorter ones) belong to John. Whereas the study, and indeed the literature, of spiritual direction has traditionally focused on monastic development, the correspondence of Barsanuphius and John redresses a balance in this regard, concentrating much of its attention on the concerns of lay persons.

The letters "call to center stage more or less all of the main actors of the *societas christiana*"[10] in the period, with the exception of women.[11] These include monks from the monastery of Abba Seridos and simple laypersons from the surrounding community, as well as high-ranking political officials and ecclesiastical leaders. For instance, bishops ask about ordinations (*Letter* 815); and there is another, or possibly more than one, from Patriarch Peter of Jerusalem (*Letter* 821). One letter concerns "the Duke, who has recently become a Christian" (*Letter* 834). Sometimes the letters address both the recipient and the scribe (*Letters* 207 and 484).

10. Perrone, "Monasticism as a Factor of Religious Interaction," in A. Kofsky and G. G. Stroumsa, eds., *Sharing the Sacred: Religious Contacts and Conflicts in the Holy Land. First–Fifteenth Centuries CE* (Jerusalem: Yad Izhak Ben Zvi, 1998), 91.

11. While there are no letters from women in the correspondence, Barsanuphius is not exclusive in his attitude toward women (*Letter* 61). The community at Thavatha welcomed female visitors (*Letter* 595) for instruction. These women stayed in specially constructed and allocated cells outside of the monastery walls. Hospitality and charity were virtues that excluded no one, irrespective of gender, in the monastery of Seridos as, earlier, in the desert of Egypt. Close contact and interaction was encouraged between the monastery and the wider society.

The letters touch on such subjects as the interpretation of dreams, conduct toward slaves, social relations with non-Christians—Jews and pagans alike (*Letters* 686, 732–735, 776–777, 836, and 821–822)—and coping with illness (*Letters* 637–646, 753–755, and 778–781). They reveal a diverse community around sixth-century Gaza, with Christians seeking direction about relations with Jews, pagans, and heretics.

When lay people inquire about illness and healing, the elders encourage them to consider the importance of spiritual health (*Letters* 637–644, 753–755, and 778–781; see also *Letters* 72–123 to a monk in illness). Other questions relate to legal and economic matters (*Letters* 667–672 and 749–756), to family relations and chores (*Letters* 764–768), to marriage and death (*Letters* 646 and 676), to property and charity (*Letters* 617–620, 623, 625–626, 629–635, 649), to the proper interaction and appropriate boundaries between monks and laity (*Letters* 636, 681–682, 712–718, 727–729, 736–742, and 751), to ascetic practices in city life (*Letters* 764–774), and to superstitions and visions (*Letters* 44 and 414–419). The seclusion of Barsanuphius and John has clearly not denied these elders the possibility and opportunity of compassion for the dilemmas of earthly entanglements.

There is also a basic structure to the text itself: letters to monastics are found in the early section of the correspondence (comprising around two-thirds of the document); these are followed by letters to lay people (comprising about one quarter of the collection); and the collection concludes with letters to bishops (including about fifty letters). In general, the correspondence is not organized chronologically, with the exception of certain letters that constitute a series or string of questions and answers. A more detailed subdivision of the letters would be the following:

1–54	Correspondence with John of Beersheba
55–71	Letters to elders and hermits
72–123	Questions from Andrew, one of the elders, who is very ill
124–131	Letters to the monk Theodore

In the correspondence Barsanuphius appears as kind, understanding, and warm; his language is clear, prayerful, and even
prophetic on occasion. He reveals a strong and supportive personality, undeterred by issues and sure about his convictions.
John is less ardent, less direct, and more guarded; his language
is concise, precise, and even conventional at times. He reveals a
thoughtful and careful personality, often deferring to his master, Barsanuphius.

4. Sources and Influence

Barsanuphius and John cite profusely from the Scriptures.
Firmly rooted in the tradition of the Church Fathers and particularly in the Alexandrian emphasis on the primacy of the Word
of God, Barsanuphius likes to adapt Scripture, both allegorical-
ly and spiritually, in order to respond to the particular needs of
each individual. For him, as indeed for the monks at Scetis, the
Word of God is a word of life.

The list of scriptural passages quoted in this sixth-century
document, whether directly or indirectly, is quite impressive.
The Book of Psalms has always been a favorite among monastics
through the ages, but the Great Old Man in particular has certain additional preferences. For instance, he refers frequently
to the Wisdom literature: to Job, to Proverbs, and to Sirach; he
also refers, though less frequently, to the Song of Songs and the
Wisdom of Solomon. Of the prophetic writings, Isaiah is men-

tioned abundantly, followed by Jeremiah, Ezekiel, and others. Naturally, the New Testament occupies a place of priority.

Barsanuphius cites all four of the Gospels, and likes to dwell on the Sermon on the Mount. His Pauline preferences include the Letter to the Romans and the two Letters to the Corinthians, yet, perhaps above all, he borrows heavily from the Letter to the Hebrews. The perspective that colors all of Barsanuphius's correspondence is that of the Kingdom of Heaven. Another favorite among monastic circles is the Letter of James; Barsanuphius is no exception here.

The *Letters* of Barsanuphius and John, which, as mentioned, date to the first half of the sixth century, frequently quote or evoke the *Sayings of the Desert Fathers*. There are at least eighty direct references to the *Sayings*, or *Apophthegmata*, themselves, while numerous phrases recommend them as a basis for spiritual practice and progress, sometimes by name (sixteen times) but mostly by implication (thirty-four times). On other occasions, the Old Men adopt alternative phrases:

"The fathers have said" (fourteen times);
"It is written in the fathers" (once);
"It is written in the elders" (once);
"It is written in the *Sayings of the Elders*" (twice);
"The *Lives of the Fathers*" (twice);
"The *Sayings of the Fathers*" (once);
"The *Sayings of the Fathers* and their *Lives*" (twice);
"The *Life of the Fathers* and the responses" (once);
"The books of the elders" (once);
"The *Gerontika*" (once).

There are at least fifty-five direct references to the *Sayings of the Desert Fathers* in the writings of Dorotheus alone. He also seems to be the first writer to designate the *Apophthegmata* as τὸ Γεροντικόν (*The Gerontikon*, or *The Book of the Old Men*).[12] Might, therefore, this Dorotheus also be one of those responsible for the collection of the *Sayings* themselves? Certainly, Dorotheus is the only ancient witness to the single saying attributed to Basil

---

12. See his *Teaching* 1.18, found in *SC* 92, 174, and PG 88.1633C.

in the alphabetical collection of the *Sayings of the Desert Fathers*,[13] while both Barsanuphius and Dorotheus refer to the *Rules* of Saint Basil.

Later ascetic leaders and authors seem to sense the importance of transmitting, even translating, their Egyptian roots for future generations in both East and West. Thus Evagrius and John Cassian included several sayings in their influential and formative treatises.[14] Abba Isaiah of Scetis inserted numerous sayings, both recognizable and original, in his *Ascetic Discourses*, possibly regarding himself as responsible for preserving and promoting the words of the elders with whom he was personally acquainted in Egypt. The abundant references to the *Sayings* in the *Letters* of Barsanuphius and John further attest to the concern of these elders that the ways and words of the ancient elders of the desert be both pondered and practiced.

Indeed, the *Letters* of Barsanuphius and John, and especially the ones addressed by and to Dorotheus of Gaza (*Letters* 252– 338), reveal yet another element that gradually disappears from the *Sayings of the Desert Fathers*, even as these begin to be collated and edited. For the original transmission of the wisdom of the Egyptian desert preserved the spontaneity of the profound advice and impressive actions of the desert fathers and mothers. During the stage of their transition from an oral culture to a written text, however, the *Sayings* inevitably become a little more static, and we begin to lose sight of the personal element that originally sparked these words. More especially, we misplace the process and struggle that initially shaped these words. What is "received" is the intense drop of wisdom, without, however, the stages that led to the final product. What is missing is the ongoing process—all of the contentions, hesitations, and limitations of the spiritual aspirant. Yet, in Barsanuphius and John, we are allowed to witness each of the painful stages unfolding in slow motion. What might normally have taken place on a face-to-face level is recorded in writing, with all of the mutual exchange of a personal relationship.

13. See L. Regnault, "Les *Apophtegmes* des Pères en Palestine aux Ve et VIe siècles," *Irénikon* 54 (1981): 328; and Dorotheus, *Teaching* 1.24, *SC* 92, 182–84.

14. Evagrius toward the end of the *Praktikos* and in chapters 106–12 of his treatise *On Prayer*, PG 79.1189–92. See also Cassian, *Institutes* 5.24–41.

Nowhere in the vast correspondence of Barsanuphius and John is there any clear or explicit condemnation or defense of the Chalcedonian definition. Their disciples are advised to abstain from such debates as well as from condemning those who chose to take sides. Other contemporary ascetics, such as Sabas (d. 532), while compassionate and non-judgmental in their outlook, are nevertheless deliberately and defensively concerned with confessional doctrine. Peter the Iberian (ca. 409–ca. 488) is actively involved in the christological controversy and openly opposed to the Chalcedonian supporters. It is no wonder, then, that an image of the Great Old Man graced the altar-cloth in the Great Church of the Holy Wisdom in Constantinople, beside those of Antony of Egypt and Ephraim the Syrian. This is perhaps why Theodore the Studite (759–826) was anxious to defend and affirm the orthodoxy of Isaiah, Barsanuphius, and Dorotheus.[15]

Yet, at the same time, the Gaza elders differ from their Egyptian counterparts inasmuch as they are overall more educated and widely read. This feature is not entirely lacking among the desert fathers, but it is the exception rather than the rule. In general, it appears to be a characteristic of Palestinian monasticism.[16] Monks in the community of Seridos were familiar with the writings of Origen of Alexandria, Didymus the Blind, and Evagrius of Pontus (*Letter* 600). Barsanuphius's answers to questions about Origenist tendencies among certain representatives of the monastic tradition, together with John's explanations of the Great Old Man's words (*Letters* 601–607), reveal two elders

---

15. The *Life of Barsanuphius and John* endeavors to handle this problem by referring to two Barsanuphii and Dorothei, one set being heretical and the other orthodox. Barsanuphius chose to adopt the rhetoric of the non-Chalcedonian party, while urging his disciples to follow a Chalcedonian bishop. See the *Testament* of Theodore the Studite in PG 88.1813–16 and PG 99.1028. These three had been anathematized by Patriarch Sophronius of Jerusalem in a synodical letter to Patriarch Sergius of Constantinople in 634: cf. PG 87, iii.3192–93. The orthodoxy of Barsanuphius was in question because of his reference in *Letter* 701 only to the first Ecumenical Council in Nicaea (325), without, however, making any mention of the fourth Ecumenical Council in Chalcedon (451). The iconographic tradition, however, is particularly interesting in light of the fact that the two Old Men permitted so few people to meet them in person.

16. In the *Life of Cyriacus* 14 and the *Life of Sabas* 83, Cyril of Scythopolis refers to the monks of Palestine as "more lettered" than others. See Price, 230 and 188.

who appreciate fine intellectual distinctions without at the same time being absorbed by these to the detriment of their prayer life. Thus, in another set of thirteen responses (between *Letters* 151 and 167) to a certain Euthymius whose mind is almost obsessed with allegorical interpretations and details, Barsanuphius will recommend humility and silence!

With the exception of scriptural references, relatively few proper names are recorded in the *Letters*. Nonetheless, as we have already observed, the *Sayings of the Desert Fathers* and the *Lives of the Fathers*, especially that of Pachomius, are recommended reading for the monks of the Seridos community. The Cappadocian theologians, particularly Basil the Great, are apparent in the teaching of Barsanuphius and John on obedience. While Barsanuphius is condemnatory of Origen, Didymus, and Evagrius, and while the two elders in general represent the anti-Origenism of the period, John appears to be the more accommodating of the pair in regard to the reading of their writings (*Letters* 606–609), and Barsanuphius reveals more familiarity with these writers than he would readily admit, possibly even being influenced by them.[17] Earlier Palestinian writers, too, clearly exerted an influence on Barsanuphius and John. For instance, Abba Isaiah of Scetis shaped the elders' appreciation of rules on eating and drinking (see *Letters* 80 and 224).

Clearly, as their immediate and most intimate disciple, Dorotheus of Gaza is decisively influenced by the Palestinian elders. It is through Dorotheus that Theodore the Studite also accepts their teachings as authoritative. Their influence is especially—although implicitly—evident in the seventh-century Sinaite tradition of John Climacus[18] and, through John, in Symeon the New Theologian and the fourteenth-century Hesychasts, Kallistos and Ignatios Xanthopouli. The fourteenth-century text by Gregory of Sinai, *On Stillness and the Two Methods of Prayer*, quotes from *Letter* 74 by Barsanuphius.[19]

---

17. Paula de Angelis-Noah, "La méditation de Barsanuphe sur la lettre *êta*," *Byzantion* 53, fasc. 2 (1983): 506–7.

18. The influence is particularly evident in John Climacus's development of the concepts of being carefree (*amerimnia*) and discerning (*diakrisis*). Barsanuphius is explicitly mentioned in the *Scholia* of *Step* 26 (PG 88.1093).

19. See PG 150.1317.

The eleventh-century anthology of Paulos Evergetinos, *Synagoge*, directly cites eighty-three letters, almost one-tenth of our correspondence, with certain modifications by the editor. Monk Nikon also refers to the *Letters* in his *Pandektes*.[20] Most of these citations (seventy of them) are from letters by John; forty-seven of them are exchanges with Dorotheus.

5. Manuscripts, Editions, and Translations

The surviving manuscripts show that the correspondence of Barsanuphius and John was early appreciated and disseminated. Although the Muslim invasions of Palestine left little or nothing in that region as reminders of the monastic or Byzantine presence and influence,[21] nevertheless the correspondence was known in early ninth-century Constantinople. The oldest manuscripts originate on Mt. Sinai and date from the tenth century. These are Georgian translations, but contain only some seventy-nine letters of the correspondence.[22] One of these (Sinai 34) is entitled, *Teachings of the Blessed Barsanuphius and John*, while the other (Sinai 35) is dated 907 and entitled, *Questions and Responses*.[23]

Several manuscripts are preserved on Mt. Athos from the eleventh through the fourteenth centuries, but also in Paris, Oxford, Athens, Moscow, Munich, Jerusalem, and Patmos. Some manuscripts have only certain letters; others only contain fragments. While there are no manuscripts from the fifteenth to the seventeenth centuries, there are several manuscripts from the eighteenth century.

Printed editions began to appear when J. Grinaeus published nine of the letters by John "the Prophet" in Basel in 1569, to-

---

20. Cf. S. Vailhé, "Les lettres spirituelles de Jean et de Barsanuphe," *Echos d'Orient* 7 (1904): 274. See also I. Hausherr, "Barsanuphe (saint)," *Dictionnaire de spiritualité* 1:1262 (Paris, 1937).

21. J. Pargoire, *L'église byzantine de 527 à 847* (Paris, 1905), 274–75.

22. The 1971 edition of the Solesmes translation also includes the letters translated from the Georgian by B. Ottier. See L. Regnault, Ph. Lemaire, and B. Ottier, trans., *Barsanuphe et Jean de Gaza: Correspondance* (Sable-sur-Sarthe: Abbaye de Solesmes, 1971).

23. Cf. G. Garitte, *Corpus Scriptorum Christianorum Orientalium*, vol. 165, Subsidia 9 (Louvain, 1956), 97 and 116–17. Also see E. Metreveli, *Collection sinaïtique de l'Institut des Manuscrits* (Tblisi, 1978), 94 and 126–27.

gether with the works of Abba Dorotheus. In Paris in 1715, B. Montfaucon published the letters relating to Origenism, and more than a century later J.-P. Migne's *Patrologia Graeca*, also published in Paris, included *Letters* 600–604 of Barsanuphius and John, which deal with Origen, Evagrius, and Didymus, as well as all of the letters addressed to Dorotheus of Gaza.[24]

The work of translating the correspondence commenced in the late eighteenth century, when several translations appeared in Moldavian, Slavonic,[25] and even in Russian. Although partial in some of their early editions, these translations were all complete by the end of the nineteenth century.

For the present translation I have used both manuscript and contemporary sources, consulting Bodleian Cromwell 18 (B) from Oxford as well as Vatopedi 2 from Mt. Athos. I have also relied on the text adopted by the most recent French edition, which is both critical and careful in its scholarship. I have, however, also consulted the partial English edition and translation of Derwas Chitty[26] as well as those of the modern Greek publication by the Monastery of St. John the Forerunner in Kareas, Athens.[27] Finally, I have referred to the edition by Nikodemus of Mt. Athos, the first complete edition of Barsanuphius and John, based on texts in several Athonite monasteries and originally published in Venice in 1816; this work was reprinted by S. Schoinas in Volos in 1960.[28]

The translation at hand is the first complete rendering in English and the first from the Greek original. A partial translation by Seraphim Rose in 1990 was based on the Russian edi-

---

24. See PG 86.892–901 for letters discussing Origen, Evagrius, and Didymus, and PG 88.1812–20 for letters to Dorotheus.

25. The Moldavian and early Slavonic translations were directed by Paissy Velichkovsky on the basis of an Athonite manuscript as early as 1794.

26. Chitty translated and published 124 letters in 1966, not long before his death in 1971. He compared Coislianus 124, Vatopedi 2, Nikodemus, and Sinaiticus 411S for his critical edition. He had, however, also prepared the draft of a translation for *Letters* 125–249. A copy of this text exists in the library of St. Gregory's House in Oxford, England.

27. Another Greek translation has been published by Byzantion Editions; see *Barsanuphius and John: Questions and Responses*, in *Philokalia*, 3 vols. (Thessalonika: Byzantion Editions, 1988–1989).

28. Nikodemus's text contains certain repetitions as well as certain errors and *lacunae*, partly corrected by Schoinas.

tion of 1855. I have endeavored to remain as faithful to the original text as possible, without, however, losing the spontaneous flavor of the letters themselves. In the instances where the Greek heading simply reads, "From the same to the same," I have elaborated, depending on the context, to say, "Letter from the same person (or brother) to the same Old Man." I sometimes refer to the responses as "answers" wherever they are juxtaposed to questions, but always as "responses" when they refer to the actual communications from the Old Men. This designation conveys the profound sense of responsibility with which the two elders speak as well as the dignity with which they treat those approaching them for spiritual counsel.

Any translation will inevitably and almost naturally resonate with the vibrant conversational style of these occasional and personal letters of the Old Men. This personal element is perhaps the most appealing to a contemporary reader. To this purpose, I have avoided—so far as this is possible—the use of foreign terms, no matter how established. Moreover, with regard to proper names, where there is a particular usage established, even to a certain degree in English translations of primary sources and existing secondary sources, such as in the case of Barsanuphius and Dorotheus, I have—in spite of seeming technical inconsistency—chosen to retain the latinized form; elsewhere I have preserved the graecized form, as in the case of Seridos and Aelianos, since there is no reason to modify these names.

Furthermore, I have translated κοινόβιον as "monastic community" rather than leaving it as *coenobium*, in order also to distinguish it from μοναστήριον (*Letter* 390) and μονή (*Letter* 582), which I have translated as "monastery." The latter terms normally refer to the monastery as a site, whereas the former term usually relates to the common life shared by the monks of the establishment, among whom may also be included the loose community of monks living either within or around the monastery proper.

LETTERS

VOLUME 1

PROLOGUE

[TITLE 1]

Letters and responses of two spiritual elders, named Barsanuphius and John, who lived in stillness near a monastic community called that of Abba Seridos in the region of Gaza;[1] these letters were conveyed through that abbot, namely, the same Abba Seridos who also ministered to them.

[TITLE 2]

Edifying teachings of the holy Barsanuphius and of John, his disciple and fellow-ascetic, which they conveyed through letters to brethren inquiring by way of Abba Seridos, who ministered to them and was himself the abbot of the monastic community in the region of Gaza, where these holy elders lived in stillness.

PROLOGUE

E ENTREAT THOSE who read this book to accept whatever is written here with gratitude, reverence, and faith, and to endeavor above all to arrive—by the grace of Christ—to the point of imitating the life and good deeds of those who spoke these words. For having trained their own life over a long period of time through endurance and faith according to God, and having, in the words of the holy Apostle, struggled "according to the rules,"[2] following the way of the holy fathers in all things, they became worthy of truly great gifts from God.

As we are about to read this book, however, we are obliged to know that some of these words were spoken to anchorites, oth-

---

1. The most specific reference in the *Letters* to the location of the community. Gaza is probably the unidentified city featured in *Letters* 792–844.

2. 2 Tm 2.5. Where my own translation of a biblical quotation appearing in these letters and responses does not differ significantly from that of the New Revised Standard Version, the latter has been used. It must be kept in mind, however, that patristic writers did not cite Scripture in a uniform way because of variations among ancient versions or because of a lapse of memory when the biblical text was not at hand.

ers to cenobites, still others to those living together, and yet others to priests and Christ-loving laypersons.[3] Moreover, some were intended for younger monastics or novices, others for those already advanced in age and disciplined in their habits, and still others for those approaching the perfection of virtue—as each was able to receive the words. For not all the same teachings are suitable for everyone. Just as in the ages of the body, different foods are appropriate for the breast-feeding child, for the adolescent, and for the elderly, the same also happens in the spiritual stages. Often, these elders responded to questions bearing in mind the weakness in the thoughts of the persons inquiring, discreetly condescending to their level in order that those asking might not fall into despair, just as we find in the *Lives of the Old Men*. So we must not receive as a general rule the words spoken in a loving way to particular people for the sake of their specific weakness; instead, we should immediately discern that the response was surely addressed by the saints to the questioner in a very personal way. For it may happen that such persons will one day come to their senses through the prayers of the saints, thereby reaching a condition appropriate for monks, and then they will again hear what is beneficial to them.

I entreat you in the Lord to remember also my humble person[4] in your holy prayers. For I have, by God's help, transmitted here in writing these responses for the benefit of those who read them with fear of God, so that the words of the saints may not be for me unto judgment, but rather that I may be protected by their prayers as well as yours, now and to the day of judgment. Amen.

---

3. The adjectival "Christ-loving" refers to a layperson, namely, someone who is neither ordained to the clergy nor tonsured as a monastic.

4. It is not clear whether the person writing is the compiler or a copyist. Indeed, it is unclear whether this person even knew the Old Men.

LETTERS TO JOHN OF BEERSHEBA (1–54)

LETTER 1

Response from the Great Old Man to Abba John of Beersheba, who asked to come and live with them in the monastic community [namely, of Seridos].

T IS WRITTEN in the Apostle: "The one who began a good work among you will also bring it to completion by the day of our Lord Jesus Christ."[1] And again our Master said to the one who approached him: "None can become my disciple if he does not give up all his possessions," and his family, "and hate his own life, too."[2] It is possible for God to inform us about the verse: "Behold, what a good and pleasant thing it is for brothers to dwell together in the same place."[3] I pray that you will attain to the measure described in Acts, that "as many as owned properties sold them, and brought the proceeds of what was sold and laid it at the apostles' feet."[4] Knowing your godly intention, I said to our beloved son, Seridos, who after God protects us from people[5]—and we hope to God that he will also protect you together with us: "Receive our brother John with much love, and do not hesitate at all; for two years ago God revealed to me that he would be coming here, and that many brothers would be gathering around us; however, I kept this revelation until I learned precisely what the Lord was doing. Now, then, that the time is fulfilled, I have also declared it

---

1. Phil 1.6.
2. Cf. Lk 14.33, 26.
3. Ps 132.1 LXX. The Psalm numbering here, as elsewhere in this volume, is that of the Septuagint.
4. Acts 4.34.
5. A reference to Seridos protecting the silence, invisibility, and inaccessibility of Barsanuphius.

to you."[6] And since you have reckoned that I should provide you with something that I wear, behold, in the presence of the same brother, I have removed the cowl from my head and sent it with him to you, saying: "Give this to him, and bring me another in its place." Keep it then until the end of your life. For it will protect you from many evils and trials. Do not give it to anyone else. For it is a blessing of God from my hands. Strive to complete your work and to be released from all obligations, just as we would do; and come settle with us, carefree, dedicating your time to God.

And I, Seridos, moreover, tell you something else wonderful. As the Old Man said this, I thought to myself: "How can I remember all these things in order to write them down? Had the Old Man so wanted, I could have brought here some ink and paper, heard his words one by one, and then recorded them." But he knew what I was thinking, and his face shone like fire, and he said to me: "Go ahead, write; do not be afraid. Even if I tell you ten thousand words, the Spirit of God will not let you write even one letter too much or too little. And not because you so wish, but because it is guiding your hand to record these things in a coherent manner."

LETTER 2

Response from the same Great Old Man to the same person, predicting the various afflictions that would befall him, including his bodily illness, as well as the progress of the soul that would follow all these, and the ensuing blessedness.

Tell brother John: "Establish your heart firm as a rock,"[7] and I am referring to the intellectual rock, in order to be able to hear what I am going to say. Pay attention then to yourself,[8] lest hearing this you become proud in your heart and fall from your spiritual promise. For boasting has ruined many people, even

---

6. Barsanuphius is characterized by the gift of foresight. See also *Letters* 4, 16, and 31.

7. Cf. 1 Sm 2.1.

8. "Pay attention to yourself" (πρόσεχε σεαυτῷ) is a phrase found frequently in the Gaza literature, and especially in the writings of Abba Isaiah. See, for example, Isaiah, *Ascetic Discourse* 27.

those who have attained to a certain measure. Rather, prepare yourself for thanksgiving in all circumstances, having heard the holy Apostle saying: "In every circumstance, give thanks."[9] Thus, whether "in affliction" or "in hardship," "in distress" or "in weakness" and bodily "labor,"[10] in all things that come upon you, give thanks to God.

I hope that you, too, are able to "enter his rest."[11] For "it is through many persecutions that we must enter the kingdom of God."[12] So do not doubt in your soul, and do not let your heart grow faint in anything, but remember the words of the Apostle, that "even though our outward person may perish, yet our inner person is being renewed day by day."[13] Therefore, if you do not endure sufferings, you cannot reach the cross. If in the first place, however, you endure sufferings, you will enter the harbor of his rest and afterward live silently and entirely carefree, with your soul established and clinging to the Lord in everything, guarded in faith, rejoicing in hope, made glad in love, and protected in the holy and consubstantial Trinity. Then, the saying will be fulfilled in you: "Let the heavens be glad and let the earth rejoice."[14] This is the carefree life of a man of God. For the Father and the Son and the Holy Spirit rejoice at the salvation of your soul, my beloved brother.

LETTER 3

Response from the Other Old Man to the same, when the latter asked to meet him.

Tell the brother: Forgive me for the Lord's sake, for I also desire to see you; but, for the sake of the others' conscience, I am not at liberty to do this. I rejoice, however, with your love at the promises sent to you by the holy Old Man.[15] And you are blessed to have been made worthy of these.

---

9. 1 Thes 5.18.
10. Cf. 2 Cor 6.4–5 and 12.10.
11. Heb 4.1.
12. Acts 14.22.
13. 2 Cor 4.16.
14. Ps 95.11.
15. See the response by Abba John to the monk Andrew in *Letter* 79.

LETTER 4

When temptation was stirred up among the monks of the place where Abba John lived before coming to the monastic community, and turmoil was again about to be stirred up while he was still there, the Great Old Man foresaw this spiritually, and wrote the following to him.

Write to brother John: Behold, I am sending you three testimonies from the power of God and from the Scriptures of the Holy Spirit, through which I am awakening your intellect to the vigilance of God and to the understanding of the Holy Spirit, so that you may know what the present time means. The first testimony is this: God said through the holy prophet Isaiah, "Come, my people, enter your chambers and shut the door behind you in hiding for a little, until the wrath of the Lord is past."[16] The second testimony is this: "Come out from them, and be separate from them, and touch nothing unclean, says the Lord; and then I shall welcome you, and I will be for you a father, and you shall be for me sons and daughters, says the Lord Almighty."[17] And the third testimony: "Be careful then as to how you live, not as unwise people but as wise, making the most of your time, because the days are evil."[18] But I tell you, run toward the things that lie before you, and complete your work quickly, remembering the Lord, who says: "No person who puts a hand to the plow and looks back is fit for the kingdom of heaven";[19] and, "let the dead bury their own dead; as for you, go and proclaim the gospel of the kingdom of heaven."[20] For I can see your life of stillness, which awaits you in Christ Jesus our Lord, to whom be glory to the ages. Amen.

LETTER 5

Response from the same Great Old Man to the abbot, when the latter was grieving that Abba John had delayed in arriving, and thought as a result that he might not come.

16. Is 26.20.
18. Eph 5.15–16.
20. Lk. 9.60.

17. 2 Cor 6.17–18.
19. Lk 9.62.

Do not lose heart, my child, nor be saddened about our brother. Even "if he is absent in body, yet he is present in spirit"[21] and is with us continually. For he is one in soul with us, and no one separates him from our love now and to the ages.

LETTER 6

Letter from the same Great Old Man written to the same Abba John, when the latter was disturbed by bodily warfare while carrying out certain duties in his region for the monastic community.

Write to our brother: While you are still outside carrying out your labor, to the best of your ability, for the sake of God and for the souls of the brothers, or rather for the sake of our and your own rest and stillness—for if the brothers find rest and protection through us, we, too, find perfect stillness through them, and the written word is fulfilled in us: "A brother assisted by a brother is like a city fortified with ramparts"[22]—do away with all relationships and excuses that you may have while you are still outside, and do not allow any excuse or relationship with any person that may draw you backward. If you do not do this, you will not be able to live in perfect stillness. For this is also how we conducted ourselves. Therefore, if you do this, I hope that your stillness will be perfect. For, with God, your lot is indeed with us, and your portion is with us forever. Let no one learn yet what we are writing to you. So when you perform your labor, if the work prospers in your eyes, give thanks to God and pray to him. For this is what is meant by: "In all circumstances, give thanks."[23]

And let us not neglect to render thanks to God, like the one about whom you once told the story that he used to go to pray in church so that he might secure food. Then he once met someone who said: "Have breakfast with me today, and then go pray," but he replied: "I cannot go; for that is what I was going to ask from God [in prayer]." Instead, whether we find what we want or not, we should offer prayer and thanks to God. And see

21. 1 Cor 5.3.   22. Prv 18.19.
23. 1 Thes 5.18.

that you bear "the death of Jesus in your body"[24] through every-thing.

Response from the same Great Old Man to the same person, when the latter was about to depart with the brothers in order to collect their handiwork, but was afraid of the desert region; and a reminder to be watchful against the bodily warfare that was bothering him; and a promise of God's assistance in the with-drawal to their community, for which he strove.

Say to him who has been called from above and by the di-vine will to dwell with us not only in this age but also in the age to come, namely, to our genuine brother, John, who is our soul mate,[25] that Christ our Master told his disciples: "Are not two sparrows sold for a penny? And yet not one of them will fall to the ground without my Father who is in heaven. As for you, even the hairs of your head are numbered. So do not be afraid. You are of much greater value than sparrows. Whoever there-fore will confess me before others, I shall also confess that per-son before my Father who is in heaven."[26]

Pay attention then to yourself with vigilance, that you may keep God before you at all times, in order that the words of the prophet will be fulfilled concerning you: "I saw the Lord before my face at all times; for he is at my right hand, so that I shall not be moved."[27] Stretch out your hands, then, with all your soul to the things that lie before you, and meditate on this continually, so that you may hear the voice of God speaking to you: "Behold, I am sending my angel before your face, to prepare your way be-fore you."[28]

The same person, having toiled a great deal, but not finding his handiwork, grew sad and wondered why an angel had not been

24. 2 Cor 4.10.
25. Lit., "of one soul with us" (ὁμοψύχῳ).
26. Mt 10.29–32. 27. Ps 15.8.
28. Mt 11.10; Mk 1.2; Mal 3.1.

sent to him for assistance, according to the Old Man's word. For he did not understand that this had been said to him in order to make his withdrawal [to the community] easier. So the Old Man writes the following to him.

Write to our brother: So long as the boat is at sea, always expect dangers and the onset of winds. When, however, it arrives in the harbor of stillness and peace, it no longer fears dangers, distress, or the onset of winds, but will be calm. Thus it is also with your love. So long as you are among people, you should expect distress, dangers, and the onset of intellectual winds. But when you reach the things that have been prepared for you, then you will have no fear.

In regard to what I told you earlier, our Master said: "Behold, I am sending my angel before your face";[29] and he was sent indeed. In regard to not finding handiwork, however, God said in the Mosaic Scripture: "For this reason, he surrounded you and chastened you, letting you hunger in that terrible desert, [testing you] to know what was in your heart."[30] Understand the things I am saying to you, and labor steadily and without hesitation, dear brother.

LETTER 9

Letter from the same Great Old Man to the same, when the latter went off on some business of the monastic community but was discouraged because he experienced great distress there.

My child, write to our brother John, greeting him in the Lord on my and your behalf, as well as on behalf of our brother John. Tell him: "Do not lose heart in your sufferings"[31] and in the bodily labors that you endure and undergo for us and for our monastic community. For this, too, is part of "laying down your life for"[32] your brothers. I hope that your reward will be great as a result of this labor; and just as God appointed Joseph to feed his brothers during the famine in Egypt, so also has he appointed you to help the monastic community with our child, Seridos.

29. Ibid.
31. Eph 3.13.

30. Dt 8.2–3.
32. Jn 15.13.

I tell you the words of the Apostle to Timothy: "You then, child, be strong in the grace of the Holy Spirit."[33]

I can see how your time of stillness is about to come; and I rejoice with you in the Lord. For so long as you dwell outside, you will experience distress and bodily labor. But when you reach the harbor of stillness, you will find rest and peace. Our Master does not lie when he says: "I will give them one hundredfold in this age, and life eternal in the age to come."[34] Therefore labor eagerly, brother, so that you may find all the more love and rest. For before the boat reaches the harbor, it is beaten and tossed by the waves and the storms. But once it reaches the harbor, it then finds itself in great calm. Perceive what I am saying, and preserve it. "And may the Lord give you understanding in all things."[35]

LETTER 10

Response from the Great Old Man to the same, when a stone fell on his foot, causing him much pain and disheartenment.

To our beloved brother John, greetings in the Lord. According to your bodily labor for our sake, and the crushing of your spirit for God's sake, may God our Master fill your soul, my beloved one, one hundredfold with heavenly blessings. Understand what I am writing to you, brother, and conceal it within yourself. I shall make you hear a heavenly joy that is sovereign and divine. For in the name of the Holy Trinity, I find that you are a co-heir of the gifts that I have been given by God. And I expect that step-by-step you will quickly acquire them. Indeed, it is possible for someone to reach the point of rest quickly through labor for God. Again it is possible for another person to reach the same thing through humility. And I hope that you will have both of these, as wrath dies in you when anger is choked from your heart. Then, the written word will be fulfilled in you: "Consider my affliction and my trouble, and forgive all my sins."[36]

And since I said that you will acquire these gifts step-by-step, look at the Gospels, how—and how often—Christ gave gifts to

---

33. 2 Tm 2.1.   34. Mk 10.30.
35. 2 Tm 2.7.   36. Ps 24.18.

the disciples, whether for the purpose of healing or casting out demons, telling them of the final perfection in regard to forgiveness of sins: "If you forgive the sins of any, they are forgiven them."[37] Therefore, if on account of your labor for the sake of God, your sins are forgiven, this is precisely the measure that I want you to attain.

If you read in this letter any words that are difficult to understand, ask Seridos, who is of one soul with you and a beloved son to me; he will explain to you the difficult passages through the grace of God. For I have prayed to God for him about this matter. "You then, as a man of God,"[38] should unceasingly run the way that is prepared for you, in order to reach with joy the harbor of Christ, which we, too, have reached, and hear the voice that is full of joy, [light,][39] life, and gladness, saying to you: "Well done, good and faithful servant; you have been faithful in a few things; I will put you in charge of many things; enter into the joy of your Lord."[40]

Rejoice in the Lord; rejoice in the Lord; rejoice in the Lord. May the Lord guard your soul and body and spirit from every evil, as well as from every opposition of the devil and every troubling imagination. The Lord will be your light, your protection, your way, your strength, "your crown of gladness,"[41] and your eternal help. Pay attention to yourself. For it is written: "Even the word that goes out from my lips will not be altered."[42]

LETTER 11

Response from the same Great Old Man to the same, advising him continually [to remember] the things written to him for his benefit and for the support of his heart.

Solomon said about his parents: "They taught me and said, 'Let our word be established in your heart.'"[43] So I also say to you, brother, let my words be established in your heart, and meditate continually on all that I have written to you, just as

---

37. Jn 20.23.
38. 1 Tm 6.11.
39. "Light" omitted from some manuscripts; see *SC* 426, 182.
40. Mt 25.21.   41. Cf. Sir 1.11.
42. Ps 88.35.   43. Prv 4.4.

God said through the mouth of Moses: "Bind them on your right hand, and they shall remain steadily before your eyes at all times; and study them when you are lying down and standing up, when you travel and sit at home."[44] Show the same progress in the perfection of your works, and my God will be with you to the ages. Amen.

LETTER 12

The same person commanded a brother to perform a task; but when the latter did not complete this task quickly, he rebuked him. When that brother grieved, he thought he should not say anything to any of the other brothers. At this, the Old Man made the following clear to him.

Tell brother John that the times are sensitive and it is with great difficulty that you will find in these times any person with a firm heart. But keep the word of the holy Apostle, who says: "Reprove, rebuke, and encourage with the utmost long-suffering and through teaching."[45]

LETTER 13

When some construction was taking place in the monastic community, he drew up the measurements of the building, since he was skilled in this. Without his knowing, however, some of the brothers thought that it was a good thing to add to these and somewhat spoiled them. When he became angry and grew faint-hearted toward them, the Old Man declared to them the following words.

Tell brother John, who is of one mind with us, that I have written many things to you through the hand of our genuine and beloved child, who loves all three of us equally, with all his soul and in perfect love. And I am not writing all this of my own will, but at the command of the Holy Spirit, entirely for the benefit and correction of the soul and conscience of the inner person, for the affliction and discipline of your body and the contrition of your heart.

---

44. Dt 6.7–8.
45. 2 Tm 4.2.

First, watch against the spirit of despondency. For it gives birth to every evil and diverse thing. If I write to you about the temptations that I have endured, nevertheless I say to you that your ears are not able to bear it, and neither perhaps are the ears of anyone else in this age. I hope, however, that you will attain to this; and, even more than this, I hope that you will see them with your own eyes, and be delivered from them by the grace of Christ through faith.

Why is your heart exhausted through weariness toward Christ's sheep? Do you not know what headaches a good teacher endures from his pupils until they reach success? As for the apostolic word that you have heard from me, namely: "Reprove, rebuke, and encourage with the utmost long-suffering and through teaching,"[46] listen and pay attention to what I tell you. Long-suffering is the mother of all good things. Look at how Moses chose for himself "to share in suffering affliction with the people of God, rather than to enjoy the fleeting pleasures of sin."[47]

When, therefore, any thought from the demon troubles you in regard to someone, tell your thought with long-suffering: "Did I become subject to God in order to subject others?" And the thought will cease from you. Run with steadfastness and strength, remembering my words, or rather the Lord's words, that you, too, may overtake us in Christ Jesus our Lord. Amen. So be it; so be it.

LETTER 14

Response from the same Great Old Man to the same because he took it to heart when he heard one of the brothers ridiculing him, saying: "Who is this man, and where is he from, that he is so distressed?"

Tell the brother, that just as "Michael" contended [with the devil] "about the body of Moses,"[48] so, too, do I struggle on your behalf until you are rid of the old self.[49] For the Jews murmured about the Savior, saying: "Is not this the son of Joseph? Do we

---

46. 2 Tm 4.2.   47. Heb 11.25.
48. Jude 9.   49. Cf. Eph 4.22.

not know his mother and his [brothers]?"[50] Understand these
things, and endure to the end.[51]

Response from the same Great Old Man to the same person,
who was not yet cleansed of this faint-heartedness.

Tell the brother that I remember the prophecy of the holy
prophet Jeremiah, who says: "Who will give water to my head,
and a fountain of tears to my eyes, so that I might weep for this
people day and night?"[52] For I expected to nourish you with solid food, but I see that you require milk again.[53] Look at what
is written: "Cleanse me from my hidden faults."[54] Watch that
the wicked dragons do not steal you and inject you with their
poison. For it is deadly. No person ever corrects good with evil;
for that person is overcome by evil. Instead, evil is corrected by
good.[55]

Behold, then, you are standing in the stadium. It is your duty
"to fight with the wild animals," as the Apostle did "in Ephe-
sus."[56] For it was after he conquered the beasts that he boasted.
You have been thrown into the turmoil of the sea, to endure
many dangers and to struggle against the storm of the waves.
And then, when you have conquered with the help of God, you
will enter with us into the harbor of calm, in Christ Jesus our
Lord, to whom be glory.

Response from the same Great Old Man to the same, when he
was about to become angry at the brothers for allowing the bricks
to be spoiled by the rain. For he attributed this to their own laziness. And foreseeing that he was also going to blame the abbot
for this, he forewarns him and alerts him to guard his thoughts,
reminding him also of the genuine love that the abbot has to-

---

50. Cf. Jn 6.42.   51. Cf. Mt 10.22.
52. Jer 9.1.   53. Cf. Heb 5.12–14; 1 Cor 3.2.
54. Ps 18.13.   55. Cf. Rom 12.21.
56. 1 Cor 15.32.

ward him, in order that through this reminder he may cast away any contrary thought.

Do me a favor, my child, and quickly bring me paper and ink. Leave aside the business for which you came here; and first write a note of greeting from me to brother John. For he is working on troubling others and being troubled by them. And tell him: Rejoice in the Lord, my brother. If the waves of the sea are many, is there no person to awaken Jesus, that "he may rebuke the winds and the sea, that there may be a dead calm" for us to perceive and worship Jesus?[57] If all is vain and temporary, why is it that our heart is still made to forget the Gospel saying: "What will it profit anyone to gain the whole world and forfeit the soul?"[58]

You should learn, my brother, that if any person causes someone distress, whether in deed or in word, that person will afterward be personally distressed one hundredfold. And I have often written the scriptural words of the Lord to you: to be long-suffering in all things and to be careful that your will is not mixed with anything else. But, if you send me the question with my beloved son, Seridos, who is always distressed when he sees you distressed, at least strive to be accurate with your thoughts, so that they do not interject a deadly poison into your heart, and so that you are not deceived in considering a gnat as being a camel,[59] or a pebble as being a stone, like the person with the beam who noticed the splinter.[60]

I have written to you as if to my own soul. For I know that your heart would rejoice in this. Indeed, it is said: "Give instruction to the wise," and so forth.[61] And you know how I hold you in the love of Christ. I hope that you are close to being carefree from now on in regard to earthly matters, and close to finding yourself occupied in the spiritual work of the fathers. For Christ my Lord will not put me to shame after I pray to him about you day and night.[62]

---

57. Mt 8.26.
58. Mt 16.26.
59. Cf. Mt 23.24.
60. Cf. Mt 7.3.
61. Cf. Prv 9.8.
62. Cf. 2 Tm 1.3.

LETTER 17

Question from the same to the same Great Old Man: "I know, father, that these things happen to me on account of my sins, and that I lack good sense and am the cause of evil. Yet the one who brings me to this distress is the abbot, because he is neglectful and overlooks things. As a result of this, they are destroyed, and I cannot bear this. So what should I do? For I respond to these thoughts and do not receive any strength [to deal with them]. And forgive me, that 'once I have spoken, but I shall not add to it a second time.'[63] Yet I marvel at how that warmth of my love for the abbot and the brothers has grown cold. Pray for me for the Lord's sake." Response.

Brother, remember what the Lord said to his disciples: "Are you also still without understanding?"[64] For I wrote to you, saying: "Be accurate with your thoughts." If you had toiled to be accurate, you would have learned that the essence of what you have just asked me I have already responded to you. So there was no need for me to write [again]. Still, I shall tell you more in regard to your questions.

First, however, I shall rebuke you. For you called yourself a sinner, but in your deeds you did not consider yourself in this way. For one who considers oneself a sinner and the cause of evil is neither argumentative nor contentious nor angry against anyone else, but always considers everyone else to be better and wiser. If your thoughts ridicule you, telling you that you are such a [sinful] person, then how is it that they move your heart against those who are better than you? Be careful, brother; you are not telling the truth. For we have still not reached the point of considering ourselves sinners. If anyone loves the person who rebukes him, then that person is wise. But if anyone [says he] loves, but does not do what he hears from that person, then this is actually tantamount to hatred. If you are a sinner, why do you blame and accuse your neighbor, claiming that he is the cause of your distress? Do you not know that one is tempted by one's own conscience, and this is what brings about personal

63. Jb 40.5.
64. Mt 15.16; Mk 7.18.

distress? That is why I wrote to you about your brothers, that "they should not make a gnat into a camel,"[65] and so on. Pray, rather, that you may be sharers in the fear of God.

As for saying about yourself that you lack good sense, do not deceive yourself, but search and you shall discover that this is not the case. If in fact you believe that it is, then you should not become angry, since you would be unable to discern whether things are right or wrong. For a senseless person is called foolish. And a senseless, foolish person implies a person lacking salt. So how can a person lacking salt season and salt others? See, brother, how we are deceived when we speak only with our mouth, but our deeds show us to be otherwise. Thus, when we respond to such thoughts, we do not receive any strength, because first we find it acceptable to criticize our neighbor, and so the strength of our spirit is weakened, and then we blame our brother when we ourselves are at fault. If you claim that everything depends on "God who shows mercy" and "not on human will or exertion,"[66] then why do you not understand and love your brother with all your heart and in perfect love? For how many have desired to acquire us as [their] elders, and strove to achieve this purpose, but were not successful?[67] Yet, while he[68] sat still, God sent us to him, and made him our genuine child. For God loves the inner disposition.

As for your claim, that "I have spoken once,"[69] and so on, if you are fighting to win, you are blessed. For this is not granted to everyone. And as for the other thoughts, refer them all to God, saying: "God knows what is best"; then you will find rest and your strength to endure will gradually return. Now, do not completely refrain from speaking. If, however, you do speak and are not heard, nor find favor in your words, do not be sad; for this is rather to your benefit. Rather, in regard to the things that

65. Cf. Mt 23.24.
66. Rom 9.16.
67. This alludes to the desire of several monastic communities to have the renowned elders, Barsanuphius and John, settle in their region. Moreover, it further indicates the established reputation, not only of Barsanuphius but also of John.
68. That is, Seridos.
69. Jb 40.5.

you admire, perfect love is without failing,[70] and one who ob-
tains it remains in its warmth, embraced in love toward God and
neighbor. Nevertheless, in regard to the prayers that you recently requested, you ought to be satisfied with [the promise] I gave
you: "I am praying ceaselessly to God for you night and day."[71]
So this, too, was unnecessary for you to write. You have divine
food from me to last you a long time. Persevere, and "wait patiently for the Lord,"[72] in Christ Jesus our Lord. To him be the
glory to the ages. Amen.

LETTER 18

Response from the same Great Old Man to the same, when the
latter asked whence the warmth, coldness, and hardness of heart
come about, as well as about bodily warfare.

On warmth and coldness, it is clear that the Lord has been
called "fire,"[73] warming and burning "hearts and minds."[74] If it
is so, then the devil is cold, and all coldness comes from him.
For if it were not so, how then is it said that "then the love of
many will grow cold"?[75] What else does the word "then" signify,
but "the times of the adversary"? Therefore, if we feel coldness,
let us call upon God, and he will come and warm our heart in
his perfect love, not only toward him but also toward our neighbor. And the face of his warmth will banish the coldness of that
hater of good.

Now if [the devil] has dried up the fountain of your heart's
tears, and has moistened your underbelly, nevertheless continue to feast the Lord "in your house"[76] and [the Lord] will dry
up the latter, purifying the fountain of your tears for the flowing of spiritual[77] water. One who wishes to attain the fear of God
does so through patience. For it is said: "I waited patiently for
the Lord, and he gave heed to me and heard my prayer." And
what else? "He drew me up from the desolate pit, and out of the
miry bog."[78] It is from such a pit that hardness of heart is also

---

70. Cf. 1 Cor 13.8.
72. Ps 26.14.
74. Pss 7.9 and 25.2.
76. Lk 19.5.
78. Ps 39.1–2.

71. Cf. 2 Tm 1.3.
73. Dt 4.24; Heb 12.29.
75. Mt 24.12.
77. Lit., "noetic" (νοητός).

thought to come. If you so desire, obtain this, and you will be saved, in Christ Jesus our Lord.

LETTER 19

Response from the same Great Old Man to the same about long-suffering.

Tell the brother: I have written to you about long-suffering, and now I tell you what our Master and God said to his disciples: "Behold, I have given you authority to tread on snakes and scorpions, and over all power of the enemy, and nothing will hurt you at all."[79] So become like Job, "drinking up scoffing like water."[80] Understand these things and meditate on them at all times.

LETTER 20

Response from the same Great Old Man to the same, when the latter asked: "If the Lord has 'given [us] authority to tread on snakes and scorpions,'[81] then how is it that I am still troubled?"

No one who has received "authority to tread on snakes and scorpions"[82] is any longer hurt or mastered by them. Therefore, examine your heart in regard to every matter. If your heart is moved even slightly, then know that you are still far from receiving authority against these. And do not neglect yourself, lest your time runs out; but whenever you see something developing—but why am I talking about things of the world, when they are temporary, instead of talking about fearful things, whether in heaven or on earth?—set God and the [final] judgment before your eyes, remembering that we have only little time to spend in this world.

And make gentleness find rest in your heart, recalling Christ, the Sheep and Lamb that was without guile,[83] and how many things he endured though he was without guilt, such as the insults, the scourging, and all the rest. Remember that we on the other hand are guilty; so why are we moved against our neigh-

---

79. Lk 10.19.   80. Jb 34.7.
81. Lk 10.19.   82. Ibid.
83. Cf. Is 53.7.

bor, when we have not been wronged by him? Remember also that "love is not arrogant" but "is long-suffering,"[84] and so on. And pray that you will attain to what is set before you, that your "labor may not be in vain."[85] Therefore, cleave without hesitation to Christ, who loves us. To him be the glory to the ages. Amen.

LETTER 21

Response from the same Great Old Man to the same, when he intended not to order anyone to do anything, but instead decreed for himself some obvious matter, so that he might only focus attention on himself.

Brother, the more I write to you, the more you should strive to understand the things that I write to you and not to invalidate them. For my words are spoken in understanding and in a stable condition of soul. You know, brother, that whoever does not endure insults does not behold the glory; and whoever does not lay aside the gall does not taste the sweetness. You have been placed in the midst of other brothers and their affairs in order to be burned and tried. For unless gold passes through fire, it is not proven. Do not give yourself any order at all, since you are already going through warfare and concerns, but with fear of God test those things that are appropriate for each moment; and do "nothing" at all "in contentiousness,"[86] but do everything you can to be foreign to wrath, becoming a model that is beneficial to all, neither criticizing nor condemning anyone, but counseling them as genuine brothers. Instead, love those who test you. For I, too, often loved those who tested me. If we are prudent, it is such people who bring us to progress.[87]

Therefore, do not set any decrees for yourself. Become obedient and humble; and be demanding of yourself each day. For the prophet also indicated what should be done daily, in telling us: "And I said, Now I have begun";[88] and Moses also said: "So

---

84. 1 Cor 13.4.   85. 1 Thes 3.5.
86. Phil 2.3.
87. Cf. Abba Zosimas, *Reflections* 3. For an introduction to and translation of the *Reflections*, see Chryssavgis, *In the Heart of the Desert: The Spirituality of the Desert Fathers and Mothers* (Bloomington, IN: World Wisdom Books, 2003), 123–50.
88. Ps 76.10.

now, O Israel."[89] Therefore, you, too, should keep this "now." If, however, it is necessary for you to give any order to someone, then test your thought to see whether this arises from some emotion. And if it still appears beneficial to you, conceal it beneath your tongue, immediately remembering the one who said: "What will it profit anyone to gain the whole world, but forfeit the soul?"[90]

And learn this, too, my brother: every thought that does not previously possess the calmness of humility is not according to God but is clearly a form of righteousness coming from the left hand. For our Lord comes with calmness, whereas all that comes from the adversary occurs with turmoil and the commotion of wrath; indeed, if they seem to put on "sheep's clothing," you should know that "inwardly, they are ravenous wolves."[91] So they are manifested by their turmoil. For it is said: "You shall know them by their fruits."[92]

May God grant all of us this understanding, so that we may not be led astray into their [forms of] righteousness. For "all things are naked and laid bare" to him.[93] Therefore, beloved, do everything that prospers in your hands, setting the fear of God before your eyes and giving thanks to him. For his is the glory, might, and power to the ages. Amen.

LETTER 22

Response from the same Great Old Man to the same, encouraging him and recalling him to spiritual gladness from the disheartenment that he variously experienced.

Address a spiritual letter to brother John in order to gladden his heart in Christ Jesus our Lord; and tell him: since "as a deer longs for flowing streams, so also"[94] do you long for us, but not as we for you; thus, "I could bear it no longer,"[95] as the most divine Apostle Paul said, and I have written to your love the following things that have been spoken by me, or rather by God.

---

89. Dt 4.1 and 10.12.
91. Mt 7.15.
93. Heb 4.13.
95. 1 Thes 3.5.

90. Mt 16.26.
92. Mt 7.16.
94. Ps 41.1.

May your vine bear fruit with trodden grapes and make spiritual wine to gladden the distressed soul; and may your land bear plentiful and good seed, like that sown "in good ground and multiplied either one hundred times, or sixty times, or thirty times."[96] May that spiritual fire burn in your heart continually, of which our Master Christ spoke: "I came to cast fire upon the earth."[97] And "let the peace of the Lord rule in your heart,"[98] according to the words of the Apostle. May your palm tree be exalted in its branches, as David says: "The righteous will flourish like the palm tree."[99] And may you be cleansed from the anger and wrath of the terrible passions, like the perfected saints, in whom even the slightest [motion] of these things does not appear. May the Lord make your soul worthy "to abide"[100] in guilelessness and gentleness, so that you may be nurtured by Christ as a guileless sheep. May you discover our footsteps like a wise tracker. May you attain to our rule, as a good inheritor of my gifts. May your eyes "see God," as one who is "pure in heart."[101] May you be long-suffering in tribulation, as one who has reached the Master's commandment, which says: "In the world you will face tribulation; but take courage, for I have overcome the world."[102] May you attain to the invincible love, which leads those who have obtained it to the royal courts and renders them brothers of Christ. "Therefore, if you suffer with Christ in order that you may also be glorified with" him,[103] and "if you die with" him in order that "you may also be raised up with" him,[104] then do not neglect the treasure that lies before you. For you have not yet understood its power.

When you attain to perfect stillness, however, then you will know Christ and admire his gift, understanding "how inscrutable are his ways."[105] For while you are still among people, you cannot understand this. But when you rest carefree like us, then you will be able to understand those things spoken of here. I pray to God day and night, that, wherever we are, you also may

96. Mt 13.8, 23; Mk 4.8, 20.　97. Lk 12.49.
98. Col 3.15.　99. Ps 91.12.
100. Ps 24.13.　101. Mt 5.8.
102. Jn 16.33.　103. Rom 8.17.
104. 2 Tm 2.11; Col 2.12.　105. Rom 11.33.

be of one heart with us in the ineffable joy of the holy ones and in the eternal light, so that you will find your portion in the promise made to the saints, where "no eye has seen, nor any ear heard, nor the human heart conceived, of the things which God [has prepared] for those who love him."[106] Be strong in the Lord. Rejoice. Amen.

LETTER 23

Question by the same to the same Great Old Man: "I ask you, father and teacher, not to be angry with my faults, but to give me a rule about how I must behave in fasting, psalmody, and prayer; and is there any distinction to be drawn in this regard between the various days?" Response.

Brother, if you had paid attention to the words of your questions, you would have understood the power of wisdom. If I am your father and teacher, why do you want me to be angry? For a father is compassionate, having no wrath at all. And a teacher is long-suffering and foreign to wrath. But as for the rule about which you inquired, you are going around in expanding circles in order to "enter through the narrow gate that leads to life" eternal.[107] Behold, Christ tells you quite concisely how you must enter.

Leave aside human rules and listen to him, who says: "The one who endures to the end will be saved."[108] Therefore, the one who does not endure will not enter into life [eternal]. So do not look for a command. I do not want you to be "under law, but under grace."[109] For it is said: "The law is laid down not for the righteous."[110] We desire that you be among the righteous.

Retain discretion, like a helmsman steering the boat according to the winds. And when you are sick, act accordingly in all things as you have written; and when you are well, again act accordingly. For when the body, too, is unwell, it does not receive food normally. Thus a rule would prove worthless in this case,

106. 1 Cor 2.9.
107. Mt 7.13.
108. Mt 10.22 and 24.13; Mk 13.13.
109. Rom 6.14.
110. 1 Tm 1.9.

too. And in regard to the various days, treat them all as being equal, holy, and good. Do everything with understanding, and this will prove to be for you unto life in Christ Jesus our Lord. To him be the glory to the ages. Amen.

LETTER 24

When a dispute arose between the abbot and him about some scriptural passage, and each of them strove to be long-suffering, the Old Man sent them this response, showing that their long-suffering was not pure of turmoil, so that they might always be watchful to attain to a state of complete absence of turmoil.

Beloved child, do not think that it was of yourselves that you understood yesterday's chapter in the letter of the Apostle Paul to the Thessalonians. But, knowing that your vaunted patience was mingled with wrath, I prayed to God that you might understand it. For in this lies the entire meaning of the letters written by me, through you, to brother John. Not only that, but pay attention to the chapters that you will read today, namely, those of the Apostle Paul and of the holy Gospel, because they possess that meaning, too. Read them three times, examining the meaning of the words for the benefit of your soul. For I utterly support you and care for you in accord with God. Therefore, join me in the toil and struggle to cut off from yourselves wrath and anger. For we need to struggle, with the assistance of God.

The chapters I am speaking about are the following: from the First Letter to the Thessalonians, from the words: "But we appeal to you, brethren, to respect those who labor among you and have charge of you in the Lord,"[111] until the end of the letter; also from the First Letter to the Corinthians, from the words: "Now concerning the spiritual [gifts], brethren, we do not want you to be uninformed. You know that when you were pagans,"[112] until: "But in the church, I would rather speak five words with my understanding, in order also to instruct others, rather than ten thousand words in a tongue";[113] and from the Gospel of Matthew, from the words: "Then Jesus went out

111. 1 Thes 5.12.   112. 1 Cor 12.1.
113. 1 Cor 14.19.

and saw a great multitude, and he had compassion on them, and cured their sick,"[114] until: "And those in the boat worshiped him, saying 'Truly you are the Son of God.'"[115]

LETTER 25

Response from the same Great Old Man to the same person as well as to the abbot, when they wanted abruptly to tighten the rule of the brothers.

I say alike to you, my child, and to the brother: I have written before to both of you about long-suffering, and now I tell you this: "If you press milk, it will produce curds; but if you press the teat, it produces blood."[116] And again the holy Paul says: "To the Jews I became as a Jew, that I might gain the Jews,"[117] and so on. Later, he says: "I have become all things to all people, that I might by all means save some."[118] For if a person wants to bend a tree or a vine branch, then that person bends them gradually so that they do not break. However, if a person pulls them suddenly and forcefully, the thing breaks at once. Understand what I am saying.

LETTER 26

Response from the same Great Old Man to the same, when the latter revealed certain things that the Old Man had ordered him to tell no one; and afterward, he fell into temptation for this reason; and about perfect long-suffering.

Tell the brother: it is written: "Anyone who does not have the Spirit of God does not belong to God."[119] Pay attention to the source of the distraction and the constraint of the affliction that arises from these thoughts, to see whether they come from betrayal, namely, from transgressing my commandment. For I have often commanded you to tell no one about this secret,[120] and yet you have openly spoken of it to many people. Am I

114. Mt 14.14.   115. Mt 14.33.
116. Prv 30.33.   117. 1 Cor 9.20.
118. 1 Cor 9.22.   119. Rom 8.9.
120. Possibly the secret assurance from Barsanuphius to John that the latter would be the co-heir of the former in the gifts received from God. See *Letter* 10.

Christ, that when he commanded people to tell none, they nevertheless spread the word very publicly[121] to the multitudes and to all people?

Not wounding the thought of our neighbor, however, is the way of Christ, who came in great mildness and gentleness for the salvation of humanity. For unless we become like crumbs, we cannot dwell among people. Observe how Christ told his disciples: "You did not choose me, but I chose you."[122] Therefore, if the calling of your love toward us is from God and not from people, then labor to achieve great patience. I have already written to you what was written of old: "By your patience you will gain your souls."[123] So make a new beginning to keep and guard whatever I tell you. For it is not yet time to reveal [these things]. Be of good cheer, then, in the Lord.

LETTER 27

Response from the same Great Old Man to the same person, when he grieved that he had taken a long time to write to him, and as a result thought he had forgotten about him.

Write to our brother, since some time has gone by: first, joy and gladness and greetings in the Lord. And tell him: Do not think, as a result of my delay in writing to you, my beloved, that my heart has consigned your memory to oblivion. I have paid attention to your behavior, and have been long-suffering until now. And be assured of the following: just as God is not forgetful of us in being merciful to the world, so, too, I am not forgetful of your love as I pray to God each day and night for the salvation of your soul, that you may attain to the measure about which I have previously written to you.

Moreover, learn this; when you are out on some service for the monastic community, my heart certainly goes with you, with God's consent. So do not grow faint in anything, my brother. I hope that all that I have written to you will come to you. For God does not lie. "And the one who endures to the end will be saved."[124] Understand what I have said and what is in store for

---

121. Cf. Mk 1.45.
123. Lk 21.19.
122. Jn 15.16.
124. Mt 10.22.

you. "For it is through many tribulations that we must enter the kingdom of heaven."[125] Therefore, "rejoice in the Lord always; again I say, rejoice."[126] So let no one learn about this secret. For it is written: "And these words seemed to them an idle tale."[127] Indeed, if one does not have a firm heart, one cannot bear it.

LETTER 28

The same [brother] had in mind to set for himself a limitation of not leaving the monastery at all during periods of fasting. And the Old Man forbade him this, so that when some need according to God might oblige him to leave, he would not grieve for transgressing this rule.

Tell the brother: Have you not heard from me that wherever you go and whatever you do for the sake of God, my heart goes with you? And now, brother, as you have already heard, do not decree anything for yourself; then, if you leave, whenever any need arises, you will not be troubled in your thought. Therefore, observe the meaning of what I have written to you; do this, and you will find rest. May peace be with you from me, or rather from God.

LETTER 29

Response from the same Great Old Man to the same, confirming his faith in the things promised to him, and leading him through such assurance to greater eagerness.

Tell the brother: be rested, and every good gift and each divine charisma will come to us through faith. Therefore, do not be insensitive to the power that daily comes upon you from God through my lowliness. And learn that your arrival here has been admired in no small way. "Run," then, toward those things which have been set before you, "in such a way that you may win"[128] them. And always remember from where God has delivered you, and render him thanks in all circumstances, praying that he may fulfill his mercy with you to the end. Amen.

125. Acts 14.22.   126. Phil 4.4.
127. Lk 24.11.
128. 1 Cor 9.24.

LETTER 30

Response from the same Great Old Man to the same [broth-
er], when he asked whether he ought to sail with the brothers
to Egypt for their handiwork.[129] For he was concerned that neither he nor the other brothers were experienced at sea or in that
city.

Tell the brother: so long as you are outside [the monastery],
you should labor for God with your brothers. Therefore, set the
tribulations of the apostles before your eyes. "For the one who
endures to the end will be saved"[130] in our Lord Jesus Christ.
Amen.

LETTER 31

They went through a great deal in Egypt before finding any
handiwork, and they endured great tribulation and distraction
in many ways; and so weariness came upon him. Since the Old
Man foresaw this spiritually, he prepared the following response
for him.

My child, write down what I am saying, or rather what God
is saying, and prepare to give this letter to brother John. First,
[convey] greetings in the Lord. Afterward, tell him: Why do you
grow weary in your tribulations, like a man of flesh, as if you
had not heard that tribulations await you, as the Spirit said to
Paul,[131] who also encouraged those who were with him in the
boat to rejoice?[132] Do you not know that "the afflictions of the
righteous are many"[133] or that they are tested in this way like
gold in fire? If we are righteous, let us be proved in tribulation.
And if we are sinners, then let us endure them as we deserve.
For "patience produces character."[134]
    Let us call to mind all of the saints from the beginning in

129. This was the practice of the Desert Fathers. See *Sayings*, Macarius of
Egypt 7, Pior 1, John the Dwarf 6 and 35.
130. Mt 10.22.
131. Cf. Acts 20.23.
132. Cf. Acts 27.21–26, 33–36.
133. Ps 33.19.
134. Rom 5.4.

order to see what they endured. For while they did good and spoke good and stood entirely by the truth, yet they were hated and afflicted by people to their very end, "praying for their enemies and for those who despised"[135] them, in accordance with the Savior's words. Have you then also been sold like the honorable Joseph,[136] or did your "hands serve in the basket,"[137] or have you been lowered into two pits?[138] Have you been badly treated like Moses from childhood to old age?[139] What have you endured, slothful one? Have you been persecuted and envied like David by Saul, or by your own son unto death, having to mourn for him when he died?[140] Or have you been thrown into the sea like Jonah?[141]

Lazy and beloved one, why is your thought growing faint? Do not fear or dread like a coward, lest you fall short of God's promises.[142] Do not be terrified like an unbeliever, but give courage to your thoughts that are of little faith. Love your tribulations in all things, so that you may become an approved son of the saints. Remember "the patience of Job"[143] and those who followed him, and be zealous in following their footsteps. Remember the dangers, tribulations, bonds, hungers, and multitude of other evils that Paul endured,[144] and say to your faint-heartedness: "I am a stranger to you."

Remember what I wrote to you: "Whether the matter at hand prospers or not, render thanks to God." Understand how things are [in this world], that they are corruptible and transitory, whereas patience according to God saves the person who has obtained it. Behold, you are struggling to secure and to perform handiwork. In order, therefore, that I may show you the apostolic word, that "this does not depend on human will or exertion, but on God who is merciful,"[145] behold, God is sending you people who have need of the world. When you receive them, do not say that I spoke at all about them, lest they be tempted by vainglory. Love them as genuine brothers, and make your thought

135. Lk 6.28; Mt 5.44.
136. Cf. Gn. 37.
137. Ps 80.7.
138. Cf. Gn 37.24 and 40.15.
139. Cf. Heb 11.25.
140. Cf. 2 Sm 1.11–27 and 18.13.
141. Cf. Jon 1.15.
142. Cf. Heb 4.1.
143. Jas 5.11.
144. Cf. 2 Cor 11.24–27.
145. Rom 9.16.

give rest to their thought. For they despise the world, desiring
to save their souls. And through me, God—I am now writing according to my foreknowledge—is drawing them here to you, in
order for you to learn that they have entirely despised it. Therefore, brother, hold my hand and walk in the "straight and narrow way that leads to life" eternal[146] in Christ Jesus our Lord, to
whom is the glory to the ages. Amen.

LETTER 32

Response from the same Great Old Man to the same, when he
asked if he should eat alone, and whether he should not come
down for holy Communion on Wednesday and Friday, and
whether he should refrain from concern about works; also, if he
happens to fall ill in his [time of] stillness, whether he should
use any treatment; and that commandments may be given to
him for salvation.

I do not wish your love to be ignorant about the benefit that
you have received from the loving God. For indeed, the pangs
have arrived, and Jesus has begun to deal with you, and to in-
troduce you in accordance with the proper order to his blessed
stillness and to blameless patience. Therefore, even if debility
or some other illness follows you, place all your hope in your
Master, and you will find rest. For I have hope in my God that
you are not far from the way of God. About eating in your cell
alone—it is to your interest and benefit. If, however, there is also
occasion to eat with the brothers, do not hesitate or be troubled, but gradually limit yourself. In regard to Communion, do
not set up any barrier for yourself, so long as you are still coming in and going out [of the monastic community]. For this sort
of thing creates a scandal for others.

And pay attention to how you practice your sitting, in humility and fear of God and unfeigned love toward all; then you "are
building your house on" firm and unshakable "rock."[147] For it is
said: "And the rock is Christ."[148] As for certain other commandments, this is not necessarily the right time. I have written quite

---

146. Mt 7.14.   147. Mt 7.24.
148. 1 Cor.10.4.

enough to you. Indeed, these words are sufficient to lead a person from the stage of a beginner to [that of] perfection. Study and remember them in order not to forget them. For they contain an entire library. Be strong in the Lord continually, remaining humble in your words, deeds, and movements.

LETTER 33

Response from the same Great Old Man to the same [brother], when his own brother according to the flesh was considering withdrawal to the monastic life, and so he asked the Old Man about this through him.

Our Lord Jesus Christ said: "No one comes to me unless drawn by the heavenly Father, and I shall raise that person up on the last day"[149] and "shall reveal myself to that person."[150] "See how the fields are ripe for harvest; and the reaper is already receiving a wage, gathering fruit for eternal life, so that the sower and the reaper may rejoice together. For here the saying holds true, that 'one sows, and another reaps.'"[151]

Brother, no one who wishes to enter a city falls asleep; no one who wishes to work remains idle upon seeing the sunrise; and no one who wishes to beautify a field is careless. For anyone who wishes to enter a city will walk more swiftly before it is too late; and anyone who sees the sunrise will rapidly depart for work in order not to be hindered; and anyone who wishes to beautify a field will strive to do so before it is ruined by rust. "Let anyone with ears to hear listen."[152]

LETTER 34

When his brother came to him again for a second time, he was troubled for his salvation, and reminded him of his former promise. He asked, however, for a sign to be given to him about this from the Old Man. And the Old Man stated the following:

In regard to the brother of whom you told me, unbelief is warring against him. And this is the sect of the Pharisees, to

149. Jn 6.44.   150. Jn 14.21.
151. Jn 4.35–37.   152. Lk 8.8 and 14.35.

whom the Lord said: "This generation asks for a sign, but no sign shall be given to it."[153] I have nothing to say to him beyond what the Apostle says: "Everything old has passed away; behold, everything has become new";[154] and: "So now, O Israel";[155] and: "You shall not tempt the Lord your God";[156] and: "If you hear his voice today, do not harden your hearts."[157] "Let anyone with ears to hear listen."[158] Pray for me.

LETTER 35

Response from the same Great Old Man to the same person, when he asked about certain brothers with physical illness and about others with spiritual illness, whether he should take them in himself; and whether he should tell the abbot to relieve the novices a little from the vigil; and also about his long silence.

Brother, the response to these three thoughts is one—do not force the will, but only sow "in hope."[159] For our Lord, too, did not force anyone, but only preached the Gospel, and whoever wanted, listened. I know that you know I am neither neglecting nor despising your love. But such tolerance is for the best. For when we also pray—and God is long-suffering in responding—he does this for the best, in order that we may learn long-suffering and not grow faint, claiming that we prayed but were not heard. For God knows what is best for us. Rejoice in the Lord, my brother, and be free from all cares; and pray for me, my beloved soulmate.

LETTER 36

Response from the same Great Old Man to the same, allowing him to begin his stillness completely carefree; and about the thought that came to him in regard to this being his final hour; and because he had conversed for a long time with one of the fathers, he wondered whether or not he had acted well.

---

153. Mt 12.39 and 16.4; Lk 11.29.
154. 2 Cor 5.17. 155. Dt 4.1 and 10.12.
156. Dt 6.16 and Mt 4.7. 157. Ps 94.8.
158. Lk 8.8 and 14.35. 159. 1 Cor 9.10.

Brother, listen to me who loves you in Christ Jesus. In regard to the cell, our Lord Jesus Christ said: "The hour is coming, and is now here, when the dead shall hear the voice of the Son of God, and those who hear shall live. For just as the Father has life in himself, so also has he granted the Son to have life in himself."[160] And I, too, say to you that the time has come for you to enter [the way of stillness] with the help of God. Establish your new cell, and enter with God as your guide. And when you are settled, do not care about anything at all. For indeed the necessity of things and your testing are calling one another.

In regard to the other thought that has been sown in you, it is idle and brings with it vainglory. For who does not know that we are in the final hour? And as for the conversation, when you see yourself almost theologizing, remember that silence is more admirable and more glorious than that. Therefore, there is nothing more that you need me to write. For I have written to you from the alpha to the omega,[161] as your love well knows. Therefore, I commit you to God. For his is the assistance and the mercy. Amen.

LETTER 37

A Christ-loving secular person sent a question to the same Abba John about some matter, and was given an answer. And when John regretted [what he had said in response], he informed the same Great Old Man, saying: "Forgive me; for I am drunk and do not know what I am doing." Response.

I often tell you: "Let the dead bury their own dead,"[162] but instead you are not even yet disgusted by their foul smell. Look at what you are saying. You do not know what you are saying. For a drunk person is ridiculed by people, is beaten, despised, does not account himself worthy, offers no opinions, teaches no one, gives no advice about anything, cannot discern between

---

160. Jn 5.25–26.

161. A possible reference to the cryptic alphabet, of which only one section survives in the collection. See *Letter* 137B.

162. Mt 8.22; Lk 9.60.

what is good and what is wrong. If you speak with your mouth, yet show otherwise with your works, then you are speaking in ignorance. Do not fall asleep, lest you suddenly hear: "Behold the bridegroom. Come out to meet him."[163] And what will your response be then: "I am busy"? He has made you carefree, and you do not want this; he has removed from you every worry, and you entangle yourself; he has given you rest, and you wish to toil. There is no time for you to mourn and weep for your sins. Remember how he told you that the door will be shut.[164] Hurry, then, so that you do not remain outside with the foolish virgins.

Pass over in your thought from this vain world to the other age. Leave behind the worldly, and seek the heavenly. Abandon the corruptible, and you shall find the incorruptible. In your mind, flee from the temporary, and you shall reach the eternal. Die completely, that you may live forever in Christ Jesus our Lord, to whom be the glory to the ages. Amen.

LETTER 38

Response from the same Great Old Man to the same person, when he wanted to receive answers from him more frequently for the assistance and salvation of his soul; and when he sought to learn whether he ought to talk with any of the brothers, or be questioned by them about thoughts.

Since I know to whom I have committed you, and what food I have offered you, if you only understood, this is why I do not write to you often. For he to whom I have committed you "knows what you need even before you ask him."[165] As you have heard, then, be carefree. For being free from all cares helps you approach the city. And not being accounted at all among people makes you dwell in the city. And dying from everyone makes you inherit the city and the treasures. Since, then, you always want to hear the same word about conversing or [testing] thoughts with the brothers, whenever necessary I shall tell you what to do. But you should care about nothing else except the completion of the journey. I greet your love unceasingly. And

163. Mt 25.6. 164. Cf. Mt 25.10.
165. Mt 6.8.

you can learn this from the gradual quenching in you of the terrible emotion of wrath. Peace will be with you, my beloved brother John.

LETTER 39

Response from the same Great Old Man to the same, when he wanted to cut off conversation even with his own attendant because he was told to be carefree in order to approach the city. And about his thought that sought the causes of the temptations rising up against him in various ways.

Say to the brother: Wait a little longer. For it is not yet time. Indeed, I care for you more than you do yourself; or rather, it is God [who takes care of you]. Brother John, do not be at all afraid of the temptations that rise up against you in order to test you. For the Lord will not surrender you to them. Therefore, whenever something like this comes upon you, do not labor in investigating matters, but cry out the name of Jesus, saying: "Jesus, help me," and he will surely hear you; for "he is near to all who call on him."[166] Do not be faint-hearted, but run eagerly and you shall win,[167] in Christ Jesus our Lord, to whom be the glory.

LETTER 40

Question from the same brother to the same Great Old Man, as to whether he ought to instruct his own attendant about the matter of orderliness; and in regard to another brother who asked about his own thoughts—but did so in riddles[168] rather than clearly—whether he had acted correctly. Response.

The most splendid teaching of our Savior is this: "Your will be done."[169] So if anyone says this prayer sincerely, he is dismissing his own will, and hanging everything on the will of God. Teaching one's brother is profitable, but the matter also results in envy. Nevertheless, it may be done gradually and intermittently, or else the matter may be entirely concealed for the

---

166. Ps 144.18.
168. See *Letters* 132–136.
167. Cf. 1 Cor 9.24.
169. Mt 6.10.

sake of the brother's conscience. As for questioning in riddles, it is self-serving, lacking in discernment, and this person needs many prayers. For signs are "not for believers, but for unbelievers."[170]

LETTER 41

Response from the same Great Old Man to the same brother, when he fell into many thoughts and cares in regard to the constitution of the monastery.

There are many things boiling inside your heart. And it is said: "I shall [try to] count them, but they are more than the sand."[171] Brother, no one knows where this place is heading except "God, who knows the human heart,"[172] and him alone. He, however, has given me assurance. Know then that the Lord will not forsake it, but will preserve and glorify it for the glory of his glorious name. To him be the glory to the ages. Amen. So stay carefree and live in stillness. For everything will happen in a timely and orderly way.

LETTER 42

Response from the same Great Old Man to the same person, when he asked where the current sickness came from; and whether he should tell the brothers who were departing for Egypt how to behave; and because he worried about them, lest they should be troubled as a result of their inexperience in travel.

Say to the brother: Those who are with you are mixed, being from Egypt as well as from Jerusalem.[173] But do not worry. For God cares for you. Simply do that which is in your heart with godly fear; and do not worry about the brothers, but only pray, and the Lord shall guide them in every matter according to his will. For nothing happens without God, especially in this place, if it is according to godly fear for the refreshment and benefit of souls.

---

170. 1 Cor 14.22.   171. Ps 138.18.
172. Acts 15.8.
173. Cf. Palladius, *Lausiac History* 21.8–9.

LETTER 43

Response from the same Great Old Man to the same, in order that he might commit all of his concerns to God.

"Everyone who drinks of the water," which I sent you through my letters, "will never thirst even to the age."[174] You ought, however, to expect and hope for refreshment through the faith of Christ. Take this bread from my food [supply], and be carefree. Do not fear anything, but receive strength and hope through the Holy Spirit. And believe that the hand of God is with you.

LETTER 44

From the blessing[175] that was sent to him, he gave some to his attendant, but not with his own hand, since he was not a priest; instead, he placed it down, and the attendant took it. When he received a blessing for a second and third time, he did the same. And doing this without supervision, he did not perceive any sin. Again, when he saw that he was relieved of the passions through the prayers of the Old Man, he said: "My passions have slackened." After this, he sent asking about a thought of blasphemy, but received no response. And while he was wondering what the cause was, God permitted a terrible apparition to appear to him suddenly—more than once, indeed twice—in order to teach him; and then, immediately, it departed. Filled with much trouble and anxiety, he remembered his oversight, but only in regard to the bread, forgetting what he had said about the slackening of the passions. And wearing the cowl sent to him some time earlier by the Old Man,[176] he fell down many times entreating to receive mercy. The Old Man writes to him about both faults, as well as about the thought of blasphemy, saying that laying down the blessings in order for the servant to take them for himself was not in fact humility, but rather arrogance and childishness.

If one knows that one is transgressing the commandment, one will show evidence of this knowledge. A person who knows can be corrected. But we are speaking simply in any case. I have committed you to the hand of God, and you turn away from this. Scrip-

---

174. Jn 4.14.   175. I.e., the bread.
176. See *Letter* 1.

ture says that the righteous "do not turn aside from the mouth of God."[177] So, what do you think that I should say? Again it is said: "Do not let arrogance come from your mouth."[178] Yet you dared to open your mouth before God and to say: "My passions have slackened." You did not say instead: "They are all laid up in me, as if in store." This is why you were abandoned for a little while, and all your wretchedness has been revealed to you. And if you did not have the covering, you would have had to labor hard. Yet, "God is faithful," it is said, "and he will not allow you to be tested beyond your strength, but with the testing will also provide the way out, so that you may be able to endure it."[179]

As for doing something in an untimely way, this comes from your own will in its arrogance. As for giving others a blessing as an archbishop would do, while you are not ordained, I do not even know how to describe this. What then? Did I not know how to send blessings to all? Or did I send them especially to you? Therefore, behold, you have been taught a little lesson about many and great matters. So be alert henceforth in order to wipe out firmly the eight alien nations,[180] and neither stay with nor be dragged along by childish matters. Acquire stringency, which is simplicity. For you have heard many times: "Do everything with counsel."[181] Pray to God about every passion and blasphemy, and he will support you and drive them away from you gradually. Henceforth be alert, and keep these things in your heart. There is no need for anyone to learn about them. Whatever has happened has happened. Therefore, Jesus will be with you. Forgive me the past, and I shall correct the future, to the ages. Amen.

LETTER 45

Response by the same Great Old Man to the same, when he fell into great illness and was overcome by very high fever, unable ei-

---

177. Cf. Prv 24.7.　　　178. 1 Sm 2.3.
179. 1 Cor 10.13.
180. A reference to the eight passions, the "nations" being peoples conquered by the Israelites. Cf. Origen, *Homilies on Joshua*, and Cassian, *Conferences* 5.17–19.
181. Cf. Prv 24.72, or 31.4 LXX. This source is frequently quoted by Barsanuphius and John.

ther to eat or to sleep for many days; and so he cried out in insult to the abbot as well as to the brothers attending him, being influenced by the devil.

Brother, how is it that your heart has been watered down, to leave the beloved and run after the enemy? You have left the voice of the Shepherd Christ, and have followed after the wolf devil. What has happened to you? What have you endured? What are these cries, which the Apostle has numbered among things of ill repute, saying: "Put away from you all bitterness and blasphemy and wrath, together with all malice"?[182] Nothing has happened to you beyond your strength, as the Apostle cries aloud: "God is faithful, and will not allow us to be tested beyond our strength,"[183] and so forth. Awaken from this turmoil of the evil thoughts, and take up the staff of the cross, with which you will drive away the wolves, namely, the demons; and remember to say: "Why are you so downcast, my soul, and why are you disquieted within me? Hope in God. For I shall again give thanks to him; he is the salvation of my countenance and my God."[184] Therefore, be sober from now on, and do not be consumed like a foolish child that has no perception. Since you ought to ascend the cross with Christ, and to be nailed with the nails and pierced with the spear, why do you carry on, poor wretch, and cry out with force against Christ and with insults against your brothers?[185] Where is for you the phrase: "Outdo one another in showing honor"?[186] Enough for now. For it is said: "Give instruction to the wise, and they shall become wiser still."[187]

Endure and be silent, and give thanks for all things. For so it is said: "Give thanks in all circumstances"[188]—which clearly means both "in hardships and in afflictions,"[189] and in illnesses and respites alike. Hold, therefore, firmly to God, and he will stay with you[190] and give you strength in his name; for his is the glory.

---

182. Eph 4.31. 183. 1 Cor 10.13.
184. Pss 41.6, 12 and 42.5.
185. See Abba Isaiah of Scetis, *Ascetic Discourse* 25.
186. Rom 12.10. 187. Prv 9.9.
188. 1 Thes 5.18. 189. 2 Cor 6.4.
190. Cf. *Sayings*, Arsenius 10.

LETTER 46

When he was relieved from illness and was once more sobered through temptation, the adversary showed him evil dreams in order to trouble him again. And failing this, again he showed him something like a monastery and a church, with many people taking refuge there in order supposedly to obtain help. The Old Man wrote to him the following for his protection.

"Glory to God in the highest,"[191] brother. "Our enemy, the devil," rages "like a roaring lion to devour"[192] you. Yet the hand of God, which always covers us, did not permit him. So when he saw that he was not permitted to do whatever he pleased, he set himself to trouble your mind, showing you some things in advance through his shameful dreams. And like a wicked one in his craftiness, when he saw that the Lord was not surrendering you to temptation, whether [bringing you] to the end or beyond your strength,[193] he made you see a monastery and a church, supposedly, of help. Therefore, safeguard your heart, sealing it[194] without turmoil in the name of the Father and of the Son and of the Holy Spirit. And I believe that he will help us trample upon [the enemy's] head. Acquire a humble heart, and give glory to the one who saved you from the snare of death. For it is from negligence that you have suffered this.

LETTER 47

Response from the same Great Old Man to the same [brother], when he fell into a temptation comprised of various thoughts, which was very strong and incomprehensible to many.

Tell brother John: I am amazed by your love, how you do not understand things. For on seeing your many trials, I have often of my own sent you a blessing,[195] so that you may receive strength through them according to God. You ought, however, always to study the 106th Psalm, where it is said: "He spoke, and a stormy

191. Lk 2.14.   192. 1 Pt 5.8.
193. Cf. 1 Cor 10.13.
194. That is, with the sign of the cross.
195. See *Letters* 1 and 37.

wind arose, and its waves were raised. They rise up to the heavens, and go down to the depths"; and again: "Their soul melted away in evils."[196] These things have come upon us, and we must endure such dangers until we reach "his desired haven,"[197] as I have written to you before. Therefore, God has not "delivered" you "to the hands of your enemies,"[198] and you, too, should not surrender to their hands. And even if you happen to do so, God will certainly not surrender you.

Do you want to be delivered from trials and not labor in them? Expect worse, and you will find rest. Remember Job and the subsequent saints, how many trials they endured; acquire their patience, and your spirit will be comforted. "Be strong and bold";[199] and pray for me, remembering my words, so that your soul may be renewed.

LETTER 48

When the abbot delayed for some reason in bringing him the above reply, he accused him vehemently, causing him great disheartenment. And when some brothers, who were attended to for their sickness, spoke to him about some matters that were being done idly and unprofitably in the monastic community, instead of admonishing and correcting them for such slander, he said that these things do not please him either. And when the abbot later told him: "I did this in accordance with the advice of the Old Man," he told him: "The Old Man lets you write and come and go according to your own will." And at this he sends him the following response, pointing out to him that those things which seem to us not to be happening correctly are being done by divine economy, and are beyond our comprehension.

Again love arouses us after some time to strike you with the rod of Christ's chastening and rebuke you, in order that the scriptural word may also be fulfilled in us, that: "The wounds inflicted by a friend are well meant,"[200] and so forth. And again, if we chasten you, do not grow faint, remembering the prov-

---

196. Ps 106.25–26.
197. Ps 106.30. See *Letters* 2, 8, 9, and 15.
198. Ps 40.2; Ezek 39.23.   199. Dt 31.6, 7, and 23.
200. Prv 27.6.

erb that says: "My son, do not despise the Lord's discipline, nor grow weary of his reproof. For the Lord reproves the one he loves and scourges every son whom he receives."[201] And even if I rebuke you, do not forget the words of the Apostle: "Reprove, rebuke, encourage."[202] Where is your mind, slothful one? Where does your thought dwell, lazy one? Why is it that the lords of your mind contradict within you the disciples of the Master, that you should not accept him to mount your mind as your Master and to enter Jerusalem[203] and cast out of the temple of God "all those who are selling and buying,"[204] putting to shame the scribes and the Pharisees? Why is it that, when you ought to dwell in Jerusalem, they drag you to Babylon? Why do you leave the water of Siloam,[205] wishing instead to drink from the murky waters of the Egyptians? Why do you move away from the way of humility, which says: "Who am I?[206] I am but earth and ashes,"[207] and prefer to walk the corrupt way, which is filled with trials and dangers?

Where did you cast my words spoken to you day and night? Where is it that I, as if talking to myself, have asked you to head, and where do you see yourself heading? Where do I want you to be, and where are you on account of your uncontrolled tongue, which you release at random? And if you give thought to your neighbor,[208] are you not scrupulous in understanding, especially in regard to the one who protects us after God, and lays down his own neck for us, whom we ought to thank and for whom we ought to pray that he might be preserved from every evil for the benefit of us and of many,[209] learning this from the holy Apostle, who gave thanks for some, saying: "Such people laid down their necks for my sake"?[210] So what do you not remember? The freedom from care, which God granted you through him? Or the re-

201. Prv 3.11–12.
202. 2 Tm 4.2.
203. Cf. Lk 19.33–35.
204. Mt 21.12; Mk 11.15.
205. Cf. Is 8.6.
206. 2 Sm. 7.18; 1 Chr 17.16 and 29.14.
207. Gn 18.27; Jb 42.6.
208. That is, Abbot Seridos.
209. Reference to the abbot as the spiritual director of the monastic community.
210. Rom 16.4.

laxation which you share in stillness as a king, while he bears the weight of those things that come to and go from us, leaving us undisturbed? For if they come because of us, it is we who ought to bear their care, and not he. Therefore, I owe many thanks to God who gave us a genuine son according to our soul, as he willed. And in return for this, you told him senselessly: "I have washed my hands of you." And you did this not once but many times, drowning his soul in much sorrow, and failing to remember the Apostle, who said: "Lest such a person be overcome by excessive sorrow."[211] Were it not for the hand of God and the prayer of his fathers, his heart would have been shattered.

Where are my commandments to you, to "weep, mourn, not seek to be counted as anything and to measure yourself as nothing"? I am drawing your love toward another direction. Pass over from the world, and henceforth mount the cross; be lifted from the earth. "Shake off the dust from your feet."[212] "Disregard shame."[213] Do not join the Chaldeans in kindling the furnace, so that you may not be burned with them[214] by God's wrath. Regard every person "as better than yourself."[215] "Weep for your dead."[216] "First take out your own log."[217] Rebuild your house, which was destroyed. Cry out: "Have mercy on me, son of David, that I may see again."[218] Learn, so "that every mouth may be silenced,"[219] "and do not speak boastfully."[220] "Shut your door"[221] against the enemy. "Put your words in a yoke, and make a bolt for your gate."[222]

You know how I speak to you. Understand my words. Labor to scrutinize them, and you will discover godly treasures hidden in them. Make them bring forth fruits worthy of God. And do not put to shame my gray hair, since I am praying for you day and night. May the Lord grant you to understand and act in his fear. Amen. And since you told him: "The Old Man lets you walk according to your own will," then I shall bear alone

---

211. 2 Cor 2.7.
213. Heb 12.2.
215. Phil 2.3.
217. Mt 7.5.
219. Rom 3.19.
221. Is 26.20.

212. Mt 10.14.
214. Dn 3.23.
216. Sir 22.11; Jn 11.31.
218. Mk 10.47–51; Lk 18.38–41.
220. Ob 12.
222. Sir 28.25.

the judgment that the Lord said through the prophet: "Truly I say to you, if you see your brother walking in a way that is not good, and you do not warn him from the evil way, I shall require his blood at your hand."[223] Do not be ridiculed, but believe the Apostle, who says that "we shall give an account"[224] for him. Yet you do not even comprehend what is happening here.

LETTER 49

Having thanked the Old Man for the correction, he begged him to write to him often about the salvation of his soul. Similarly, about a thought that he sought to tell the abbot, he entreated the Old Man to tell him. Response.

Brother John, I do not know what this is. I have written to you from A to Z, from the beginner's stage to that of perfection, from the outset of the way to its very end, from the "putting away of the old self with earthly desires"[225] to the "putting on of the new self created according to God,"[226] from becoming estranged from the sensory world to becoming a citizen of heaven and an inheritor of the spiritual land of promises. Ruminate on my letters, and you will be saved. In these, you have the Old and the New [Testaments], if only you are able to understand. And if you understand them, you will have no need of any other book. Shake off forgetfulness, and move away from darkness, so that your heart may be at peace with your senses, and all this will come to you. Let the smoke of the idol sacrifices from your spiritual Nineveh disappear, and the fragrance from the incense of your spiritual repentance will spread throughout its streets, preventing the wrath that was threatening destruction.[227]

Why do you sleep? Why are you tossing these responses regarding your salvation as if they were pillows, when they are for the salvation of those who study them with faith? Stop dreaming; wake up from your deep sleep. Quicken your pace. Take over Zoar, so that the destruction of the five cities may not overtake you.[228] Do not turn backward, in order not to become a pil-

223. Ezek 3.18 and 33.8.   224. Heb 13.17.
225. Eph 4.22; Col 3.9.   226. Eph 4.24; Col 3.10.
227. Cf. Jon 3.   228. Cf. Gn 19.22.

lar of salt.[229] Become "wise as the serpents,"[230] so that your enemies may not lead you astray; but be "innocent as the doves,"[231] so that requital may not war against you. Become a genuine servant of one master; otherwise, you will be enslaved to many. Do not separate yourself from him. For the unfaithful servant received condemnation for this. Watch even how you sit. Say to yourself: "Why am I sitting like this? What have I gained from this sitting?" And the loving God will enlighten your heart to understand. Behold, now he has made you carefree, free from every earthly concern. Give heed to yourself, and watch where you are and what you want, and God will assist you in everything, my brother. And as for the thought that you asked me to tell my son, I could of course tell him. Unless, however, you tell him with your own mouth, you are estranging yourself from genuine and perfect love toward him; if you are of one soul and one heart according to Scripture,[232] then no one hides anything from one's heart. Wake up to yourself; for you are still heavy-hearted. The Lord will forgive you.

LETTER 50

Response from the same Great Old Man to the same [brother], when he asked whether he ought perhaps no longer to converse with anyone after the Holy and Great Week.

After the Feast [of Pascha, or Easter], be silent for five days a week, and then meet with others two days a week, as necessity arises. Again I am telling you what to do. Do whatever is in your power to be free from all cares. For God provides what is best for every person, whether he pricks someone's heart personally, or whether he awakens one for one's benefit by means of others.

LETTER 51

After the Feast [of Pascha, or Easter], a certain bishop came and sought to speak with him. Some of the other novices also wanted

---

229. Cf. Gn 19.26.
231. Mt 10.16.

230. Gn 3.1; Mt 10.16.
232. Cf. Acts 4.32.

to question him about thoughts. So he sent a question to the
same Great Old Man. Response by Barsanuphius.

You know that we have never placed a bond on anyone, let
alone on ourselves. So since I have told you: "Be silent for five
days a week, and then meet with others two days a week," you
should be free from this care, too, as well as when I tell you
to meet with others. Moreover, when you do meet with others,
be carefree as to what you say and speak. For Christ said: "The
Spirit of your Father will be speaking through you."[233] As for the
brothers about whom you tell me, when necessity arises, do not
refuse them; and God will help you. Amen.

LETTER 52

Response from the same Great Old Man to the same person,
when he spoke about disorder in the world.

Brother, "while we have the opportunity,"[234] let us give heed
to ourselves, for everything is in disarray; and let us practice silence. And if you wish to find rest in all things, become dead
with regard to every person, and you will indeed have rest. Observe that it is about thoughts, as well as about every matter and
conduct and care, that I am telling you to be still in peace.

LETTER 53

Following this response, he sought to cut off conversations completely; one brother was very much troubled by this and entreated him that he might converse with him, if need arose. Out of
compassion, he promised that he would. And he asked about
this, as well as about a cowl sent to him by some other brother,
whether he should accept it. Response by Barsanuphius.

Brother, I sent you a word: "Be carefree." What else do you
want? Pay attention to yourself. "The harvest is plentiful."[235] Do
not abandon it and start "gleaning" grapes "after the grape-
pickers."[236] Instead, leave everything behind, and spend your
time harvesting and gathering, so that you may have your fruits

233. Mt 10.20.   234. Gal 6.10.
235. Mt 9.37; Lk 10.2.   236. Sir 33.17.

from the corn and the wine,[237] in order that your heart may be strengthened and gladdened in the Lord.[238] Study the letters, which I have written to you; for they are not fruitless. And in regard to the cowl, if the brother desires with all his heart to give it to you, then accept it, condemning yourself as being unworthy.

LETTER 54

A brother who was going through very great warfare, and was ashamed to confide boldly in the abbot, sent [a letter] imploring the same Abba John to receive him and to hear his thought, without the abbot's knowledge. So the [Old Man] was troubled in two ways, neither wanting to receive him without [the abbot's] consent, in order not to scandalize the others, nor again wanting to grieve the brother. Wondering what to do, he questioned this thought with the same Great Old Man, asking whether he should lock his door. Response by Barsanuphius.

Tell the brother: Who is so lacking in understanding as to choose something harmful and more painful for himself, instead of whatever is easier and more tolerable with humility and prayer? Do not lock the door. For mortification is not found in the locking of the door, but rather in the locking of the mouth.[239] I embrace you "with a holy kiss."[240]

237. Cf. Ps 4.7; Dt 33.28.   238. Cf. 1 Sm 2.1.
239. Cf. *Sayings*, Macarius 16.   240. Rom 16.16; 1 Cor 16.20.

LETTERS TO AN EGYPTIAN MONK
AND TO PAUL THE HERMIT (55–58)

LETTER 55

A certain elderly Egyptian man came to live in the monastery where the fathers were, and addressed a letter written in Egyptian to the Great Old Man (for he, too, was Egyptian) requesting prayer and counsel for the benefit of his soul, and asking whether it would be possible to be allowed to meet him. He wrote back his response in Greek, as follows.

INCE I HAVE promised myself not to write to anyone personally, but only to respond through the abbot, this is why I have not written to you in Egyptian as you wrote to me, but was compelled to tell him to write to you in Greek. For he does not know Egyptian. If you have ranked me in your letters as being your beloved father in the Lord, who understands the labor and the needs and the dangers of your soul, then, if I am your father as you write, I give you a commandment not to bother me about meeting. For I do not show favoritism to anyone in my life. If I open up for you, then I should open up for all;[1] and if I do not open up for you, nor do I open up for anyone else. I have written this to you since you wrote saying: "If it is possible, make me worthy of your gentleness, and be merciful to my suffering soul." And again, since you said in the same letter: "My sin has separated me from you, my master," I have not been separated now from you by the grace of Christ, the Son of God, but I am always with your love in the Spirit.

As for what you write to me later in the same letter, namely, "Pray for my sins," I also say the same to you: pray for my sins. For it is said: "In everything, do to others as you would have them do to you."[2] Now I, though a wretched man and the least

---

1. See *Sayings*, Arsenius 8.   2. Mt 7.12; Lk 6.31.

of all people, nevertheless do whatever I can for the sake of him who says: "Pray for one another, so that you may be healed."[3] Brother, we are foreigners, and so let us become foreigners, not counting ourselves as being anything, so that no one counts us as anything; and then we shall find rest. But since you have entered our monastery, wrestle in order to endure. For it is said: "The one who endures to the end will be saved."[4] And above all, strive to die unto all people, and you will be saved. Say to your thought: "I have died and am lying in the tomb." Trust me, beloved one, that, being compelled by the love of God, I have transcended my boundaries in speaking these things to your love. For who am I, the least of all? This is why I ask for forgiveness, saying: "Servant of God Abramios, for the Lord's sake forgive my babbling, and pray for me."

LETTER 56

Response from the same Great Old Man to Abba Paul, an old man living in stillness and seeking to receive a blind brother in order to attend to him.

Brother Paul, there is a proverb that says: "If you see a young person running, then know that an elderly person has ensnared him." For us, then, the elderly person ensnaring us is Satan; and, out of envy, he wants to throw us into evil days on the pretense of our having rights.[5] Moreover, we do not know how many of those who wanted to pull people out of the river have themselves been drowned with them. Look at how long he has wanted to ensnare you; and when you ask questions and receive answers, he sets his trap in a different, a worse manner. God does not require you to do good to your neighbor beyond your ability. For it also says: "Do not withhold good from your neighbor, in accordance with the resources at hand."[6] So, say the blind man comes, and

---

3. Jas 5.16.

4. Mt 10.22.

5. "Pretense to rights" (τὸ δικαίωμα) is a phrase derived—albeit implicitly—from the Desert Fathers (cf. *Sayings*, Antony 4) and used by Barsanuphius to signify self-justification, self-trust, and self-deceit. It implies assuming the pretext that we are doing what is right. See *Letter* 477.

6. Prv 3.27; Sir 29.20.

you also fall gravely ill. Who will attend to the two of you? Even if someone attends to you joyfully, nevertheless whoever brings you these justifications is always saying to you: "See, you have brought a burden on the community." And as you know, another person is difficult to bear, as the Scripture says: "Who can bear a shriveled soul,"[7] and especially that of an elderly man? But if you need to experience some evil days, do as you please.

Had I not been asked, I would not have spoken. And again, what I have spoken, I have done so for the love of Christ, so that my brother may not be led astray. If, however, you feel compassion toward him for God's sake, and believe that God is able to help him, then pray to him, and he will do with him as he wills. I have not bound you, brother, nor have I offered you a commandment, but only an opinion. Therefore, do as you please. Moreover, forgive me for the Lord's sake; and pray for me, the least one.

LETTER 57

Response from the same Great Old Man to the same [brother], when he initiated a conversation with someone else on matters of faith; but not being qualified for such an inquiry, he was troubled by the discussion.

The divine Apostle, moved by the Holy Spirit, said: "God is faithful, and will not let us be tested beyond our strength, but with the testing will also provide the way out, so that we may be able to endure it."[8] My genuine soul-mate and beloved brother, be assured in the Lord that, seeing the sorrow and the turmoil of the temptation that has come upon you, I have so terribly ached as never before, especially when I remembered the Apostle saying: "Who is weak, and I am not weak?" and so on.[9] And again: "If one member suffers, then all suffer together with it."[10] For if even I do not do as the Apostle says, nevertheless I have heard him saying: "Weep with those who weep, and rejoice with those who rejoice."[11] Yet, glory to the most high God, who has

---

7. Prv 18.14.
9. 2 Cor 11.29.
11. Rom 12.15.

8. 1 Cor 10.13.
10. 1 Cor 12.26.

not allowed the enemy, that hater of good, to fulfill in you all of his evil according to his own will. For he desires to swallow people alive, as Peter, the chief of the apostles, bears witness, saying: "Like a lion, he roars, looking for someone to devour."[12] My master, let us not hastily accept the turmoil of evil thoughts, in order thus to be moved and troubled against our neighbor. For this is of the devil's doing, and nothing else. And what have we done with the saying: "Blessed is anyone who endures temptation. For such a person has stood the test,"[13] and so on?

Therefore, I have not written these things to your love as if you need teaching. For if you search the Scriptures, you will have greater soberness and understanding than I. Indeed, I am wretched and weak, having only an empty name.[14] Out of pain of heart and out of greater love for God, however, "I have written [to you] with many tears."[15] Therefore, may he establish your heart in his fear, "who firmly established the heavens and fixed them in place."[16] May he found your building upon the firm rock,[17] "who has spread out the earth on the waters";[18] and may he rebuke your trials, who "rebuked the winds and the sea."[19] May he set far from you the forgetfulness of the commandments, who set far "the east from the west."[20] May he take pity on your soul "as a father has compassion for his sons";[21] and may he illumine your heart, who illumined the things that formerly were dark.[22] May he grant you patience to dwell in peace with me, your beloved, until your last breath, even as some time ago he revealed to us through his grace; for he said: "The one who endures to the end shall be saved."[23] May he give us peace with each other to the end, that peace which he gave to his own disciples.[24] May he grant us to come to his perfect love, who said: "If you love me, [you will] keep my commandments."[25]

---

12. 1 Pt 5.8.
13. Jas 1.12.
14. That is, a reputation and nothing more.
15. 2 Cor 2.4.   16. Is 42.5.
17. Cf. Mt 7.24.   18. Ps 135.6.
19. Mt 8.26.   20. Ps 102.12.
21. Ps 102.13.   22. Cf. Eph 5.8.
23. Mt 10.22.   24. Cf. Jn 14.27.
25. Jn 14.15.

And again he said: "By this shall everyone know that you are my disciples, if you have love for one another."[26] If we had such love, nothing would separate us from each other until death.

It is, however, also written: "So now, O Israel";[27] and again: "If the spirit of the ruler rises against you, do not leave your post."[28] I tell you the word of Ruth: "Do not let me be separated from you, for [only] death shall come between and separate me from you."[29] Yet if you upset any of these things, I am innocent in every way. You shall see and answer to this on the fearful day. For I gladly offer my soul to death for you, my brother. And there is no commandment. Be silent and confident, wondering and glorifying God, who redeemed you from great dangers and sorrows and diverse trials. To him be the glory to the ages. Amen. Forgive my great babbling. For it is out of much sadness and great joy that I have extended my word to you. May the Lord be with you, beloved.

LETTER 58

On receiving this response, he declared the following to him by way of a reply: "Master father, forgive me for the sake of the Lord, and pray for me. About my sadness and turmoil, however, which you said are as if from the devil, you know, master, that from childhood I have accepted the faith of the 318 holy fathers,[30] and have never accepted any other teaching but this, yet I am still troubled. So if you know, father, that I am troubled in an inappropriate manner, then give me a word that my Lord will account for me to God, and that no hurt will come to me, and I will cease from my sadness and turmoil. I am terribly tormented about these things. For I am a simple person, full of foolishness, and tempted by many sins. Therefore, do not react against me, master, but write back to me offering forgiveness, and help me in these matters through your prayers, which are well received. Indeed, I trust in God that you will gain favor for my wretched soul." Response from the same Great Old Man to the same.

---

26. Jn 13.35.
27. Dt 4.1 and 10.12.
28. Eccl 10.4.
29. Ru 1.16–17.
30. A reference to the fathers of the First Ecumenical Council in Nicaea (325 C.E.). Abba Paul is possibly non-Chalcedonian.

If you have understood what has been written to you by me, you would have learned that I wrote this of my own accord. For to say: "I offer my soul on your behalf" may be interpreted as: "I am accountable for your love." I am not ashamed to tell you, my brother, that you are not able to explore those matters concerning the faith. So since you cannot do it, do not explore them; otherwise, you are drawing sorrow and trouble to yourself. Even if a faithful person speaks or argues with heretics or unbelievers, yet this person is never vexed to the ages. For this person has Jesus within, the "Prince of Peace"[31] and of calm. Such a person can argue calmly and lovingly, bringing many heretics and unbelievers to the knowledge of our Savior Jesus Christ. So then, brother, since it is beyond you to explore these matters, keep the royal way, namely, the faith of the 318 fathers, into which you were also baptized. For it contains everything with precision for those who understand its completeness.

Be silent, then, and give heed to your sins, and how it is that you must encounter God. And if you so hold to my commandment, or rather God's, I confess that I shall give account for you on that day when "God will judge the secret thoughts of all."[32] Therefore, do not hesitate, thereby bringing yourself to worse things. For the enemy turns sweet things into bitter; but the Lord Jesus will abolish him from us. First of all, from now on, do not be concerned about other things. For the Lord has removed from you all care. And when the evil demon saw that you had been delivered through the prayers of the saints, he sought to leave with you some of the smoke from this temptation. Pray for me, brother, that he may not also say to me: "You, then, that teach others, will you not teach yourself?"[33] And again, do not stumble in these things and grieve me, your beloved. May the Lord protect us under his wings. Amen.

---

31. Is 9.6.   32. Rom 2.16.
33. Rom 2.21.

LETTERS TO ABBA EUTHYMIUS (59–71)

LETTER 59

An old man, called Abba Euthymius, who lived in stillness, asked the same Great Old Man in the form of a prayer, saying the following: "Giver of light, the way of those in darkness, illumine us also who are in the fog. For you, Holy One, have said yourself: 'Ask and you shall receive; knock and it shall be opened for you.'[1] And since you also desire to open for us a door of salvation, make haste; for you have made a beginning. If you had not desired to save us, you would not have declared to us that the things which are impossible with us are nevertheless possible with you who are God.[2] You have declared to us, Holy One: 'Cleanse yourself, if you want me to come.' And I told you, Holy One, that clay cannot cleanse itself. And again you told us, Master: 'Whoever wishes to be counted worthy of my gifts, let that person observe my footsteps in all things.' And how is it possible for the person who is blind from birth[3] to observe these things, unless his eyes are opened? A blind person looks for someone to lead him by the hand, so that somehow he might at least meet his small needs. For even Timaeus, the son of Bartimaeus, sat by the road asking for alms. And when he heard that the light of righteousness was passing by that way, he cried out, saying: 'Son of David, have mercy on me.' And when the crowds rebuked him, he cried out all the more saying: 'Son of David, have mercy on me.' When your goodness had compassion, and you called him toward yourself, saying: 'What do you want me to do for you?' he said: 'Teacher, I want to see.' And at once your goodness said: 'See,' and he did; and he saw your footsteps and followed you.[4] I, too, want to cry out, but the one who always wants to darken the eyes of the seeing rebukes me. If your goodness wants to call me also toward yourself and to say: 'What do you want me to do for you?' then like

1. Mt 7.7.
2. Cf. Mt 19.26; Mk 10.27; Lk 18.27.
3. Cf. Jn 9.1.
4. Cf. Mk 10.46–52.

him I, too, shall cry out: 'Lord, let my eyes be opened.'[5] For if the leper had been able to cleanse himself, he would not have cried: 'Lord, if you choose, you can make me clean,'[6] but he would have cleansed himself. Like him, I, too, cry out. Speak to me also in the same holy voice: 'I do choose; be made clean,'[7] and at once the leprosy will leave me. And having seen and been cleansed, then I shall observe your footsteps in order to walk after you; for you are the way of those who have strayed. Therefore, I entreat you, as my father: 'Yes, father, pray to our Master Christ, that he may open my eyes; for I have you to lead me by the hand and bring me to my Master Jesus.' For his is the glory with the Father and the Holy Spirit, to the ages of ages. Amen." Response by Barsanuphius.

"EHOLD, NOW IS THE acceptable time"[8] to chant the words of the Gospel: "Those who are well have no need of a physician, but those who are sick."[9] Therefore, if a sick person visits a doctor, that person must follow carefully the prescription of the doctor, according to the saying: "But whoever approaches God must believe that he exists and that he rewards those who diligently seek him."[10] For faithful is the one who said: "I shall give them one hundredfold now in this age, and eternal life in the age to come."[11] Those who approach the great doctor are illumined by him; and he heals all their spiritual passions. Let us, therefore, not boast by saying that we are faithful, since we are judged as hypocrites and unfaithful. For the things that are visible also reveal the faith that is invisible, which dwells in the innermost secrets of the heart. If we believe the Savior, who says: "Let it be done to you according to your faith,"[12] let him now also say to the soul that dwells in our body: "Take heart, daughter, your faith has saved you."[13]

So, then, it is not so much saying or proclaiming something that constitutes our faith; rather, our perfect faith is revealed in the healing itself. Therefore, if you have believed and been healed, then walk and do not stumble. You have been healed; so

5. Mt 20.33.
7. Mt 8.3.
9. Lk 5.31.
11. Mk 10.30.
13. Mt 9.22.

6. Mt 8.2.
8. 2 Cor 6.2.
10. Heb 11.6.
12. Mt 9.29.

do not limp. You have been healed; so do not carry any spot of leprosy. You have been healed; so show that your issue of blood has ceased. And if you have these things, O human being, you are close to hearing the Savior saying to your most pure and beautiful soul: "You are altogether beautiful, and there is no flaw in you,"[14] and again the Apostle saying: "Not having any spot or wrinkle or anything of the kind."[15] The door then is open to us, and the way made plain before us. But let us observe that "the gate is narrow and the way strait that leads to life,"[16] and that: "It is through many tribulations that we must enter the kingdom of heaven."[17] And let us persevere in the work of our labor. For truly: "The sufferings of the present time are not worth comparing with the glory about to be revealed to us."[18] And: "God is not unjust, so as to overlook [our work]"[19] in such labors, if we endure patiently to the end. For it is said: "The one who endures to the end shall be saved,"[20] in Christ Jesus our Lord. Amen.

LETTER 60

Question from the same person to the same Great Old Man in the form of a prayer, about unclean thoughts and about the resurrection: "O 'Life and Resurrection,'[21] visit us; for we are your creation; and cleanse us from the legion of evil, Holy One; for you have shown compassion on your creation, and cast out the legion, when the demons sought to enter the swine. Whether it was in the irrational swine, or in me who am rational, for I have received them and have gone over the cliffs into the sea[22] where the waves beat me—I do not know. But now someone is pricking me from within to awaken the Helmsman[23] so that he may give me his hand and snatch me up from the deep, as he did with Peter, and that he may say to me also: 'You of little faith, why did you doubt?'[24]

"And since you promised me, through the responses of your servant Barsanuphius, to lay us in the same grave, shall we therefore also rise together? For I fear the one who said: 'Then two

---

14. Song 4.7.
16. Mt 7.14.
18. Rom 8.18.
20. Mt 10.22.
22. Cf. Mk 5.9–13.
24. Mt 14.31.

15. Eph 5.27.
17. Acts 14.22.
19. Heb 6.10.
21. Jn 11.25.
23. Cf. Mk 4.38; Lk 8.24.

shall be in the field; one will be taken, and the other will be left. Two women shall be [grinding] at the mill; one will be taken, and the other will be left.'[25] And since, from the creation of the world, people have been falling asleep and the bodies of the saints are often found together with those of the sinners in the same tomb, shall they then rise together in the resurrection, when your chosen angels come to raise all the righteous? Or shall they not, but only the elect? It is for this reason that I am afraid and entreat you, through your servant, that, just as you have shown that we shall lie together in one grave, so also you may show that you shall raise us together. And I entreat my father, Barsanuphius, since the two of us have received fields to reap, and since I have fallen ill and cannot reap, that he may strive so long as he is strong to bring to you, the Master, sheaves of righteousness also on my behalf. We have also seen in the ancient fathers such an example; for three went out to reap and one fell ill, like me, and returned to his cell; and the others took strength and gathered the harvest. And when they had completed the harvest and returned to their homes, they obliged him to receive his wage. But he objected: 'What wage, when I have not labored, but only you have labored?' And when they took him to [spiritual] court in order for him to receive the wage, the fathers ordered him to take it; and their judgment was counted blessed.[26] Therefore, Master Christ God, validate this prayer of mine; for yours is the glory to the ages. Amen." Response.

Just as someone who is master of his house sets in place his own faithful stewards, giving them both his keys and his possessions as well as his household, and it depends on the faithful steward how to sleep or how to feed or how to be rewarded by his own master, or with whom he will keep company, whether with drunkards or with people of modest conduct—and for the one is stored up "woe," while for the other a blessing—so also our God has set for himself certain faithful people as stewards, and has given them his keys, namely, free will, to shut and to open. They are faithful, because all Christians are baptized; and the good management of things entrusted to them clearly signifies the works of Baptism for their own salvation. Therefore, if

25. Mt 24.40–41.
26. See *Verba Seniorum* 17.20, PL 73.976–77.

any one of these turns away from this straight way, his portion[27] comes to be with the drunkards, with those who are drunk with the wine of lawlessness. This person is counted as a rational swine; and you know what happens to such a person when the Master arrives! If, however, he manages well the affairs entrusted to him, everyone knows the word of blessing to him from the Master. For it is said: "Their voice has gone out through all the earth, and their words to the ends of the world."[28]

As for the resurrection, however, this age is a threshing-ground, and the tares are found together with the wheat.[29] Therefore, when the resurrection takes place, the voice of the Gospel teaches us that they are raised mixed together; for it is said: "And he will separate people from one another, as the shepherd separates the sheep from the goats,"[30] and so on. And when he spoke about the two women and the two men in regard to the end of the world, he was referring to faithfulness and faithlessness, indicating that afterward, one is taken while the other one remains. And as for the reaping of the brothers, good is actually constituted by both. The one who was ill had the good intention of working, but it was illness that prevented him; the others held that the Lord had strengthened them through the prayers of the brother who was ill, and so the grace of the Holy Spirit came upon both of them. Therefore, as the Lord said to the apostles: "Do not rejoice at this, that the demons submit to you, but rejoice that your names are written in heaven,"[31] so we, too, should not seek to know whether we shall all be raised, but whether we shall hear: "Come, you that are blessed by my Father, inherit the kingdom prepared for you from the foundation of the world,"[32] and whether we shall be together with Jesus, as he said, "in the Father."[33] For to him is the glory to the ages. Amen.

LETTER 61

Question from the same person to the same Great Old Man in the form of a prayer: "Lord Jesus Christ, Physician of wounded

27. Cf. Mt 24.49, 51.
29. Cf. Mt 13.15–20.
31. Lk 10.20.
33. Jn 17.21.

28. Ps 18.5; Rom 10.18.
30. Mt 25.32.
32. Mt 25.34.

souls, we offer you prayers from your holy words, which [we ask] that you accept through your servant. For you have said, Holy One: 'Those who are well have no need of a physician, but those who are sick.'[34] Your servant Paul also mentioned this: 'So that what is lame may not be put out of joint, but rather be healed.'[35] Holy One, in one of these responses, you said: 'If you have been made whole, then why are you limping?'[36] One who has been made whole does not limp, but walks straight. As for me, since I am lame and wounded, this is why I cry out, so that you may visit me, too, just as you visited him who was traveling down to Jericho and fell among the thieves (for I, too, have fallen among the same thieves, and have been wounded), that you may also bind my wounds, and set me on your holy animal, namely, on good faith, bringing me into your holy inn[37] in order to take care of me where you care for all those who are troubled. Master, the woman with the issue of blood came up behind you, and was healed by touching your garments.[38] Yet I receive healing daily from your holy members, namely, your body and blood, and the water that issued from your holy side,[39] and still my illness swells. Since you said, Holy One, that anyone who visits a doctor and wants to be healed does whatever is prescribed by the physician, then send me, Master, whatever medicines, cauterizations, and plasters you want; but please stop my stinking issue of blood, namely, my unclean thought. You also said, Lord, that the door is opened; yet the dogs are watching on all sides, not allowing anyone to approach the door, and the good housemaster sees the poor man coming from afar and being troubled by the dogs, and so he sends the doorman to drive away the dogs in order that the poor man may approach and receive alms from your goodness. Father, what does it mean when you wrote to us: 'Anyone who lives seven years[40] shall see things that have not happened since the foundation of the world'? And what are we younger ones doing? How are we to be saved? Pray to the Lord that he might show us where the holy mountains are to which he told us to flee[41] in order to be saved, and what kind of mountains they are. Are they spiritual mountains? Or are they visible mountains? We,

34. Lk 5.31.   35. Heb 12.13.

36. See *Letter* 59.   37. Cf. Lk 10.30–34.

38. Cf. Mt 9.20–22.   39. Cf. Mk 5.22–34; Jn 19.34.

40. Or, "several." The expression literally reads: "a week of years" or "seven years" (ἐτῶν ἑβδομάς).

41. Cf. Mt 24.16; Mk 13.14; Lk 21.21.

too, should know that when the hour comes we may flee there
and be saved, in the name of the Father and the Son and the
Holy Spirit, to the ages. Amen." Response by Barsanuphius.

Brother, let us understand what we are saying here, and we
shall see that we have reproof from our own words. For unless
the person who comes to the doctor is disciplined according to
the prescription of that doctor, that same person cannot be rid
of suffering. And since you have spoken about also receiving
other healing and medicines, I am amazed by how your love
does not comprehend the wisdom of our great Doctor in every
art, how he has cut off all occasion [of sin] from every person
who asks him. Indeed, in opening up every book of healing to
all those who seek to look in them for salvation, he has demon-
strated us to be without excuse. For even when women every-
where chant: "I am a worm, and not human; scorned by others
and despised by the people,"[42] what shall the men do? I am not
speaking as one who abhors women—far be it from me! For we
have not been thus commanded. Yet although from the beginning they were the cause of transgression, God did not exclude
them from the divine teaching. So if this medicine pleases us,
why do we throw it away, even if we are so deceived as to think
that we have not thrown it away but that we still have it? Therefore, we speak in form, but not in fact. For it is true—and if
we examine our inner being, then we shall truly discover it to
be so—that we bear neither reproof nor insult, nor again anni-
hilation or shame. And from the thought that you have today,
in which I once tested you, you may learn—for afterward you
regretted that you had not actually learned—that I did those
things about which you know because I wished to test your love,
but I found the old nature still dwelling in you. Nevertheless,
I think that your love has benefited quite a lot from this. Our
Lord, then, is perfect, and desires all of his people to be perfect. For it is said: "Be perfect, therefore, just as your heavenly Father is perfect."[43] So one who bears these cauterizations is
saved. For whoever has his own foul smell in the nostrils can

42. Ps 21.6.
43. Mt 5.48.

sense no other smell, even if he stands over numerous dead things. And whoever has been plundered by thieves has nothing to share with others.

Do you see, then, beloved one, how those of us who are held captive by freedom from care do not wish to be entirely care-free, in order to regard ourselves as we are—as earth and dust? Instead, we have grown old nourishing vainglory in ourselves. For if we feel that our work is pleasing to God, and that our settlement edifies everyone, and that we have been rid of judging and condemning, this is the ultimate vainglory and nothing else. Therefore, if our great and heavenly Physician has granted us cures and plasters, through what else is the cause of our destruction to be found other than through the weakness of our own free will? Above all else, he has granted us humility, which banishes all pride and "every proud obstacle that is raised up against the knowledge" of the glory of the Son of God;[44] he has granted us obedience, which "is able to quench all the flaming arrows of the enemy";[45] he has granted us the excision of our will in all things before our neighbor. All this gives rise to imperturbability in the heart and to a brighter, more joyful outlook, as well as to greater stability in our vision. As for the great plaster, which braces all our limbs and "cures every disease and every sickness,"[46] he has granted us a love like his. He himself has become our model. For it is said: "He humbled himself, becoming [not just] obedient, [but even] to the point of death."[47] And laying down his life for us, he taught us, saying: "Love one another just as I have loved you," and: "By this shall everyone know that you are my disciples, if you have love for one another."[48]

So if you do not want to walk with a limp, then take up the staff of the cross, and set your hands firmly on it, and die, and you will no longer walk with a limp; for a dead person never walks with a limp. And if you hold this staff, then there is no need for a door-keeper. For with this staff you can drive away not only the dogs, but also that chief of the wild beasts, the roar-

---

44. 2 Cor 10.5.
45. Eph 6.16.
46. Mt 4.23 and 9.35.
47. Phil 2.8.
48. Jn 13.34–35.

ing lion.[49] Jacob said: "With my staff, I crossed the river";[50] and again: "he worshiped above this [staff]."[51] Moses performed signs with the staff. And the person who is nailed to the staff surely sheds streams of fluid. For the person who dies, dies to sin. And what hope is expected after this, except resurrection on the third day? It is sufficient for the crucified person to be raised up with Jesus. As for the matter of seven[52] years, there will be diverse tribulations and upheavals. And about the mountains that you mentioned, let us understand them to be the holy Mary the God-bearer and the saints in succession, and such persons as in those times are found firmly to have the seal of the Son of God. For he saves many people on account of them; and to him is the glory to the ages. Amen.

LETTER 62

Question from the same [brother] to the same Old Man: "Trinity inseparable, do not be separated from us. 'Out of the mouths of babes and infants, you have prepared praise for yourself.'[53] Father, you are truly a good disciple of the true Physician. Indeed, you have given us medicines and antidotes. And the first cauterization has greatly pricked my heart, so that I cannot bear the pains. For you wrote to us that we should sing: 'I am a worm, and not human.'[54] And truly I sing and worship and glorify and exult to the ages, but I do not dare say: 'I am a worm, and not a human being.'[55] For I am a human being that is wounded by the corruptible worm. What, then, is the force of this incorruptible worm? This worm came for my sake to deliver me from the corruptible worm, which corrupts the human race. And since this corruptible worm, which corrupts and is corrupted, goes down into the wounds and works therein infection and stench, the incorruptible worm came, of which it is said: 'I am a worm, and not human.'[56] And just as this worm enters our wounds, so also the incorruptible worm goes down 'into the lowest parts of the earth,'[57] and thence begins to corrupt all the impurity of the old

49. Cf. 1 Pt 5.8.
50. Gn 32.10.
51. Gn 47.31.
52. Or, "several." See p. 79, n. 40.
53. Ps 8.3; Mt 21.16.
54. Ps 21.6.
55. Ibid.
56. Ibid.
57. Eph 4.9.

worm; and having thus cleansed them all, it leads them up, while itself remaining incorrupt. This is the worm that cleansed Job of the corruptible worm, and that said to him: 'Arise, gird up your loins like a man.'[58] This worm also 'drew out the dragon with a hook,'[59] while hanging on the wood. To this worm 'all things are put in subjection, except the one who subjected all things to himself. For he has subjected all things beneath his feet.'[60] The corruptible worm corrupts all things, and there is nothing anywhere on earth, neither wood nor food nor earth nor flesh, which it does not consume, except salt and oil. And what is this salt and oil, except the Father who has subjected all things to himself, and who seasoned his creation with his mercy, who also gave salt to the apostles that they might season the world from the stench of the idols, and come to the fragrance of the true God? Amen. And what is the force of the mustard, to which he likened the kingdom of heaven,[61] instead of to the olive tree or the palm tree or any of the great trees, preferring rather the insignificant one? It is because the mustard is very harsh, and stiffens our hearts. Yes, father, pray that the Lord may show us this mystery of the worm and of the mustard, so that we, too, may glorify the Father and the Son with the Holy Spirit, to the ages. Amen.

"Father, since you have reminded me of previous matters, I, too, have not forgotten but always remember those things which the enemy did not do but instead was enraged when he saw fruit produced in this place; but your patience and God's loving-kindness did not allow his foul will to come to pass, and so we are even until now glorifying God. Since you told me that: 'You repented afterward, after the deed,' would that it were even afterward, that I may not persist in it completely. And since you told me that 'one who falls among thieves and is plundered has nothing to share with another,' for this reason I pray in hunger, in order that you, who have something to share, may throw me your crumbs, so that I, too, may receive food like the dog beneath the table[62] from you that have [something to offer]. And since you said: 'Pride and pretentiousness have aged with you,' pray for me, that they may depart from me in the name of the Lord. Amen." Response by Barsanuphius.

---

58. Jb 38.3 and 40.2.   59. Jb 40.19–25.
60. 1 Cor 15.27.
61. Cf. Mt 13.31; Mk 4.31; Lk 13.19.
62. Cf. Mk 7.28.

David earlier spoke, saying: "My wounds grow foul and fes-
ter"; but why is this? "Because of my foolishness."[63] So then,
foolishness is a storehouse of all evils. For foolishness has giv-
en birth to disobedience, and disobedience to a wound; and after the wound, the same foolishness gave rise to carelessness,
and carelessness to infection, and infection brought about the
stench, and the wretched flesh was filled with worms and was
corrupted. Thus corrupted, it was thrown into the sea, and became food for the great fish, being installed in its bowels, until
there came a heavenly worm, nailed on the hook of the cross,
and was let down into the bowels of the great fish, bringing up
through its mouth the food that it had swallowed, together with
its entrails. And taking the flesh, he anointed it with oil and
washed it with water and cooked it with fire; for it is said: "The
same shall baptize you with the Holy Spirit and fire";[64] and he
fed it with bread and gladdened it with wine, and seasoned it
with salt, thereby changing it from corruption. In addition to
this, he added to it mustard, contracting all the corruption and
stiffening the nostrils of the dragon, so that he [the dragon]
was rendered unable even to smell it, and disturbing his eyes so
that he could not look upon the perfection of its humility.[65]

Therefore, knowing all these things, let us not overlook his
counsel, lest the word also be fulfilled in us: "If salt has lost its
flavor, how will its saltiness be restored?"[66] And what does the
lack of these things signify? Nothing other than: "The fool said
in his heart, there is no God."[67] So if you have not forgotten the
previous things, and you know the last things, listen to him who
says: "One who knows the will of his master but does it not, will
receive a severe beating."[68] So, if we say: "We know," but we are
careless, we are not far from the "woe" that belongs to those
who sin in knowledge. If, however, we understand that we are
"earth and ashes,"[69] we are like Abraham and Job, and to the
ages we shall not be plundered, but shall always have something

---

63. Ps 37.6.
64. Mt 3.11; Lk 3.16.
65. Cf. Abba Isaiah, *Ascetic Discourses* 2 and 11.
66. Mt. 5.13.   67. Pss 13.1 and 52.1.
68. Lk 12.47.   69. Gn 18.27; Jb 42.6.

to give others also—neither gold nor silver,[70] but a model of humility and patience and love toward God. To him be the glory to the ages. Amen.

LETTER 63

The same person did not eat bread, and so he asked the Great Old Man about his diet. Response.

Brother, rejoice in the Lord. Entreat God to grant me perfect patience. For I begin something but do not bring it to completion. Instead, I am immediately diverted from my course. I long to make a beginning and come to some end, hearing the Apostle, who speaks about the beginning and the end: "The one who began a good work among you will also bring it to completion by the day of our Lord Jesus Christ."[71] Yet, even though I, the wretched one, do nothing pleasing to God, on account of your command I am offering an opinion, as if to a brother.

Take four vegetables a week, if you can, and every Sunday either drink their juice or boil them for your physical weakness, and I think you will eat well enough. Yet, as to whether I speak in foolishness, I know not. For one who does not direct oneself cannot possibly direct others. Forgive me, brother. I ought to entreat you to give orders to me; nonetheless, pride still entreats me, as the root of all evils. Pray, brother, that we may cross the way that lies before us. For it is full of storms and dangers, yet I am laughing and indifferent in my foolishness. Nevertheless, I do not lose hope. For I have a merciful and compassionate Master. So give me your hand for the sake of love, and draw me toward him; and through you he will save me, the wretch. To him be the glory to the ages. Amen.

LETTER 64

The same [brother] did not practice the diet recommended to him by the Old Man, and so he asked him the same question a second time. And he responded to him as follows. [Response.]

70. Cf. Acts 3.6.
71. Phil 1.6.

Brother, since you found me happy to be ordered by your love, perhaps this is why you have ignored my words. Indeed, the cause of this does not come from you but is derived entirely from me, inasmuch as my words are fruitless. For they do not come from the sweat of practice, and so they do not have any force. One who asks and disobeys angers God; for on account of the question, the envy of the enemy also follows. To this day we have not learned the craftiness of the demons. The Apostle ceaselessly preaches, saying: "For we are not ignorant of his designs."[72] Take heart, my brother; unless you were my soul-mate for the sake of the love that is according to Christ, I could not give you any response. For as I have also told you before, I am not up to this measure.

Yet since God has glued me to your love, again I speak in foolishness: limit yourself to four vegetables a week, as I told you, and each Sunday either drink their juice or boil them on account of your weakness. Do not believe in your heart, however, that I have given you a command. It is not a command, but the opinion of a brother. The way is open before us. "Let us run in such a way that we may win";[73] for we are corruptible people, and have only a short time on this earth; let us find mercy at that fearful and terrible hour, in Christ Jesus our Lord.

LETTER 65

Response from the same Great Old Man to the same person, indicating the significance of the response.

Brother, what else have I to say about this, I who have done absolutely nothing? Even if you say: "You have done, and are doing something," yet I never myself remember doing anything except always angering God in my works. Therefore, I expect nothing for my works. On account of his loving-kindness, however, I hope to be saved. For he died "to save sinners."[74] So I am sitting here by virtue of his name, until he personally comes and tells me: "What do you want me to do for you?"[75] so that

72. 2 Cor 2.11.   73. 1 Cor 9.24.
74. 1 Tm 1.15.   75. Mk 10.51.

I, too, may say with that other person: "Lord, let me have my sight again."[76] Even if I had works as well, I would not dare to speak, for fear of the condemnation of the Pharisee.[77] Nevertheless, I tell you, brother, that all my life and hope hang upon him, and I entreat him night and day to be cleansed from my visible and hidden passions. What, then, do I have to say about achievements, when I hear: "Every mouth shall be silenced,"[78] and so forth; and again: "Let the one who boasts, boast in the Lord"?[79] And blessed is the one who has been cleansed from wrath and the rest of the passions, who has "kept all of the commandments,"[80] and who says: "I am a worthless servant."[81] Yet, if we achieve one thing and then lose it through another, what has it profited us daily to build up one and tear down another? If anyone thinks nothing of [both] glory and disgrace, such a person can be saved in Christ Jesus our Lord; to him be the glory. Amen. Commend me to the Lord, and remain confidently in your stillness, praying for me, the wretched and lowly one.

LETTER 66

Question from the same [brother] to the same Great Old Man: "Father, pray for me; for I am toiling. Before I began speaking to you, anything I seemed to do, I was doing it without any toil on my part; but since you have given me a word, I am toiling to the point where I am falling into sickness. And prior to this, I wrote to you about this word, and you actually reckoned me to have proud thoughts, telling me about the Pharisee.[82] Yet I, father, did not speak to you out of pride, but only out of necessity. I entreat you, offer a prayer so that the Lord may reveal to you that which is in me." Response by Barsanuphius.

Brother, divine Scripture says: "Do all things with counsel,"[83] and: "Do nothing without counsel."[84] When you were acting without counsel, namely, from your own will, you were not toiling with your intellect. For there is no one who does not need

---

76. Lk 18.41.
77. Cf. Lk 18.10–14.
78. Rom 3.19.
79. 1 Cor. 1.31.
80. Mt 19.21; Lk 18.21.
81. Lk 17.10.
82. Cf. Lk 18.10–14.
83. Prv 24.72, or 31.4 LXX.
84. Sir 32.19.

a counselor, except God alone, who created wisdom.[85] When, however, you sought in accord with God to cut off your own will and come to humility, and to take me, your least brother, as your counselor, then you provoked envy in the demon who hates good and is always envious of all people. Do you see the crookedness of the devil?

Of myself, I have not commanded you in any way; when you asked me, I advised you as a brother; and having heard me, you left and accordingly added to your actions. Moreover, I spoke to you about the Pharisee. For he, too, was boasting when he said what he said. You asked for some assurance, yet this is nothing else but pride. Pay attention, and you will see clearly how, when you make a beginning, he immediately brings you some pretext, and so you interrupt the beginning; and again you recommence, and immediately you stop. And you do not remember that "the one who endures to the end will be saved,"[86] or that "he who began a good work among you will also bring it to completion by the day of our Lord Jesus Christ"?[87] If you find rest in acting by yourself, as you have been doing, I am not disappointed. For I do not want to become anyone's spiritual elder or teacher. I have the Apostle offering me reproof: "You, then, that teach others, will you not teach yourself?"[88] Brother, those who are being saved "melt away the soul as a spider."[89] Therefore, we need much patience, until we enter into the kingdom of God through many tribulations,[90] in Christ Jesus our Lord. Amen. Forgive me, brother, and pray for me.

LETTER 67

Question from the same person to the same Great Old Man: "O Jesus, who sought the wandering sheep,[91] teach us also how to seek the Shepherd. Father, there is one more question that I wish to ask you. Since it is written: 'Seek the Lord and his strength; seek his presence continually,'[92] how can a sinful person seek the Lord forever? Teach us this word for the sake of him who gave

---

85. Cf. Prv 8.22.
87. Phil 1.6.
89. Cf. Ps 38.11.
91. Cf. Mt 18.12.

86. Mt 10.22.
88. Rom 2.21.
90. Cf. Acts 14.22.
92. Ps 104.4.

you wisdom, so that we, too, may forever seek the face of the Lord; for to him is the glory to the ages. Amen." Response by Barsanuphius.

Brother Euthymius, I entreat your love, toil with me in prayer to the kind and loving God. For your love has also asked me to write to you about how we may seek the Shepherd. And from the very first day until now, I am praying to God about your request; and he tells me: "Cleanse your heart from the thoughts of the old self, and I shall grant you your requests. My gifts are received by and granted to those who are pure. For as long as wrath and remembrance of evil and other similar passions of the old self trouble your heart, wisdom will not enter it. If you sincerely desire my gifts, remove from yourself the vessels of the enemy,[93] and mine will come to you quite naturally. Have you not heard: 'No slave can serve two masters'?[94] Therefore, if you serve me, then do not serve the devil; and if you serve the devil, then you can never serve me. So if anyone wishes to be counted worthy of my gifts, that person will follow my footsteps. For as a guileless sheep, I accepted all the sufferings, not responding in any way,[95] and I told you to be 'as innocent as doves.'[96] Instead of this, you still have the fierceness of the passions. Look at how I do not say to you: 'Walk in the light of your fire.'"[97]

Therefore, having heard these things, I mourn and moan, until his goodness is also compassionate toward me, and he delivers me from the terrible passions of the old self, so that I may follow the footsteps of the new self, and accept all things that come upon me with great patience. For you know that "patience produces character."[98] The Apostle has made mention of this. So pray, my brother, that it may come to pass in me. And reprove me for the sake of love, if anything escapes me, so that I may correct this. For, indeed, I am foolish. Nevertheless, I love those who teach and reprove me, knowing that their teaching will be for the salvation of my soul. Again, pray that I may avoid the pitfall of pretending to have rights; for I am troubled in ev-

---

93. Cf. Neh 13.8.   94. Lk 16.13; Mt 6.24.
95. Cf. Is 53.7.   96. Mt 10.16.
97. Is 50.11.   98. Rom 5.4.

ery way. And forgive me for all the ways in which I am always
putting you to work. Nevertheless, this matter deserves great reward in Christ Jesus our Lord. Amen.

LETTER 68

Question from the same person to the same Great Old Man: "Father, my labors, which I give to you, you have assigned to yourself. And this is what the wise do in order to bear the burden of
their neighbor. Yet, since I asked you about the response, I did so
not only for my sake but for the sake of many others, whose souls
will benefit from it; especially since you, in your great compassion, father, encourage us to ask about the [right] way of life. But
I pray, since the Lord has sent you to me as a haven and refuge,
be merciful and entreat the Master that he may show his mercy
to me and reveal to me any slight matter wherein I may fall without knowing. Indeed, [I ask that you] reveal this to me as you revealed it the first time, so that I may repent. And afterward, show
me the way that I should walk; for you have assumed responsibility for my soul." Response by Barsanuphius.

Brother, I speak to you as to my own soul. For the Lord has
bound your soul to mine, saying: "Do not leave him"; so it is
not for me to teach you, but rather to learn from you. For I fear
him who says: "You, then, that teach others, will you not teach
yourself?"[99] since it also says: "A nod is sufficient for a wise person,"[100] although it was not sufficient for you,[101] but you wanted
to hear more explicitly. If a fool sins by word, he receives forgiveness from all; for he is a fool and does not know what he
says. If, however, a wise person sins, he does not receive forgiveness; for he is wise and has sinned intentionally. Therefore, the
same happens if any of the brothers living outside sins by word;
that brother receives forgiveness, for he is outside, with everyone else. If, however, we sin, we who are considered as reclus-
es and hesychasts and virtuous among people, what forgiveness
can we receive?

Moreover, since you want to know about this matter openly,

99. Rom 2.21.
100. Cf. Prv 9.9.
101. Using the variant reading, σοι; see SC 426, 330.

I shall tell you. You are sitting within, as one who has died to the world. How then, when you converse with someone, do you change from love and joy to exasperation and remembrance of evil, blaming your neighbor rather than yourself, instead of saying: "It is I who am unworthy," even reckoning yourself as being someone?[102] For when occasion arises, you say: "Speak; for I have spoken and they have gladly heard." What! Do you really think that they gladly receive your word? Are you Elijah the prophet? Blame yourself, and learn that everything that happens to you does not happen without the will of God, whether it is a matter of rest for which you give thanks, or of trial which you must endure. Where is the word that is written: "You endure it when someone gives you a slap in the face,"[103] and so on? This is why we are far from God.

So if you want to learn the [right] way, it is as follows: regard the one who strikes you as the one who cherishes you, and the one who dishonors you as the one who glorifies you, and the one who insults you as the one who honors you, and the one who afflicts you as the one who refreshes you.[104] And whether it is by oversight or by choice that people behave toward you in their customary way, do not be troubled, but rather say: "If it was the will of God, then they would come." And when they do come, receive them with joyful face, rejoicing that: "although I was unworthy, the Lord was merciful to me," as Daniel said when the Lord visited him; he simply said: "God has remembered me,"[105] believing that he was unworthy. And put aside the pretense to rights; for if you say anything, you will say: "My speech was good," and when you think of something, you will say: "It was good that I thought of it." Good? Good? Where is the good in this? Why do we not understand that God will come to our assistance in everything, if only we do not trouble anyone whether by word or by deed? You were struggling to reveal your

---

102. "Not reckoning oneself as something" (τὸ ἀψήφιστον) is a phrase derived from the Desert Fathers (see *Letter* 604) and frequently used by Barsanuphius and John to signify the way of extreme humility or disregard of oneself. See *Letter* 272.

103. 2 Cor 11.20.

104. Cf. Abba Zosimas, *Reflections* 2–3.

105. Dn 14.38 LXX.

thought to the brothers, preferring to fulfill your will, thinking: "What if the work is not done today?"—and you wounded the feelings of some of the younger ones who say: "What are two more days, that the old man cannot wait?" Tell me truly: was the work done? Did you ascend to heaven? Rather, you were simply struck in an untimely way by the devil. Brother, from now on let us "leave the dead to bury their own dead," and let us "proclaim the kingdom of God"[106] in Christ Jesus our Lord. Amen.

LETTER 69

Question in the form of a prayer from the same person to the same Great Old Man: "Life of the desperate, do not overlook me; for I lie in despair. 'The unfolding of your words gives light; it imparts understanding to the simple.'[107] You have declared to me, Holy One: 'Purify yourself, and cast away from you the old self.' But can clay purify itself? Or can a building decorate itself, unless its builder decorates it? Or can a pot shaped by the potter bake itself, unless the one who molded it places it in the fire to test whether it can be used? So if you, Holy One, wish to save what you have fashioned, send down your divine fire, that it may bake the pot molded by you, that it may receive your oil and not leak; for yours is the glory and the mercy to the ages. Amen." Response by Barsanuphius.

Brother, do not compel me to speak when I desire to embrace stillness and silence. Now, then, fix your heart on the Lord, and persevere without being shaken. For the one who envied Adam from the beginning, casting him out of paradise, envies also our concord in Christ. He who said, however: "I watched Satan fall from heaven like a flash of lightning,"[108] will abolish him from us and tear up his nets. Therefore, do not be caught up in any of his tricks, by being shaken from your place. This is how he tricked Malchus.[109] For he is terribly bitter against us. Yet if we are humble, the Lord will abolish him. Therefore, let us direct the blame for everything upon ourselves; for this is victory.

As for thinking about departing to the desert, the fathers

---

106. Lk 9.60.   107. Ps 118.130.
108. Lk 10.18.
109. Cf. Jerome, *Life of Malchus* 3 in PL 23.55.

have said: "There are three chapters; whoever keeps these is able to dwell both among people and in the deserts, and any other place. These are blaming oneself, leaving behind one's own will, and regarding oneself as being beneath all creation."[110] And your love should learn that all the effort of the devil aims precisely at separating us from one another. For he sees the Scripture accurately fulfilled in us, namely, that "a brother assisted by a brother is like a city fortified with ramparts."[111] May the Lord not grant him the fulfillment of his will in us; instead, may he "crush" him, in accordance with the word of the Apostle, "swiftly under our feet."[112] So do not doubt. For I hope that the two of us shall be laid together in a single grave, as I have already told you. This is why God has brought us together, in order that we may profit from one another. So all these trials will become models for the benefit and support of many others. Be still, then, brother, and pray that we may traverse this passage, in order that we may not spend our days in vain. For the time has drawn near, and the enemy is raging. Therefore, God has not rendered your labor vain; far be it! Rather, the one who "desires everyone to be saved and to come to the knowledge of the truth"[113] also desires that you may enter into perfection. For he said to the apostles: "Then, say that we are worthless servants."[114] Let us preserve ourselves, and he shall work his mercy with us for the sake of his name, which has been invoked upon us. To him be the glory to the ages. Amen.

LETTER 70

When distrust had been sown by the envy of the devil in the thought of the questioning elder against the same Great Old Man, in regard to the benefit of his responses, the latter knew what was in his heart and stated the following to him.

First, and before all else, I glorify the holy and consubstantial Trinity, and say: "Glory to the Father and the Son and the Holy Spirit, both now and always, and to the ages of ages. Amen." It

---

110. Cf. *Sayings*, in *Sentences Nouvelles*, 333.
111. Prv 18.19.   112. Rom 16.20.
113. 1 Tm 2.4.   114. Lk 17.10.

was not inappropriate that I should begin with such a doxology, but I do so in order to show the demon, that hater of good, that in the fantasies that derive from him there is nothing like this doxology, but only turmoil, sorrow, and disheartenment. Therefore, brother, let us offer thanksgiving to God for our redemption from the great temptation which came upon us in our lack of understanding, and for the fact that his loving-kindness did not allow us to be destroyed to the end. For he is always true, who said: "As I live, says the Lord, and I have no pleasure in the death of sinners, but rather that they should turn from their ways and live."[115]

Now, then, let us give constant thanks to the one who has saved us and who always saves us; for to him give thanks the angels, the supra-worldly powers, the heavenly hosts, the Cherubim and Seraphim, with most dignified voices, ceaselessly and endlessly shouting and crying out, saying: "Holy, holy, holy,[116] Lord of Sabaoth,"[117] and so forth. Let us then perceive this, giving thanks to him "who has heaven as a throne and the earth as a footstool,"[118] "whom all creatures serve."[119] And let us begin from this scriptural prototype, likewise giving thanks ourselves to the Father; for he had mercy on "the world, and was not sparing" in sending "his only begotten Son as Savior"[120] and Redeemer of our souls. Let us give thanks to the Son; for "he humbled himself, becoming obedient to the point of death, even death on a cross"[121] for our sake. Let us give thanks to the Holy Spirit, the Giver of life, which spoke through the Law, the Prophets, and the Teachers; which instructed Peter to repent, and commanded him to go to Cornelius,[122] and glorified him, giving him power to raise the dead, such as Tabitha;[123] which always anticipates and crushes the snares of the enemy for those who call upon him, according to the prophecy of David, who

---

115. Ezek 18.3, 23.
116. The "thrice-holy hymn" or *Trisagion* was frequently adopted in liturgical usage from the early fifth century.
117. Is 6.3.
118. Is 66.1.
119. Jdt 16.14.
120. Jn 3.16; Rom 8.32; 1 Jn 4.14.
121. Phil 2.8.
122. Cf. Acts 10.19–20.
123. Cf. Acts 9.40.

says: "The snare is crushed, and we have escaped; our help is in the name of the Lord, who made heaven and earth."[124] Behold, then, he has had mercy on us and healed us from such great sickness. Let us hear him saying: "Behold, you have been made whole; do not sin any more, so that nothing worse happens to you."[125]

Moreover, let us seek to attain humility in all things. For the one who is humble lies on the ground; and the one who lies on the ground has nowhere to fall. It is clear, however, that the one who is on high ground easily falls. So if we have been turned back and corrected, "this is not from our own doing; it is the gift of God."[126] For Scripture says: "The Lord lifts those who are bowed down, and enlightens the blind,"[127] and so on. When, however, you write to me: "Who shall separate us from the love of Christ?"[128] this word is of great measure. Behold, we very nearly cut off the cord of Christ's love, as a result dying and forsaking Christ's ship. Nevertheless, in order not to break the seal and talk too much, it is good for me to stop here. For someone is pricking me, saying: "Where there are wise persons, do not display your wisdom."[129] So I shall cease speaking. I have written as to a truly beloved one. By doing this, you will attain the way that leads to eternal life, which is in Christ Jesus our Lord, with whom to the Father with the Holy Spirit be glory, honor, and might, to the ages. Pray for me, brother.

LETTER 71

On receiving this, the old man gave himself over to mourning and tears for many days. And the Great Old Man writes to him the following in order to comfort him.

Brother, let us cast behind us whatever has passed, according to the apostolic word that says: "Everything old has passed away; behold, everything has become new."[130] Let us yoke ourselves with one mind in the easy yoke of Christ,[131] and establish our-

---

124. Ps 123.7–8.
125. Jn 5.14.
126. Eph 2.8.
127. Ps 145.8.
128. Rom 8.35.
129. Sir 7.5.
130. 2 Cor 5.17.
131. Cf. Mt 11.29–30.

selves in the love of Christ. For it is said: "God is love."[132] Therefore, if anyone claims to possess love, let that person possess
nothing hated by Christ. Let us strive to cleanse our hearts from
the passions of the old self, which God hates. For "we are his
temples,"[133] and the divine does not dwell in a temple stained by
passions. Let us then enter and attain our small stillness. For we
have done what is sufficient. And let us pray that our life of stillness may be according to his will, glorifying the holy and pure
Trinity. Enter then, and commend me to God. And no longer
trouble me about these things, whether through questions or
letters. For I am very busy now.

I have sent the scapular[134] at your command, knowing that I
am nothing but earth and ashes. Therefore, I have not sent it to
you because I am good enough—for I am unclean and a debtor
in all things—but that I may not overlook the commandment
that says: "Give to everyone who asks from you."[135] And I have
sent it also for the love that is in Christ. So when you receive
it, pray for me; and pray that "our labor may not be in vain,"[136]
but in Christ Jesus our Lord. To him be the glory to the ages.
Amen.

132. 1 Jn 4.8.
133. 2 Cor 6.16.
134. The *analabos* is a monastic garb of the Eastern Church, depicting (once,
or many times: *polystavrion*) the symbol of the cross. It is made of fabric or, originally, leather. Here I have translated it as "scapular," although the correspondence with the Western scapular is by no means precise.
135. Mt 5.42.
136. 1 Thes 3.5.

LETTERS TO AN ELDERLY MONK
NAMED ANDREW (72–123)

LETTER 72

An old man who was ill, named Andrew, who was living in still-ness in the monastic community, declared some of his secret faults to the same Great Old Man, while at the same time giving thanks for the fact that he had been counted worthy to dwell near such a person; and about his bodily illness. Response by Barsanuphius.

F YOU TRULY believe that it is actually God who has brought you to this place, then entrust him with all your cares[1] and cast on him all your concerns; and he will dispose your affairs as he wills. If, however, you hold back from him in regard to any matter at all, whether about some bodily illness or the passions of the soul, then you are obliged to deal with these as you see fit. For when someone has discharged everything to God, and that person experiences even the slight-est affliction, duplicity always leads that person to say: "If per-haps I had taken care of my body, I would not have to be afflict-ed in this way." Therefore, one who gives oneself to God must surrender oneself to him unto death and with the whole heart. For God knows, far more than we do, what is good for our soul and body. And to the degree that he allows you to be afflicted in the body, he accordingly lightens the burden of your sins.

God, then, demands nothing from you but thanksgiving and patience and prayer for the forgiveness of sins. See how proud I am, that while I am ridiculed by the demons, thinking that I possess love according to God, I am reduced to telling you: "I now bear half of your burden;[2] and for the future God is again

1. Or, "seal" (σφραγίς).
2. Cf. *Sayings*, Antony 16.

able to help you." I have spoken as someone beside himself. For I know that I am weak and incapable and naked of every good work. Yet my shamelessness does not allow me to despair. For I have a compassionate Master, one who is merciful and loving, who stretches out his hand to every sinner until his last breath. Cleave unto him, and in [every] matter he will do "far more than all we can ask or imagine."[3] To him be the glory to the ages. Amen. Forgive me, my brother, and pray for me.

LETTER 73

Having heard this from him, namely, the words: "I bear half of your burden," grieving that he did not promise him complete forgiveness, he entreated and begged him urgently for a second time, that through Christ he might grant him this completely. Response by Barsanuphius.

I am astonished by your love, brother, because you do not understand the affairs of love that is according to God. In the first place, God knows how I regard myself as earth and ashes, being nothing at all. Yet, if I say something to someone beyond my measure, or beyond my power, I do so moved by the love of Christ, knowing—as I said—that I am nothing but a worthless slave. Since, then, you did not understand what I told you, namely, that I bear half your sins, I have made you my partner. For I did not say to you: "I bear one third," leaving you to bear more and be burdened more than I. And again, I said what I have said in order to banish self-love; this is why I did not speak to you of bearing two-thirds, showing myself to be stronger than you; for such conduct would be vainglory. Nor did I say: "I bear the whole." This belongs to the perfect, to those who have become brothers of Christ, who laid down his own life for our sake, and who loves those who love us and do this for us in perfect love. And again, I would have rendered you a stranger to spiritual labor if I had not spoken in this way. So I am not vainglorious, as if ascribing to myself the whole; nor am I envious, by making you a partner in this good conversion. If we

3. Eph 3.20.

are brothers, then let us share equally in our Father's property,[4] and injustice will not divide us. If, however, you wish to cast on me the whole burden, then for the sake of obedience I accept this, too. Forgive me that great love leads me to speak nonsense. Yet may it be to you your gladness in Christ Jesus our Lord, to whom be the glory to the ages. Amen.

LETTER 74

Request from the same person to the same Great Old Man, that he might pray for him on account of an illness that befell him. Response by Barsanuphius.

Scripture says: "We have passed through fire and through water, and you have brought us out to a place of refreshment."[5] Those who wish to please God must pass through certain afflictions. How shall we call the holy martyrs blessed on account of the sufferings they endured for the sake of God, if we are unable to bear a simple fever? Say to the afflicted soul: "Is not the fever better for you than [the fire of] hell?" Let us not despair in illness; for the Apostle said: "Whenever I am weak, then I am strong."[6] Observe how "God directs hearts and minds."[7] Let us endure, let us bear, let us become disciples of the Apostle who says: "Be patient in suffering."[8]

Let us give thanks to God in all things, that the saying may not be fulfilled in us too: "He will give you praise, only when you do well for him."[9] And if you required bodily care, or for the sake of your testing have found a little tribulation, why do you not remember Job's words: "If we have received the good from the hand of the Lord, shall we not also endure the bad?"[10] Notice how those who in all things desire comfort shall hear: "During your lifetime, you received your good things."[11] Let us not slacken. For we have a merciful God, who knows our weakness better than we. And if in testing us he brings upon us illness, we nevertheless have the Apostle softening it for us by say-

4. Or, "essence" (οὐσία).
5. Ps 65.12.
6. 2 Cor 12.10.
7. Ps 7.9.
8. Rom 12.12.
9. Ps 48.19.
10. Jb 2.10.
11. Lk 16.25.

ing: "God is faithful, and will not allow you to be tested beyond your strength, but together with the testing will also provide for you the way out, so that you may be able to endure it."[12]

The Lord will strengthen alike the sick person and those who serve that person; and both these tasks will be for the glory of God. Look to the end of your patience, and do not grow despondent or weary. For God is nearby, saying: "I shall never leave you or forsake you."[13] Believe me, brothers, [when I say] that vainglory has gained control over me. Never have I in sickness laid down to rest or put down my handiwork; and yet great illnesses have come to me. Recently vainglory has been tricky, ever since I have entered its cell, and it does not allow illness to come to me. And I am grieved, because I desire patience, and I do not know what I can endure. No affliction comes my way, and so I melt when I hear: "Whoever endures to the end will be saved."[14] Nevertheless, pray that I may continue to hold fast the hope of salvation in Christ Jesus our Lord, to whom be the glory. Amen.

LETTER 75

The same old man was still sick and entreated the same Great Old Man to pray for him, that he might receive help from God. Response by Barsanuphius.

Since you have God, do not be afraid, but "cast all your anxiety on him,"[15] and he will take care of you. Do you not know that "if the earthly tent we live in is dissolved, then we have a building from God, a house not made with [human] hands, one which is eternal in the heavens"?[16] Believe then without hesitation, and God will help you. For he is merciful. To him be the glory. Pray for my own weakness for the sake of love.

LETTER 76

The same old man lived with a certain brother, and both of them fell ill; so he asked the Other Old Man to pray for them. Response by John.

12. 1 Cor 10.13.   13. Heb 13.5.
14. Mt 10.22.   15. 1 Pt 5.7.
16. 2 Cor 5.1.

The Lord said: "By your patience, you shall gain your souls."[17] And the Apostle follows suit, saying: "For you need patience."[18] And the prophet: "I waited patiently for the Lord, and he inclined to me and heard me."[19] And again, God our sweet Master said: "Whoever endures to the end will be saved."[20] Both of you should live in patience, giving thanks and looking to the holy power of God that comes to you from on high. For the purpose of all these things is to test you. Be vigilant in our words: "Prove me, Lord, and test me."[21] Pray for me, I entreat you, for the sake of the love that is according to God.

LETTER 77

Question from the same person to the Great Old Man: "Since my thought tells me that I cannot be saved, pray for me, merciful father, and tell me what I should do when I am prevented from fasting." Response by Barsanuphius.

May the God of heaven and earth grant you and my unworthy self to find mercy at that hour, and to stand with boldness before his awesome and glorious seat of judgment. Beloved brother, since you have such a merciful God, do not cast yourself into despair. This brings great joy to the devil. So be confident in the Lord; for no one who endures to the end[22] in this place is cast out of the fold of the sheep of Christ our God. Indeed, there are some in this fold who have great boldness before God. And they are shameless in entreating him, that those who dwell with them in this blessed place may not be separated from them; they entreat him that, as they dwell together in "the place that God has chosen for his name to be invoked therein,"[23] so also may they be together in the future. Therefore, do not be afraid, most worthy one. For if I, who am weak and the least of all, have therefore been assured that you have been numbered and enrolled into the blessed flock of Christ, how much more so have the fathers, who are saints of God and worthy of him, been as-

17. Lk 21.19.
19. Ps 39.1.
21. Ps 25.2.
23. Dt 12.11.

18. Heb 10.36.
20. Mt 10.22.
22. Cf. Mt 10.22.

sured of this! "Wait, then, for the Lord,"[24] and "hope in him."[25]

And in regard to material fasting, do not grieve. For it is nothing without spiritual fasting. Indeed, "there is nothing outside a person that by going in can defile," with the exception of sensual pleasure, "but the things that come out"[26] of that person are what defile. And again, God has granted discernment as a guide for the monk. Therefore discern, beloved, from whom it is that God requires almsgiving. Is it from the poor or from the rich? For Scripture says the following: "Do not withhold good from those who need it, according to the resources that you have at hand."[27] God does not require asceticism from those who are physically ill, but only from those who are able and healthy in body. So condescending a little to your body is not a sin. For God does not require this of you. He knows the illness that he sent you.

In every circumstance, therefore, give thanks to him, because thanksgiving intercedes before God for one's human weakness.[28] So "put away the old self with its lusts, and put on the new self, created according to the likeness of God";[29] and rejoice, being glad in the Lord, and always being joyful with his saints. Who can imagine, who can possibly fathom the ineffable joy of the saints, the inexpressible gladness, the incomparable light, how it is that he reveals to them—while they are still here[30]—his mysteries, his wonders, the glory that awaits them, and the refreshment that redirects their mind away from this world, so that they are always seeing themselves in heaven with Christ and the angels? They are not afflicted by hunger, by thirst, or by any other earthly matter. For they have been freed from all the faults and passions and sins of this life. And I quote the scriptural word differently: "Where their treasure is, there also is their heart."[31] One who has attained to these knows what one hears. And so what can I do, who have done nothing good? Yet I do not despair. For God is able to count us with those who shall find mercy in Christ Jesus our Lord, with whom to the Father with the

24. Ps 26.14.
25. Ps 36.5.
26. Mk 7.15.
27. Prv 3.27.
28. Cf. *Sayings*, Nau 637.
29. Eph 4.22–24; Col 3.9.
30. That is, still living.
31. Cf. Mt 6.21.

Holy Spirit is the glory to the ages. Amen. May the Lord hear his genuine servants and swiftly send to you his great mercy, granting to me the understanding "to come to the knowledge of the truth."[32] Pray for me, and greet your brother and concelebrant, entreating him to do the same for my humble person.

LETTER 78

Question from the same [brother] to the same Great Old Man: "Since I have severe rheumatism in my feet and hands, and fear that this might come from the demons, tell me, father, if this is so, and what I should do. For I am greatly in distress, being unable to fast, and instead being compelled to consume food many times. And what does it mean, when I see wild beasts in my dream? I entreat you, master, for the Lord's sake, to send me a small blessing from your holy food and drink, that I may receive some comfort from them." Response by Barsanuphius.

Do not grieve, my beloved one. For this is not of the demons, as you think, but it is an influx of God's discipline for our improvement,[33] in order that we may give thanks to God. Was not Job a genuine friend of God? And what did he not endure, giving thanks and blessing to God? Yet the end of his patience led him to incomparable glory. Therefore, you also should be a little patient, and "you will see the glory of God."[34]

As for fasting, do not grieve. For as I have already told you, God does not require of us anything beyond our strength. What else is fasting but discipline of the body, in order to enslave a healthy body and weaken it on account of the passions? For he says: "Whenever I am weak, then I am strong."[35] Illness, however, is greater than mere discipline, being reckoned as a substitute for the regular [ascetic] way;[36] and it is even of greater value [than asceticism] for the person who endures it with patience and gives thanks to God. That person reaps the fruit of salvation from such patience. Therefore, instead of the body being weakened through fasting, it is weakened in and of itself. Give thanks

---

32. 1 Tm 2.4.
34. Jn 11.40.
36. Greek, πολιτεία.

33. Or, [spiritual] progress (βελτίωσις).
35. 2 Cor 12.10.

that you have been exempted from the toil of regular [ascetic] behavior. So, even if you eat ten times, do not grieve, for you are not condemned. For this is a result neither of demonic action nor of slack thought; rather, it is happening to us in order to test and benefit the soul.

In regard to the dreams about wild beasts, they are demonic fantasies, which want to deceive you through these in order to make you believe that your suffering comes from the demons. "The Lord," however, "destroys them with the word of his mouth,"[37] through the prayers of the saints. Amen. And do not grieve. "For the Lord disciplines those whom he loves, and chastises every child whom he accepts."[38] Yet I also believe in regard to this bodily suffering that God will do with you as his mercy wills. May the Lord strengthen you and fortify you in order to endure. Amen. I have sent you a little water from the vessel of our holy father, the blessed Euthymius. I have also sent you a small blessing from my own food, so that you may bless my food. Pray for me, dearest one.

LETTER 79

Question from the same person to the Other Old Man: "Pray for my most unbearable illness, father, and declare to me about diet, whether it does not perhaps cause a scandal that I readily and continually eat. And tell me about psalmody, how I should abridge it. For I have no strength to recite the Psalms. Plant me, master, and water me.[39] And reveal to me whether that which our holy father has said, namely, that 'the Lord will work his mercy with you,' referred to my death." Response by John.

Although I have kept silent, I did so because I had no word to speak or anything good to offer you. Yet, why do you ask bread of one who eats carobs?[40] I am telling you this because, even though I am nothing, I congratulate you on what our blessed father wrote to you. Behold, then, he is offering you the solid food of spiritual bread. Why do you need my very watery milk, which

---

37. 2 Thes 2.8.   38. Heb 12.6; Prv 3.12.
39. Cf. 1 Cor 3.6–8.
40. A carob-pod or bean-pod, an indirect reference to the parable of the Prodigal Son (Lk 15.16).

only creates distaste? Neither Scripture nor the fathers have forbidden condescension toward the body, when it is brought about not by sensual pleasure but with discernment. Therefore when, as he has already told you, you eat and drink neither with waste nor with self-indulgence, then these do not bring condemnation to you or scandal upon others. For the Lord said about these: "They do not defile a person."[41] As far as psalmody or liturgy are concerned, however, do not be distressed. For God does not require these of you on account of your illness. One who gives heed to one's self is distressed in ascetic struggle[42] for the sake of the Lord and for one's own salvation. But you have the affliction of illness in the place of distress through ascetic struggle.

And about your illness, again do not grow weary. The Lord does not forsake you, but allows the illness for your best interest, which he knows, so that you may not be afflicted beyond your capacity. The Old Man, however, did not speak about death at this time, but about the mercy that God will work within your love. So I implore you to endure as he told you, and you will truly see the glory of God. In regard to the planting, if it is altogether true that "the one who plants and waters"[43] is nothing—and you have ascribed both of these to me—instead of me, who am nothing, you have "God who increases" and protects and works within you according to his mercy. Therefore, rejoicing in his goodness, "be strong and bold"[44] in him, and pray for me that his mercy may also come to me.

LETTER 80

The same old man was suffering from illness, and again he asked the same Old Man to pray for him. Response by John.

Your illness has been given in order to test you. Endure it thankfully, and God will swiftly show you his mercy. I greet you[45] in the Lord, imploring you to pray for me.

41. Mt 15.11; Mk 7.15.
42. Abba John uses the term πολιτεία, namely, "way of life," as did Abba Barsanuphius in the previous letter.
43. 1 Cor 3.6–8.
44. Dt 31.6.
45. Plural, referring to the community.

LETTER 81

The same person again asked the Great Old Man the same question. Response by Barsanuphius.

Behold, brother John has said that God will swiftly show mercy on him.[46] What do I, who am the least, have to add? I am very happy today, and I believe that God is sending him relief today through the prayers of his saints. Pray for me, beloved ones.

LETTER 82

Following this response, he immediately became healthy on the same day. And he sent a letter of thanks to the [Great] Old Man, announcing the mercies of God, which came through him. Response by Barsanuphius.

Our Lord Jesus Christ told his disciples and apostles, granting them joy: "Do not rejoice at this, that the demons submit to you [in my name], but rejoice that your names are written in heaven."[47] Likewise, then, if we, too, cry out with joy at the help that has come to our body in the name of our God and Protector of our souls, Jesus Christ, what should we do when we receive complete purification from all the passions of our soul through his fearful, glorious name? How many voices, tongues, mouths, hearts, and thoughts will ever be able to repay him with the proper doxology? I reckon that the appropriate doxology cannot be found even among the bodiless [angels]. For the divine is incomprehensible. To him be the glory, the authority, and the power, to the ages. Amen.

LETTER 83

A certain brother said to this old man: "Behold, old man, you have been restored [to health] through the prayers of the saints." And he answered, saying: "Whenever you have spoken this word to me, and this is now the fourth time, I have observed that de-

---

46. Barsanuphius is addressing the monk in the third person, because he is responding through the monk's abbot, Seridos.

47. Lk 10.20.

mons wear down my body." So the Other Old Man was asked about this. Response by John.

This matter contains envy and lack of faith: envy, because the demons are not happy that a person should benefit; and lack of faith, that on seeing the illness he is doubtful in his heart.

LETTER 84

Question from the same person to the same Old Man: "Tell me, father, how this is possible. Is it because we lack faith? Or is it because the demons bring us to such lack of faith?" Response by John.

The demons sow lack of faith through their envy. Therefore, if we accept this, we become their accomplices and partners.

LETTER 85

Question from the same person to the Great Old Man:[48] "Father, when I am relieved of illness, how should I spend each day?" Response by John.

"Rejoice in the Lord; again, I say rejoice."[49] You have now gladdened me with your question; or rather, you have gladdened God and his angels. As for those things that you wrote, the Lord said: "You ought to have practiced these without neglecting the others."[50] You ought to recite the Psalms a little, to repeat [the verses of the Psalms] by heart a little, to examine and watch your thoughts a little.[51] For one who consumes many types of foods during one's meal is gluttonous, whereas someone who eats daily from only one food is not only lacking in greed, but in time perhaps even develops a distaste for that food. So this also applies in your case. Yet it belongs to the perfect to grow accustomed to eat each day of the same cooked meal, without feeling any distaste. Therefore, in regard to psalmody and repeat-

48. In fact, the letter is addressed to the Other Old Man, John.
49. Phil 4.4.
50. Mt 23.23.
51. Cf. *Sayings*, Antony 1.

ing [verses] by heart, do not bind yourself with strict rules, but do whatever the Lord gives you the strength to do. And do not neglect your reading and prayer; little by little, you will gradually spend the day pleasing God. For our perfect fathers were not limited by any particular rule. Indeed, their daily rule included singing Psalms a little, repeating [verses] by heart a little, examining their thoughts a little, taking a little break for food, and [all] this with fear of God. For it is said: "Whatever you do, do everything for the glory of God."[52] May the Lord Jesus guard us from all evil. Amen.

LETTER 86

Question from the same person to the same Old Man:[53] "How should one examine the thoughts? And how does one avoid captivity?" Response by John.

The examination of one's thoughts follows this pattern: when a thought comes, you pay attention to what it produces. Let me give you an example. Suppose that someone has insulted you, and your thought troubles you in the matter of responding. Say to your thought: "If I respond, I disturb him and he is grieved against me. Therefore, be a little patient, and it will pass." If, however, our thought is not against some other person, but is an evil thought in itself, then you must examine the thought and say: "Where is this evil thought leading?" and then your godly thought will respond to you: "The evil thought leads to hell," and it will cease. Do the same in regard to all your thoughts. When the thought enters, examine it immediately and cut it short. As far as captivity is concerned, great vigilance is required; so, then, as the fathers have said, if this leads your intellect to fornication, you should lead it to sanctification; if it leads your intellect to gluttony, you should bring it to asceticism; if it leads your intellect to hatred, you should bring it to love; and so on, and so forth. Do not grieve; for you will find mercy, according to the promises that you have received. "For if we live, we live to the Lord; and if we die, we die to the Lord."[54]

52. 1 Cor 10.31.   53. That is, Abba John.
54. Rom 14.8.

LETTER 87

Question from the same person to the same Great Old Man: "Tell me, father, about unceasing prayer, and in what measure it is to be found, and whether I am obliged to have a rule." Response by Barsanuphius.

Rejoice in the Lord, brother; rejoice in the Lord, beloved; rejoice in the Lord, fellow heir. Unceasing prayer[55] is in accordance with the measure of dispassion. Then, the coming of the Spirit is known, and it teaches us everything itself. If it teaches us everything, then it also teaches us about prayer. For the Apostle says: "We do not know how to pray as we ought. But that very Spirit intercedes for us with sighs too deep for words."[56] Therefore, what should I now say to you about the buildings of Rome, when you have not yet been there? A person living in stillness, especially one that is bedridden, has no rule. But be rather like a person who eats and drinks as much as he pleases. Thus, when you happen to be reading, and you see compunction in your heart, read as much as you can. Do the same when you recite the Psalms. Moreover, hold on to thanksgiving and the prayer: "Lord have mercy," as much as you can. And do not be afraid. "For the gifts of God are irrevocable."[57]

LETTER 88

The same person, after regaining health, felt pain in the stomach. And he sent to the same Great Old Man, imploring him to pray for him, saying: "From midnight, my mouth and eyelids and hands and feet grow dry; and when I wake up, my whole body trembles for up to an hour, beginning from my stomach. And then I feel weak, and become like clay. I want to recite a Psalm, but I cannot do so with my mouth; and if I want to do so in my heart, I am overcome by sleep. Therefore, what shall I do? For I do not know what to do, and I see myself hindered in the way of salvation. So I implore you, father, for the sake of the Lord: pray for me, and declare to me what this means." Response by Barsanuphius.

55. Cf. 1 Thes 5.17.   56. Rom 8.26.
57. Rom 11.29.

This matter concerns a small illness of the stomach. Yet it also is heavily involved with the activity of the demons. Therefore, despise both of them. For it is said: "Those who belong to Christ Jesus have crucified the flesh with its passions and desires."[58] Behold, then, the elders are praying for your love. You, too, should weep a little in prayer, giving thanks to God and praying for mercy; and he will have mercy on you. For we have a greatly merciful Master and compassionate Father. And no one is sufficient, either of the powers above or of the genuine servants below, to express his goodness appropriately or to say how it is that he yearns to have mercy on the human race. Yet this is why he is long-suffering toward us, that he may multiply our patience for salvation, as he has taught us: "By your patience you will gain your souls."[59] Therefore, brother, do not become weary. For Jesus has begun to work his great mercy within you. To him be the glory. Amen. Pray for me.

LETTER 89

Question from the same person to the Other Old Man: "What did our father mean when he said: 'Jesus has begun to work his great mercy within you'?" Response by John.

He was speaking about [spiritual] progress and the great benefit to the soul. He meant that you would find yourself in such a company that you will rise on that day with great joy, if you hold on to patience and thanksgiving until the end.

LETTER 90

Entreaty from the same person to the Great Old Man: "I believe that 'whatever you bind on earth will be bound in heaven, and whatever you loose will be loosed.'[60] I am entreating you, father, for the mercies of God; help my weakness; for I am maimed in soul and body. And I am distressing the brothers with whom I dwell. Ask God to grant me to perform my needs by myself, so that the brothers will not carry my burdens. For I believe that whatever you ask of God he grants to you. Be compassionate with

58. Gal 5.24.   59. Lk 21.19.
60. Mt 18.18.

my weakness, father, and forgive me." Response by Barsanuphius.

Brother, your little key opens my door.[61] For I am a fool, and
I cannot bear to conceal the wonders of God. So if someone is
surprised by hearing my words, he says nothing else but: "He
is beside himself." And, in so thinking, he does not know that
"all things are possible for God,"[62] and nothing is impossible for
him. Therefore, as he acted through the first [disciples], and
raised the paralytic[63] as well as Tabitha,[64] who had died, so is he
also able to act now. I speak before him and do not lie: I know
that a certain servant of God in this present generation, in this
time and this blessed place, is able even to raise the dead in the
name of our Master Jesus, and to cast out demons, and to heal
incurable illnesses, and to perform other works of power no less
than the apostles, as the one who gave him this gift, or rather
these gifts, bears witness. For what is this, that even such things
occur in the name of Jesus? Indeed, he does not use his own
authority. He can even abolish wars, as well as open and shut
the heavens just like Elijah. For our Lord always has genuine
servants, whom he no longer calls servants but sons. And if the
enemy is envious, by the grace of Christ he can cause no harm.
For the ship has passed through storms, the soldier through
wars, the helmsman through winter, the farmer through rough
weather, the merchant through thieves, and the monk has been
perfected in stillness.

Who is it that, on hearing these excessive words, will not say
that I am out of my mind? And, in truth, I am out of my mind.
I am not, however, bearing witness about myself, but about another. So if anyone wants to say that I am beside myself, as I
said, let him say so. If, however, anyone desires to strive toward
reaching this measure, let him not shrink away. I have said this
to your love in order to assure you that what you desire can indeed occur. For if we have requested for you the heavenly blessings, ineffable and eternal, which "no eye has seen, nor ear

61. Cf. *Sayings*, Peter the Pionite 2.
62. Mk 10.27.   63. Cf. Acts 9.33–34.
64. Cf. Acts 9.40.

heard, nor the human heart conceived, that God has prepared for those who love him,"[65] and God has granted these things to you—and these things shall be yours if you keep the traditions—then how much more so is it not difficult in regard to the bodily passions to ask God and to receive the grace that you not be sick or afflicted even for a single day? Nonetheless, Jesus knows better than we what is profitable and beneficial for us: whether we should receive the reward of patience like Job, or whether we should receive the reward of service like Eulogius the former lawyer.[66]

So, then, ask nothing else of God or through his servants, except assistance and patience. For "the one who endures to the end will be saved"[67] in Christ Jesus our Lord. He is concerned about us to the ages. Amen. Do you not know what the Lord said to the holy Paul, when he asked that the affliction should be taken from him? "My grace is sufficient for you."[68] Did he say this because he hated him? Or did he know what was good for him? Remember: "I consider that the sufferings of this present time are not worth comparing with the glory about to be revealed to us."[69] Forgive me, and pray for me, the worthless servant, that I, too, may maintain these measures to the end. For the one who maintains them has already become the brother of Jesus. To him be the glory to the ages. Amen.

LETTER 91

Entreaty from the same person to the same Great Old Man about finding mercy on that day. Response by Barsanuphius.

Brother Andrew and beloved friend in Christ, I am amazed that your love, or rather your simplicity, doubts as you do about what was promised. The Lord said to Philip: "Have I been all this time with you, Philip, and still you have not known me?"[70] Believe me, brother; you shall receive all that was promised; and if you so desire, even more. For there is small mercy to find, and there is great mercy to find. And David chose the great mercy.

---

65. 1 Cor 2.9.   66. Cf. *Lausiac History* 21.3–14.
67. Mt 10.22.   68. 2 Cor 12.9.
69. Rom 8.18.   70. Jn 14.9.

Therefore, one who desires great mercy shall find it through humility, gentleness, patience, and the like. So finding mercy depends on the prayers of the saints. Whether it is great or small mercy, however, depends on you. Choose, then, whatever you will. Dwell in peace, in holiness, in humility, and support your neighbor, becoming a model for him as a monk and as one who has advanced. And keep your brother beside you as a child and a servant. If he should slip or spoil anything, advise him and show him his mistake in order that he might be corrected. And pray for me.

LETTER 92

[Question] from the same person to the same Great Old Man: "Father, give me the rule of a beginner, who has not yet received the habit. And pray for me, because my brother afflicts me, while nevertheless at the same time comforting another person." Response by Barsanuphius.

Dearest brother, you have written to me about a matter beyond your power, namely, that I should command you in something that you are not able to bear. For you have said that I should give you the rule of a beginner, who has not yet received the habit. Yet the discipline for a beginner is as follows. He should walk in great humility, without either regarding himself as being of any account in anything, or else saying: "What is this?" or "What is that?" Rather, he should walk in great obedience and submission, neither regarding himself as being equal to anyone, nor saying: "This person is honored; why am I not honored? That person is comforted in everything; why am I not comforted?" When he is despised in all things, he does not become annoyed. Such is the behavior of a genuine beginner, who truly desires to be saved.

Now these things are difficult for you to bear, on account of both your bodily weakness and your maturity of age. For you have sought to bear the heavy burden. I am laying on you, however, the lighter one, not so much by way of obligation as by way of counsel. Regard your brother as your child, as I told you, and as indeed you do regard him in this way. And if, through temptation, he comforts someone else more than you, or perhaps it is God who wants to comfort that person and to afflict you—offering him the assurance to do so—then endure this, and do not be afflicted. For it is by endurance of afflictions that we gain our souls.[71] And we do not become "fellow-sharers in" Christ's "sufferings"[72] except by endurance of sufferings.

Hold onto thanksgiving in all circumstances, because this will intercede for any weakness before God.[73] Your rule is to sit down and pay attention to your thoughts and to have fear of God, considering: "How shall I encounter God? How have I spent the time that has passed? I will repent even now, for my departure has approached; and I shall endure my neighbor and the afflictions and trials that come from him, until the Lord grants mercy to me and brings me to the state of lack of anger, banishing from me the vice of envy, which is the offspring of the devil."

Let your last few days be spent in the search of your thoughts, and contradict those thoughts that bring you turmoil, advising your son with fear of God, reminding him of his mistakes, knowing that he, too, is only human and subject to temptations. May the Lord Jesus Christ, the Son of the living God, give you a peaceful condition and a life according to his fear. I am surprised by how you can read the Scripture that says: "Brethren, whenever you face trials of any kind, rejoice,"[74] and yet such minimal temptations trouble you. Know at least where you are, and what power you have, and may those who are iron-necked be humbled. May the peace of God be with you. Forgive me and pray for me, that I may not hear the words: "You, then, that teach others, will you not teach yourself?"[75] And what shall I do out of love? Yet mercy is from him, God our Master.

LETTER 93

Question from the same person to the same Great Old Man: "My thought tells me: 'You have spoken once, and even ten times, to your brother. So leave him alone now to do as he wills; and be carefree, as the fathers have said.'"[76] Response by Barsanuphius.

---

71. Cf. Lk 21.19.
72. 2 Cor 1.7.
73. Cf. *Sayings*, Nau 637.
74. Jas 1.2.
75. Rom 2.21.
76. Cf. *Sayings*, Nau 318.

Dearest brother and soul-mate, may the peace be yours which the Lord gave his disciples. For he first gave them peace,[77] banishing from them every fleshly thought and every diabolical concept, in order that their hearts may be found pure, and that they themselves may also receive in purity the lessons and commands of their own Master. Therefore, beloved, on receiving this awesome peace, which comes not from me but from the Savior Jesus Christ, prepare yourself also intelligently and without anger to hear and to act. For you know how much I want to take you and send you on wings to heaven. The devil is moving on every side to trouble you, whether by envy or by anger, but he has found no place. Yet, in things that are unimportant, he has found you ridiculed, declaring war on you through these things, and troubling also your brother through you.

Nevertheless, what I wrote to you in previous letters, to tell your brother of his mistakes and to admonish him, either I did not say it clearly enough and you did not take it seriously, or else I did say it clearly but you were defeated in the struggle. Now, then, the devil rejoices against you and approaches with bitter justifications, saying to you: "You have spoken once, and even ten times; but let him do what he wills, and be carefree, as the fathers have said." And they are ridiculing you even in this. For you are as far from this measure as heaven is from earth. Furthermore, do you want to learn what the Lord has said about the trees, that they also bring forth fruit?[78]

Learn, then, what the silence that comes from the devil produces for you, namely, much turmoil and anger. For when you hasten to do something on your own, without asking anyone, you are quickly ensnared. This is how the simple suffer from their ignorance. And I will make it clear to you that your long-suffering is not godly, and that after storing up your treasure for many days, you suddenly open your purse and it is found to be empty. Godly long-suffering, however, does not speak at all until the very end, whereas, with your brother, you resemble a master in his behavior toward his servant. Instead of giving him a mere slap each day, telling him of his mistakes and—behold—mak-

---

77. Cf. Jas 1.2.   78. Cf. Mt 7.17–19.

ing peace, you are long-suffering for many days, but then afterwards you give him a single blow on the back and take his life.

The same person asked the Other Old Man the same question,
whether he ought to leave his cell for another place, and if perhaps then the warfare would cease. Response by John.

If you had listened and followed the response given by the
[Great] Old Man, when he told you to count yourself as nothing and not to seek equality with any other person, then you
would have found rest instead of being troubled; and then,
there would have been no need for [you to consult] me or
any other person. Do you see, brother, how you are mocked by
the demons? You say that the brother's faults are true. But tell
me, do you know accurately that they are true? For in speaking about someone's faults out of suspicion, sometimes those
faults are found not to be true. What kind of sins, then, was the
Lord speaking of when he said: "Truly I say to you, if you do not
forgive others their sins, then neither will your heavenly Father
forgive you your sins"?[79] What sins was he talking about: true
ones, or suspected ones? Surely, about true ones. So how do
you judge and condemn your brother for his faults over the last
three weeks? Do you not know that you are casting yourself into
great condemnation? For indeed, if you call your brother to account for these trespasses, God will call you to account for your
own sins from your youth to this day. What happened to: "Do
not let the sun go down on your anger"?[80] Where is: "Bear one
another's burdens"?[81] Where is the letter from the [Great] Old
Man, which could serve as your rule? Instead of giving thanks,
you offer this? Do you not know what is said: "They repay me
evil for good,"[82] and so on? How does the brother minister to
you? Is it not for the sake of God and his love? So how can you
wound his thought?

Pay attention, for your departure is near, as you have both

79. Mt 6.15.   80. Eph 4.26.
81. Gal 6.2.   82. Ps 34.12.

heard and confessed, and the demons do not let you steadfastly count yourself as nothing in order that you may find rest. Declare war against the thoughts that bring you turmoil, as the good [Great] Old Man informed you, and you will find assistance. If, however, you turn instead to ten thousand devices, if you do anything whatsoever, if you migrate [elsewhere] when there is warfare and temptation, then it does not depart from you unless you wrestle against the thoughts, so that, from your own toils, you may acquire a little to mingle with the prayer of the saints. For when it is "powerful, it is effective."[83] Say to your thought: "Tomorrow, you are dying." Count yourself steadfastly as being nothing, and you will find rest. May the Lord give you his peace. Amen.

LETTER 95

Question from the same person to the same Old Man: "Father, I admonished my brother with godly love; but he did not accept it, and I was troubled. So what should I do? And if I meet the brothers whom you ordered me to meet, assure me that no one will suffer from thoughts about it." Response by John.

The trouble is that we do not pay close attention to what we say. Every counsel that allows turmoil to enter a person's heart is not godly counsel, but comes from the action of the devil mingled with the pretense to rights. If you have counseled your neighbor in a godly way, how is it that you were troubled? For godly sorrow lets no one be troubled. Even if the one who is counseled goes away and speaks against the one who counsels, the latter is not troubled but instead bears the burdens of the former. And it has also been revealed to you that it was a temptation, that God has abolished it and continues to abolish it. May the Lord grant you health of soul and body to understand the machinations of the evil one and to escape from them. Pray for me. Now, as for meeting with the brothers of whom you spoke, when this also happens in godly love, it does not allow scandal to enter, but only edification.

83. Jas 5.16.

LETTER 96

Question from the same person to the same Old Man: "Abba, the brother altogether afflicts me. If it were possible, I would be glad to change him. My thought tells me that if I were alone, I would not have affliction, but rather find salvation. So, tell me if this is good." Response by John.

Brother, do not let your pretense to rights afflict you by saying: "If I were alone, I would not have affliction, but rather find salvation," because you are ignoring the Scripture that says: "Many are the afflictions of the righteous,"[84] and again: "Many are the torments of the wicked."[85] So whether you are righteous or whether you are a sinner, you ought to bear the burden of the blame. For we cannot be without affliction; it teaches us patience. And we have an excellent teacher in the Apostle, who says: "Be patient in suffering."[86] Indeed, tribulations are set before those who wish to be saved. For the Lord said: "In the world you will have tribulation,"[87] and again: "It is through many tribulations that we must enter into the kingdom of heaven."[88] Observe, my brother, that it is because he wills you to be saved that he said: "My soul is deeply grieved, even to death."[89] It is he who allows you to be afflicted a little, so that you may find therein mercy from him in return for your patience at that fearful hour. For if in all things we desire rest, we shall certainly hear: "During your lifetime, you received your good things."[90] Our Master endured all the sufferings for our sake. So how is it that, when we remember them, we still do not endure, instead of becoming partakers with him? See how we have been commanded: "Give thanks in all circumstances,"[91] so that the hater of good may not attract us to ingratitude with the result that we lose everything.

In regard to taking another brother, it is not difficult for the abbot to give you another. Moreover, it is all the same in the end. So if you make haste to take another, and he, too, is found to trouble you in anything, then what would you do? For even

---

84. Ps 33.19.
85. Ps 31.10.
86. Rom 12.12.
87. Jn 16.33.
88. Acts 14.22.
89. Mt 26.38; Mk 14.34.
90. Lk 16.25.
91. 1 Thes 5.18.

if the brother is limited, yet he still has some integrity. I am not saying this to you in order to prevent you from taking another brother, but I advise you to "test everything, and hold fast to what is good."[92] Indeed, just as someone ministers to you for the sake of God, so also should you bear that person's burdens, so that you may in return "fulfill the law of Christ."[93] Is it because I do not want you to have rest? God knows that, if I were able, I would minister to you all my life. But what shall I do, for I am entirely worthless? Let us despise bodily comfort, which is an abomination to God,[94] so that it may not alienate us from God. I am writing this to you as to a soul-mate, that it is God's will for us that we should be a little troubled. For without tribulation, there is no progress in the fear of God. Forgive me, man of patience, and pray for me that I may make a new beginning. For I am now near my end.

LETTER 97

Response from the Great Old Man to the same person.

Rejoice, brother, and be of good cheer. Do not let the devil trouble you in things that are of no benefit. What does your love think? That it is without God's permission that anyone is tempted or troubled? No, but God permits these things to occur for the benefit of the soul; and when the devil sees that this is what has occurred, he twists things in such a way for us, just as he did at the beginning, until he had cast us out of paradise. For what has he not changed for us? Instead of holy peace, has he not placed in us a wicked wrath? Instead of hatred that is from God, namely, to hate evil things, has he not placed within us an evil hatred, namely, to hate good things and even God himself? Yet we do not understand this; and we do not realize that, in order to cut off from us every shameful consideration and every evil and soul-corrupting thought, God has told us "to pray for our

92. 1 Thes 5.21.
93. Gal 6.2.
94. Cf. *Sayings*, Poemen 38. Abba Poemen is particularly popular in the *Letters* of the Other Old Man. See *Letters* 654, 96, 279, 287, 316, 347, and 500. For Poemen in Barsanuphius, see *Letters* 604, 237, 244, 347, 433, 492, and 541.

enemies, and to bless those who curse us," and commanded us "to love our enemies."[95] And if we have been commanded to love our enemies, who render us no service either out of zeal or out of carelessness, then what forgiveness will we have if we do not love those who do us good and offer us service, even if the demons show us the service that they have rendered us out of carelessness?

If you desire to be saved, and have entrusted your soul to God and to us, then do not place any trust in your thought. For the demons sow an evil seed, giving us one thing instead of another. Therefore, continue and you will learn the way of God. For he said: "If you are willing and obedient to me, you will eat the good of the land,"[96] and so on. So then, it is up to us whether we will eat or not eat. Why do we blame our neighbor? Do not allow any pretext to anyone in anything at all, but in all things be pleasing. And do not think of anything evil against anyone, because in this way you become evil yourself. For the evil person thinks evil things, and the good person thinks good things. To suspect any people, however, of "speaking against me," this is the warfare faced by novices.

So then, from this perspective, if there are two people praying in one cell or counseling one another, it could be said about them that they are doing just the opposite. And if some people think in this way, that does not mean that such people are thinking truthfully, but simply gaining destruction for themselves through such foolishness. Do not behave in this way. For your brother believes that he is finding mercy through you. Even if you are afflicted a little on account of him, in order to obtain peace, "rejoice and be exceedingly glad, for great is the reward"[97] of patience. And before this, you have already learned from brother John that, without God, we are not permitted to be troubled for our benefit. So do not trust the demons in anything against your brother. For [God] has nothing to do with this, but it is the demons that want to trouble you. The Lord will abolish them. And as for your thought, that "I have come to be the servant of all people," this does not come from humility. The Apostle boasted that he be-

95. Mt 5.44; Lk 6.27–28.   96. Is 1.19.
97. Mt 5.12.

came the servant of all,[98] and you also dare to say this? When did you come to this measure of humility? You do not know what you have said, brother. May the Lord forgive you.

LETTER 98

Response from the same Great Old Man to the same.

I am astonished how some people, who have spent many years in schools, are yet still learning the alphabet and syllables, when they really ought by now to be accomplished teachers. In the same way, I am also astonished at how those who have spent a long time in the monastic life, and ought to be able to discern the deeper thoughts of others, are nevertheless still besieged by the warfare of novices. You ought to be guiding into the straight way those who have gone astray, as if you were perfected; and yet, instead of bearing the burdens of the weak, you burden them to the point of drowning on account of sorrow.

Pay attention to yourself, brother. I wonder, does this not inflict harm on your soul at all, that you trouble the thought of your neighbor? For once he has performed some labor for God's sake, you bestow on him further thoughts, such as: "You have done as you wanted to do." Would a mature person speak in this way to a novice? This was not your role; instead, your role was to counsel, to direct, fearing him who said: "Do not place any stumbling-block or hindrance in the way of your brother."[99] Why was it necessary to say anything sorrowful to your neighbor? And why do I say this to you, and behave in this way toward you? My foolishness does not allow me to bear inside me any word, until I express it and end up troubling the soul of my brother. Whenever the devil sows evil thoughts in you (for this is his work: to sow one thing instead of another, and never to allow us to remember death), why are you so troubled by trivial matters, as novices and eccentrics are? Where is the phrase: "We are destitute, we are persecuted, we are tormented"?[100] Our fathers chose afflictions for themselves, and we are not even ashamed in seeking every comfort. Let us learn, wretched as we are, that all of these things

98. Cf. 1 Cor 9.19.   99. Rom 14.13.
100. Heb 11.37.

have been written in the records above and will be required of us with full precision. I am writing these things because I desire to remove from you every bit of rot. If, however, I am causing [you] distress, then forgive me, and I will trouble you no longer. Pray for me, that I may come to the knowledge of life. And as far as your death is concerned, I have often told you, and I will tell you once again, that you do not have very long to live in the body.

LETTER 99

Question from the same brother to the same Great Old Man: "Father, you know that I would not dare in any way at all to contradict your command. For whatever you say is life for us. But pray for me, because the brother is altogether troubling me." Response by Barsanuphius.

Rejoice, my beloved, rejoice in the Lord. I know, and I am convinced in the Lord, that even if I tell you to live in a prison for an entire year, you will not contradict my word, knowing how and to whom I am speaking, namely, to my fellow-servant and soul-mate. Do you not know how Job says: "Do not human beings have a harsh ordeal in their sojourn on earth?"[101] So be prepared always for trials and afflictions; and forget everything that lies behind you, as the Apostle says, but stretch forward instead to what lies ahead of you,[102] so that when you speak again in this way against your brother, no remembrance of evil will occur within you. The Lord "will swiftly crush Satan under our feet."[103] May the grace of God, his peace, and his love be with you until the end. Amen. And may he grant us joy, gladness, holiness, gentleness, humility, and love, which "never fails,"[104] so that we may support one another in the fear of God. For death will not be long in coming.

LETTER 100

Question from the same person to the same Great Old Man: "Tell me, father, what humility means; and pray that the end of my life may be peaceful." Response by Barsanuphius.

101. Jb 7.1.
102. Cf. Phil 3.13.
103. Rom 16.20.
104. 1 Cor 13.8.

Humility means regarding oneself as "earth and ashes,"[105] in deeds and not just in words, and saying: "Who am I?[106] Who counts me as anything? I have nothing to do with anyone."

As for your death, wait on the Lord for just a little while longer, and he will glorify the end of your life in great joy. Pray for me, my brother. I greet you in the Lord.

LETTER 101

Question from the same person to the same Great Old Man: "Abba, behold, my brother is rudely opposing me, showing no compassion toward me. Therefore, what do you command me to do?" Response by Barsanuphius.

Brother Andrew, I am surprised at your simplicity. Do you simply imagine that the devil rests calmly, without tempting anyone? Can we blame those whom the demon causes to fall and foam at the mouth? So it is also with those whom the devil leads to contradiction and lack of compassion; we cannot blame them but only their passion. Pay careful attention to what is being said. For the devil is influencing you, too, to act; so you do not consider your own faults, but instead see your neighbor's clearly. Behold, you have described your brother's faults, but you do not speak of your own.

Only a few days ago, you were asking about humility, and you heard that you must regard yourself as "earth and ashes,"[107] not counting yourself as being anything. Now, earth and ashes, and not reckoning oneself as being anything, require compassion from a person, especially from someone in whom the hater of good is still working. This is because you are more advanced than he, in age and in monastic experience as well as in ordination; and the one who is more advanced should bear the one who is less advanced, saying: "I am the unworthy one." If, however, you say this and do not endure patiently, then you are saying it inappropriately. For who are you, that you have eyes to behold the passions of another person, when you have heard the gospel on matters that surpass human understanding? If you

105. Gn 18.27; Jb 42.6.   106. Cf. 2 Sm 7.18.
107. Gn 18.27; Jb 42.6.

preoccupy yourself with these matters, then you ought to forget even to eat your meals! Nevertheless, you have not even tasted of these matters, and they have not become as desirable to you as they should. Remember Lazarus[108] and how long he endured, giving thanks to God. Do not forget these matters about which I have often said to you: "It is the envy of the devil," who knows what is in store for you. I trust in God, however, that the devil will not have overpowering strength.

LETTER 102

Question from the same [brother] to the same Great Old Man: "Pray for me, father; for I have fallen into fantasies." Response by Barsanuphius.

Brother Andrew, let us cry out with the holy Paul: "O the depth of the riches and wisdom and knowledge of God! How unsearchable are his judgments and how inscrutable his ways!"[109] How God also cuts us short in order for us not to boast in our bow, and in order for us not to suppose in our mind that our "sword is saving us,"[110] rather than the grace of his goodness! For he says: "You are being saved by grace."[111] This is why he allows us to fall into fantasies and other passions, so that we may come to know our weakness and where we still are. Out of his goodness, he allows this for our benefit, in order that the conviction of our hope may be from God and not from ourselves. Watch, however, that you do not think it is the will of God that we fall into fantasies and other passions. For it is on account of our negligence that he permits us to suffer these things, while out of his loving-kindness he makes use of our wrongdoings to bring us to humility, which leads to our salvation. What then? Should we attribute our salvation to our evil passions? Surely not. Rather, we should attribute it to his mercy and shrewd wisdom. Therefore, observe how from all sides God arouses our mind, in order that we might remember to say: "If the Lord had not been my help, my soul would soon have lived in Hades,"[112] and so forth.

108. Cf. Lk 16.20.
110. Ps 43.6.
112. Ps 93.17.

109. Rom 11.33.
111. Eph 2.5.

Knowing, then, that we are suffering these things on account of our weakness and negligence, we should do all that we can in order not to fall into such fantasies. And it is up to his mercy to deliver us from them. He did this with Peter and Paul, withholding his power a little from them, in order that they might recognize that they are human. One fell into denial,[113] while the other was let down in a basket,[114] that they might learn not to trust in themselves but only in the Lord of all. You also, then, should learn what you are and where you are, pardoning your fellow servant and condemning yourself. Become truly humble, not only before God but also before people. And "cast all your anxiety before him,"[115] "who is able to accomplish far more than all we can ask or imagine."[116] He shall fulfill all of his promises to you. He will not refuse those who genuinely ask, his very own and honorable brothers, who have through him and in him liberated themselves entirely of the old self and heard from him with ineffable joy: "Whatever you bind on earth shall be bound in heaven,"[117] and so on. He also granted them "all authority in heaven and on earth."[118] Therefore, "serve the Lord with fear, and rejoice in him with trembling."[119] Give thanks to him with unceasing mouth for showing mercy on you and many others through his servants. To him be the glory. Amen.

LETTER 103

Response by the same Great Old Man to the same person, when the latter asked for a prayer.

May the compassionate God, the highest and merciful one, grant [all of] you strength from above always to meditate on the words that we have addressed to you and to perform true spiritual work, namely, to struggle against the thoughts that disturb us. May you be found among those who received the talents and doubled them,[120] that you may hear what they heard. May you also wrestle to bear one another, and may your earth

---

113. Cf. Mt 26.69–75.
115. 1 Pt 5.7.
117. Mt 18.18.
119. Ps 2.11.

114. Cf. 2 Cor 11.33; Acts 9.25.
116. Eph 3.20.
118. Mt 28.18.
120. Cf. Mt 25.14–30.

bring forth good and seasonable fruits for God, "some one hundredfold, others sixty, and others thirty."[121] This is my prayer to
God: that you may keep all these things and that I may see you
in the kingdom of my God as his genuine friends, rejoicing in
the Lord.

LETTER 104

Question from the same [brother] to the same Great Old Man:
"Tell me, father, how did this temptation arise within me? And
what does it signify? And how can it be abolished? Pray that I
may be delivered from it." Response by Barsanuphius.

The devil, that hater of good, who knows the benefit of our
soul and that there is no other settlement of our salvation than
"bearing one another's burdens,"[122] has become envious and is
struggling to sow his seed within you to tempt you. So this is
how the temptation arose in you, which the Lord will abolish.
Such a temptation is abolished through "bearing one another's
burdens"[123] and by praying for the person through whom the
temptation has occurred.[124] Without struggle accompanied by
such reasoning,[125] there is no way out of the temptation. Sowing
[the thought of] withdrawal from this place is also a temptation
that arises from his envy, resulting from your pretense to rights,
in order to rend the love of the saints, who are praying for you,
as well as deprive you of their help. Behold, I have shown you
the way into and the way out of this temptation. Endure a little and you will be relieved of your burden in Christ Jesus our
Lord. Amen.

LETTER 105

Response by the same Great Old Man to the same person, when
he grew weary before the temptations that assailed him.

My brother and soul-mate Andrew, do not grow weary. For
God has not forsaken you; nor will he forsake you. This is the

---

121. Mt 13.8; Mk 4.8.   122. Gal 6.2.
123. Ibid.   124. See Abba Zosimas, *Reflections* 3.
125. That is, inner reflection (Greek, συλλογισμός).

Master's promise to our common father, Adam, and it will not pass away: "You shall eat your bread by the sweat of your face."[126] Just as he decreed for the outer nature, so also does this apply to the inner nature, so that in asceticism we may cooperate with the prayers of the saints. Moreover, these prayers accomplish a great deal, so that no one remains fruitless. For just as gold is fired in the furnace and held by means of tongs, being beaten into shape by the hammer and thereby being tested and proving acceptable for a royal diadem, so also a person—who is supported by the prayer of the saints, which is able to and indeed does accomplish a great deal—is fired by sorrow and beaten by temptation. If such a person endures with thanksgiving, then that person is shown to be a son of the kingdom. Therefore, everything happens to you for your benefit, in order that you, too, may have boldness among the saints on account of your own toils. So do not be ashamed to offer up the first-fruits of these toils. Do not add grief to yourself instead of spiritual joy. And trust in him, who has made a promise; for he will fulfill it.[127] Beloved, keep strong in the Lord.

LETTER 106

Response by the same Great Old Man to the same person, when he fell into deep depression.

Brother Andrew, may our kind and loving God not grant the enemy who hates good to sow his sadness and depression in you, so that he may not lead you to despair even about those things promised through the Holy Spirit to you, as the beloved one of the blessed God. Rather, may he open your heart to understand the Scriptures, just as he opened the heart of those around Cleopas.[128] How is it that God tested the holy patriarch Abraham even after making promises to him? For it is said: "And after these things had been said, God tested Abraham."[129] After which words? I think it is after the promises. His friend, who offered the voluntary sacrifice to him upon the altar, who

---

126. Gn 3.19.
127. Cf. Heb 10.23 and 11.11.
128. Cf. Lk 24.32.
129. Gn 22.1.

did not deserve to suffer anything terrible, whose faith was reckoned as righteousness,[130] this same person was allowed by God to fall into temptation in order to be tested, so that the powers of darkness may be defenseless and so that he may prove to be a model for the faithful, who will only "enter the kingdom of God through many afflictions."[131] It is through patience that these will gain their souls,[132] by rendering thanks in all circumstances.[133] In addition to all this, also bear in mind the saintly Job, that genuine friend of God, "who was truly blameless and upright, one who feared God and turned away from every evil deed";[134] how could such a person, who did not deserve to suffer anything evil, be given over to temptation for the testing of his virtue, until he brought shame upon his enemies and accusers, who could offer no defense against his charges?

Furthermore, take for the support of your faith the example of "the pioneer and perfecter of our salvation, Jesus,"[135] who delivered us from the curse that was given;[136] when he faced the time of the cross, he showed us a way of patience and salvation, saying: "Father, if it is possible, let this cup pass from me; yet, not what I want but what you want."[137] This he did for our sake; for he rebuked Peter when the latter said: "God forbid it, Lord! This will never happen to you,"[138] because he was prepared and willing to suffer. Nevertheless, for the sake of our weakness, he prayed that the cup might pass, in order that we might not be weak in our prayer, especially when we are not heard immediately for the sake of our testing. Therefore, let us closely examine the sufferings of the Savior who became human, enduring with him the shame, the stigma, the humiliation, the contempt of the spitting, the insult of the cloak, the false glory of the crown of thorns, the vinegar of bitterness, the pain of the fixing of the nails, the piercing of the spear, and the water and the blood. In this way, you should take heart in your own pain. For he will not let your toil be in vain. Rather, in order that, at the time when

---

130. Cf. Gn 15.6; Rom 4.3.
131. Acts 14.22.
132. Cf. Lk 21.19.
133. 1 Thes 5.18.
134. Jb 1.1.
135. Heb 12.2.
136. Cf. Gal 3.13.
137. Mt 26.39.
138. Mt 16.22.

you see the saints bearing the fruits of endurance and boasting of their afflictions, you may not feel that you have no share with them, he allows you to endure the labor for a while in order that you may partake with them and with Jesus, having boldness before him in company with the holy ones. Therefore, do not be sad. For God has not forgotten you, but cares for you as his true son, not as an illegitimate one. You shall be in good standing if you pay careful attention to yourself, so that you may not fall away from fear of and gratitude to God. You shall be blessed if you have truly become a stranger and a pauper. For these shall inherit the kingdom of God.[139] "Be strong and bold"[140] in the Lord. I do not shy away from repeating the same things to you; may the Lord grant them to you. Pray for me.

LETTER 107

Request from the same person to the same Great Old Man in regard to establishment of heart and forgiveness of sins committed since his birth. Response by Barsanuphius.

The Lord Jesus Christ will be the healing and eternal support for your soul and body. He shall establish your heart, so that you may not be dominated by the devil, who hates good and who hates people. As for the forgiveness of your sins from birth to this moment, God will grant you this after forty days because through your little patience you actually share in my supplications about this gift. Therefore, "be strong and bold"[141] in the Lord. May the Lord be with you, that great Healer of souls and bodies. Peace be to you in the Lord, brother.

LETTER 108

Response from the Other Old Man to the same person.

If in worldly matters, people praise someone who has acquired wealth, how much more do I praise your love that has gained wealth in God through the supplications of our blessed

139. Cf. Mt 5.3.   140. Dt 31.6.
141. Ibid.

father. Indeed, had his prayer not anticipated you by saying: "Take heart, and be strong and bold,"[142] then you would have succumbed to a dangerous illness on account of your little negligence and cowardice that prevent you from maintaining long-suffering and patience with your thoughts as well as with your fellow-servants, remembering the words of the Apostle: "Bear one another's burdens, and in this way you will fulfill the law of Christ."[143] Therefore, it was out of love that the Lord chastened you with mercy through the prayer of his servant, in order that through this small discipline you may cooperate with his supplication. This is reckoned as work for you, so that the mouth of the enemy might be blocked, that he may not say: "If he had been tested for the sake of discipline, he would have surrendered." Therefore, do not be grieved. For whatever you have heard from the Old Man will occur to you. So be strong, in accordance with his word, and be bold.[144]

LETTER 109

The same elder was delivered from temptation through the prayers of the holy [Great] Old Man and his spiritual teaching. So he sent a word of thanks to him. Response by Barsanuphius.

Let us render all glory to the God of glory; and let us sing to him unto the ages. Amen. For glory does not belong to us, but is only proper to his Son and his Holy Spirit. God has led your love toward our frailty in order that we may be of assistance to one another, in his desire also to fulfill the Scripture that says: "A brother assisted by a brother is like a city fortified with ramparts."[145] May all of us be assisted by our elder brother, and I mean Jesus; for he was well-pleased to make us his brothers.[146] And so we are his brothers and are praised by the angels for the kind of brother that we have, who is able to strengthen us, capable of dividing the spoils with us;[147] a chief captain who can crush our enemies in war; a physician who can heal our passions; a general during time of peace in order to set our inner

---

142. Ibid.
144. Cf. Dt 31.6.
146. Cf. Heb 2.11.
143. Gal 6.2.
145. Prv 18.19.
147. Cf. Lk 11.22.

nature at peace with the outer nature when it has been submitted to him; a nurse who can nurture us with spiritual food, able
to grant us life with his life, mercy through his mercy, and compassion through his compassion; a king endowing us with roy-
alty; and a God who deifies us. Knowing, therefore, that everything lies in him, pray to him. "For he knows what you need
even before you ask him,"[148] and he will grant every request of
your soul, if you do not stand as a hindrance. Always offer glory
to him; for to him is due glory, to the ages. Amen. Pray for me,
brother, that I may know my weakness and be humbled.

LETTER 110

Request by the same person to the same Great Old Man about
the lack of rain and about his long silence. Response by Barsanuphius.

God does nothing in an untimely manner, but does everything for the benefit of people. If he prevented the rain for
their discipline, then he will again show compassion and send
rain. In the same way, if he has prevented my words for a time
so that some people may understand this, then if people have
not understood, God will once again allow me to speak in accordance with people's need and for the sake of their benefit.

LETTER 111

Request from the same brother to the same Great Old Man: "I
implore you, holy father, to fulfill for me your holy promises
about the forgiveness of sins." Response by Barsanuphius.

"Blessed is the God and Father of our Lord Jesus Christ, who
has blessed us with every spiritual blessing in the heavens,"[149] in
that, if you prepare yourself to receive your requests, you will receive them through your great toil and through my own weakness. For I consider the gain and profit of every person and
every soul also to be my own. I am even glad to be burned in
sacrifice[150] for the sake of your souls, as God knows who alone

---

148. Mt 6.8.   149. Eph 1.3.
150. Cf. Phil 2.17.

knows our hearts. I know and I am convinced that we have not lost our labor. Therefore, have confidence that you will receive your requests. When, however, you receive them, make sure that the grace remains with you. For many people have reached the point of receiving their requests; then, after they received them, they fell away [from grace] because they did not protect what they received in godly fear.

So, become a desirer and preserver of good things, a pleasing servant for your Master, a humble disciple of the one who humbled himself for you, obedient to the obedient one, forbearing before the forbearing one, long-suffering for the long-suffering one, merciful as the merciful one, bearing the burdens of your neighbor, just as he bore your own burdens, loving all people sincerely in the manner that he loved us, following him in everything until he receives you in his great rest, where "no eye has seen, nor ear heard, nor the human heart conceived, what God has prepared for those who love him."[151] To him be the glory to the ages. Amen. Pray for me, monk.

LETTER 112

The same person addressed the same request to the same Great Old Man. Response.

Brother Andrew, may the one who said: "Ask, and you shall receive"[152] grant you all that you request. Only prepare your house with much cleanliness in order to receive these gifts. For they are stored in a house that has been cleansed, and they offer their sweet fragrance where there is no stench. When someone tastes of them, that person becomes a stranger to the old self, being crucified to the world and having the world crucified to that self,[153] always living in the Lord. And no matter how much the waves of the enemy beat against the vessel, yet they do not break it. Rather, henceforth, that person becomes fearful to the adversaries through the mere sight of the holy seal. The more one becomes their enemy, the more genuinely friendly and beloved one grows toward the great king. Therefore, broth-

---

151. 1 Cor 2.9.   152. Mt 7.7.
153. Cf. Gal 6.14.

er, show complete hatred in order to acquire complete love; show complete estrangement in order to acquire complete intimacy; abhor adoption in order to receive adoption; surrender your will in order to perform your will; cut yourself away and bind yourself; put yourself to death in order to give life to yourself; forget yourself and know yourself. Then, behold, you will have the works of a monk.

LETTER 113

The same person asked the same Great Old Man the same question. Response.

Brother and beloved of my soul, Andrew, if you knew the gift of God in the way that you should, then every hair on your head would become like a mouth and you would be unable to glorify and give thanks to him sufficiently. Nevertheless, I believe that you are learning. And, as God himself knows, there is not a blink of the eye or a moment when I do not have you in my mind and in my prayer. And, if I love you so much, then the God who created you loves you still more. I implore him to guide and direct you in accordance with his will. Thus he is directing you for the benefit of your soul. If he should be long-suffering toward you, yet he is multiplying the benefit of your soul. Therefore, sit and offer thanks to him for everything, reckoning yourself as nothing at all and believing that all you have been told will occur, in Christ Jesus our Lord. Amen.

LETTER 114

Response by the Great Old Man to the same person, who was asking the same things as well as about receiving prudence from God.

Brother Andrew, our Master Christ said to Martha: "If you believe, you shall see the glory of God."[154] You, too, then, should believe, and you shall see Lazarus rising from the dead and dining with Jesus.[155] You will see Mary sitting at his holy feet, released

154. Jn 11.40.
155. Cf. Jn 12.2.

from Martha's distraction.[156] And believe that everything that God is requested through my unworthy self to provide to your love will come to you. Therefore, God requires nothing else from you but patience and thanksgiving; and he shall open for you the treasures of his wisdom and prudence. I embrace you in the Lord, in whom you may enjoy health of soul and body. Pray for me.

LETTER 115

Response by the same Great Old Man to the same person.

Beloved brother, Andrew, listen. If those who receive sterling coins from the king preserve these with zeal and care, then they shall remain bright and clean. If they neglect them, not only will they become rusty, but they may even be lost. This is why one wise person said: "Lock up your silver and gold."[157] Indeed, I am telling you not only to bind it with unswerving faith but also to seal it with humility and with the long-suffering of patience, through which the one who endures is saved.[158]

I am telling you something bold, by the God who permits me. The great Mediator, Jesus, the Son of the blessed Father, the one who bestows the holy and life-giving Spirit, tells you through me, the least [of all]: "Your many sins are forgiven you,"[159] namely, [your sins] from birth to this moment. Therefore, receive this great and ineffable joy, love him with all your strength, "bearing fruit worthy of repentance,"[160] crying out with the holy Paul those melodious words: "Who will separate us from the love of Christ? Will hardship, or distress, or persecution, or famine, or nakedness, or peril, or sword?" Say with him: "For your sake, we are being killed all day long; we are accounted as sheep to be slaughtered. No, in all these things, we are more than conquerors through him who loved us. For I am convinced that neither death, nor life, nor angels, nor rulers, nor authorities, nor things present, nor things to come, nor powers, nor height, nor depth, nor anything else in all creation will be able to separate us from the love of God in Christ Jesus our Lord."[161]

---

156. Cf. Lk 10.39–42.
158. Cf. Mt 10.22.
160. Mt 3.8.
157. Sir 28.24.
159. Lk 5.20 and 7.47–48.
161. Rom 8.35–39.

Show that you are meditating on these things not only with your words but also with your works. For he says: "By your patience, you will gain your souls."[162] You have assumed great dignity; show great and worthy works of patience and thanksgiving, through which comes the expectation of perfection. Let us become worthy of this perfection in the name of the Father and the Son and the Holy Spirit. Amen. Soften these things continually and consciously, and you shall taste their sweetness. How they render fragrant your soul and the souls of those who are able to entertain them! Be bold in the Lord and be strong, most pious one.

LETTER 116

Response by the same Great Old Man to the same person.

Brother Andrew, the Lord said: "Elijah has already come."[163] And I tell you that your spiritual Lazarus has already been raised and loosed of his bonds,[164] while these words have been fulfilled for him: "You have loosed my bonds."[165] Therefore, you, too, should offer a sacrifice of praise to him who loosed [Lazarus], so that he may not fall again through indolence into the former bonds, in accordance with the words of the Savior: "Behold, you have been made well; do not sin any more,"[166] and so forth. Give thanks to God. For he is concerned about you and cares for you and looks after you in all things, if you continue to desire this. Enjoy health in both soul and body; and pray for me.

LETTER 117

The same person, who received such a great gift, also requested a commendation for himself as well as for those with him. Response.

Andrew, servant of the most high God and fellow-servant with me, who am the least, peace be with you and with the rest of our fellow-servants from God the Father and our Lord Jesus Christ.

162. Lk 21.19.
163. Mt 17.12.
164. Cf. Jn 11.44.
165. Ps 115.16.
166. Jn 5.14.

I am making it clear to you that, even before your request, I had already commended you to the holy, worshipful, consubstantial, and life-creating Trinity, which is without beginning, in a commendation for your protection from all evil. I do not, however, wish you to be ignorant also of the fact that there is another commendation, more fearsome and more necessary and awe-inspiring, more desirable and beloved, more honorable and more glorious. Listen to what that commendation is. When our enemy, that hater of good, is shamed by hearing that blessed and life-creating voice of our Savior addressing us, that voice which is full of joy and gladness and exultation, which illumines with ineffable brightness and says: "Come, you that are blessed by my Father, inherit the kingdom prepared for you from the foundation of the world,"[167] then the great commendation comes: "When the kingdom shall be handed over to God the Father."[168] This is it, and outside of this, there is no other. Now, listen to how this comes about. As each of the saints brings to God the sons whom they have saved, they say in clear voice, with much and great boldness while the holy angels and all the heavenly powers express their wonder: "Behold, here I am, with the children whom God has given me,"[169] commending not only them to God but also themselves. Then "God becomes all in all."[170] Therefore, pray that we may reach that point. For blessed is the one who expects and attains. Pray for me, my beloved ones.

LETTER 118

The same person endured fantasies and temptations from the demons and wondered how, after receiving such loving-kindness and the promises of good things to come, he should still be enduring these. So he asked the same Great Old Man about this, and if the seals of the promises still hold. Response by Barsanuphius.

"Those who love the Lord have great peace, and nothing can make them stumble."[171] You shall have peace in God, most hon-

---

167. Mt 25.34.
168. 1 Cor 15.24.
169. Is 8.18.
170. 1 Cor 15.28.
171. Ps 118.165.

orable and like-minded brother Andrew. Do not let the throng of demonic passions and fantasies break you down, but trust that they accomplish nothing by their thronging and tempting except to multiply virtue, so long as we pay very close attention and try to retain a little patience. For it is said about the righteous person that is saved: "If one should draw back, my soul has no pleasure in such a person."[172] Therefore, let us not slacken the rope, lest we lose what has been given to us by the kind, loving, and merciful God. For to him belongs the giving, and to us the keeping. Do not be surprised that, although the holy promises and the "gifts of grace are irrevocable,"[173] the dishonored passions again mobilize themselves against you, expecting to plunder the boundless treasure. Rather, remember their shamelessness according to the witness of God our Master about the glorious Job, who is among the saints, and how many temptations and tricks they set in motion in order to cast down the tower. Yet they were unable to do so; nor were they able to plunder the treasure of his bright faith and thanksgiving. For conversation with fire shows up the gold even brighter; that is to say, excessive temptations show up the righteous person even brighter. For God allowed and permitted his servant to be tempted, in accordance with his own testimony about the righteous person, for the sake of greater testing and for the glory of the Master, as well as to render the enemy defenseless. Therefore, do not grow faint. For the seals of the promises hold true. Rather, endure for the Lord. "For the one who endures to the end will be saved"[174] in Christ Jesus our Lord. Amen.

LETTER 119

Response by the same Great Old Man to the same [brother], when a thought was sown within him that not abstaining from food was preventing him from reaching what had been promised him.

It is not because I wish to abolish abstinence and the monastic discipline that I am always telling your love to perform the

---

172. Cf. Hab 2.4.   173. Rom 11.29.
174. Mt 10.22.

needs of your body as necessary—far be it from me! Rather, I am saying that, if the inner work does not come to our assistance after God, then one is laboring in vain on the outward self.[175] For that is why the Lord said: "It is not what goes into the mouth that defiles a person, but it is what comes out of the mouth that defiles."[176] Indeed, inner work with labor of heart brings purity, and purity brings true stillness of heart, and such stillness brings humility, and humility renders a person the dwelling-place of God, and from this dwelling-place the evil demons are banished, together with the devil, who is their captain, as well as their shameful passions. Then that person is found to be a temple of God, sanctified, illumined, purified, endowed with grace, filled with every fragrance and goodness and gladness; and that person is found to be a God-bearer, or rather is even found to be a god, according to the one who said: "I have said, you are gods, all sons of the Most High."[177] Therefore, do not let the thought, or rather the evil one, trouble you, so that bodily foods prevent you from attaining to the promises. No; for they are holy, and evil cannot issue from good. But, of those things that come from the mouth, the things that are dispatched from inside the heart[178] are the ones that prevent and hinder a person from arriving swiftly at the promises that lie before us. Therefore, when you carry out your bodily needs, do not have any doubts, but do whatever your inner nature can do to labor and humble its thoughts. Then God will open the eyes of your heart in order to see "the true light"[179] and to understand the words: "I am saved by grace"[180] in Christ Jesus our Lord. Amen.

LETTER 120

Question from the same person to the same Great Old Man: "Master, since you know that I am weak in soul and body, I implore you to entreat God, that he might grant me power and assistance for patience in order that I might thankfully endure whatever comes upon me." Response by Barsanuphius.

---

175. Cf. *Sayings*, Arsenius 9.   176. Mt 15.11.
177. Ps 81.6; Jn 10.34.   178. Cf. Mt 15.18–19.
179. Jn 1.9.   180. Eph 2.5.

Brother Andrew, I want your love to learn that all the gifts of grace are given through the advent of the Holy Spirit, and they are given "in many and various ways."[181] For sometimes God gave the Spirit to the apostles to cast out demons, while at other times to perform healings; sometimes to foresee and at other times to raise the dead. The perfect gift, however, was to forgive sins and to set souls free from darkness and bring them to the light. Behold, then, I pray to God that, after the liberation of your soul, he may grant you the Holy Spirit for patience and thanksgiving, "that our opponent will be put to shame, having nothing" as a case against us.[182] You, then, should also cooperate a little in your struggle to obtain this, and "God, who is rich in mercy,"[183] will give it. Pray for me, brother.

LETTER 121

Question by the same [brother] to the same Great Old Man: "I entreat you, Master, always to remember me. And declare to me how I should treat our brother who dwells nearby." Response by Barsanuphius.

Brother, it is written: "If I forget you, O Jerusalem, let my right hand be forgotten,"[184] and so on. So much for the matter of remembering. As for how one should treat the brother, however, one who wishes to please God cuts off the will for the sake of a neighbor, doing violence to oneself. For such a person says: "The kingdom of heaven suffers violence, and the violent take their inheritance by force."[185] Learn, then, how your brother is refreshed and do precisely that. Then you, too, shall find refreshment from God, in Christ Jesus our Lord. To him be the glory to the ages. Amen.

LETTER 122

The brother who lived near this elder, who was unwell, had compassion on his illness and asked the Great Old Man to pray for him. Response by Barsanuphius.

181. Heb 1.1.
183. Eph 2.4.
185. Mt 11.12.

182. Ti 2.8.
184. Ps 136.5.

Trouble-rousing brother, "if only you knew the gift of God"[186] and why, from time to time, he chastens his servant Andrew like a compassionate father, you would have glorified God in order that he might protect him from the foul mouth of the dragon so that he might not find any excuse [to speak out] against him on the day of judgment for the sake of the great promises offered to him by God through me, the least and most unprofitable of his servants. What then? Do you think that I do not have compassion on him more than any other person? I do. For where are the words: "If one member suffers, then all the members suffer together with it"?[187] If he truly knew the brightness of the things that were in store for him, then he would be making melody with Paul, giving thanks, exulting, and saying: "The sufferings of this present time are not worth comparing with the glory about to be revealed to us."[188] God will strengthen him and send him his great mercy. I greet you in the Holy Spirit, beholding with God your progress in Christ Jesus our Lord. Amen.

LETTER 123

The same brother sought to minister personally to the elder, according to his strength and with the help of his own attendant. The elder, however, hesitated and did not wish to be ministered to by him because of the words of Abba Theodore of Pherme, who did not tolerate even commanding his own disciple.[189] [Therefore,] he asked the Other Old Man about this. Response by John.

The God of heaven and earth shall add to your faith, most honored and dearest brother; and he shall strengthen your love in his fear in order to fulfill your good purpose toward your neighbor. So if you labor a little in accordance with your strength, God will not deprive you of the reward for your labor. Therefore, do whatever you can to refresh the elder; for this pleases God even more than worship. If there is anything that you cannot do, let the brother do it. The elder, however, should not hesitate when he is ministered to by you because he

186. Jn 4.10.
188. Rom 8.18.
187. 1 Cor 12.26.
189. *Sayings*, Isaac of the Cells 2.

is ill. Rather, he should give thanks to God and pray for you. For being ill, he should not apply to himself the word of Abba Theodore, who said about the brother: "I am not the head of a monastic community in order to command him. If he wishes to do whatever he sees me doing, then let him do it." For Abba Theodore used to say this because he was able to carry out his own bodily needs and to minister to others. Nevertheless, this particular elder is unwell. And each person ought to live in accordance with one's limits and condition in the fear of God, thanking God always that, through his means, others also receive their reward. Therefore, he should not hold a grudge against anyone who wants to hear the words: "I was sick and you took care of me."[190]

As he has often heard, God does not require anything from the ill person except thanksgiving and patience. For these intercede for one's powerlessness before God.[191] So let the elder not hesitate when he is ministered to by any brother who wishes to labor for God; he should not say: "I am a burden on this brother," or: "I am a source of grief for this brother." Rather, let him say: ["This person can be equal to the one who ministers to those who are ill."][192] Since, then, God has granted him the assurance to receive his reward through me, may the Lord strengthen him and not condemn me." Let the elder keep these things, and then you shall live in peace, by the grace of Christ our God. Above all, "bear one another's burdens, fulfilling in this way the law of Christ."[193] Furthermore, let us remember in regard to these matters that death will not delay in coming. Therefore, "serve the Lord with fear"[194] as well as your neighbor, that by your neighbor you may inherit immortal life in Christ Jesus our Lord. And, having your hope in him, "do not worry about tomorrow."[195] For he cares for us; and, if "we cast our anxiety on him,"[196] then he will take care of us as he wills. To him be the glory. Amen. I salute you in the Lord, entreating you to pray for me for love's sake.

190. Mt 25.36.
192. Manuscript variant.
194. Ps 2.11.
196. 1 Pt 5.7.

191. Cf. *Sayings*, Nau 637.
193. Gal 6.2.
195. Mt 6.34.

LETTERS TO THE
MONK THEODORE (124–131)

LETTER 124

Question from a monk named Theodore to the Great Old Man: "How can I know which thoughts are from God, which are natural, and which are from the demons?" Response by Barsanuphius.

Y CHILD, THEODORE, WHEN YOU ask a question, you should understand what you are asking and prepare yourself for work. For it is written: "Do not be haughty, but give yourselves to humble tasks."[1] Your questions, brother, belong to someone with high measures. Therefore, unless the inner eye is purified by means of much sweat, you cannot be detached from thorns and prickles in order to seize the grape that strengthens and gladdens the heart. If one does not reach this measure, then one is unable to discern whether one is ridiculed and deceived by the demons in trusting them. For they transform matters as they desire, especially for those who are not familiar with their tricks. Therefore, beloved one, hope in the Lord, "and he shall give you the desires of your heart."[2] Cut off your own will, and in all things say to the Lord: "Not as I want, but as you want,"[3] and then he shall treat you in accordance with his mercy.

Child, listen to the way of discerning the three thoughts, about which you have inquired. When your thought suggests that you are doing something according to the will of God, and you find joy in the matter but also find affliction resisting you, learn that this is from God and struggle to endure, according to the words of Paul: "I punish my body and enslave it, so that after proclaiming to others I myself should not be disqualified";[4] so just fulfill the will of God.

1. Rom 12.16.
3. Mt 26.39.

2. Ps 36.4.
4. 1 Cor 9.27.

Now, if a natural thought should come to you, pay close attention and you will discern the difference. For it is said: "Therefore, a man leaves his father and his mother, and cleaves to his wife, and the two become one flesh."[5] Since, then, the Apostle knew that it was the will of God not only to leave that which comes from the demons but also to abandon that which is natural for the sake of eternal life, he said: "The flesh is useless."[6] "Whoever is united to a woman is one flesh with her; one who is united to the Lord is one spirit with him."[7] Therefore, for those who desire to be spiritual, he advised the rejection of the flesh. For whatever is not beneficial is also harmful; and whatever is harmful must be rejected. For those who live in the world and desire to lead a pious life, he proclaimed: "Marriage is held in honor,"[8] and so on.

As for the thoughts that come from the demons, first of all these are troubled and filled with sadness; they also subtly and surreptitiously drag one backward. They dress in sheep's clothing, that is to say, they suggest thoughts of righteousness; "but inwardly, they are ravenous wolves,"[9] that is to say, they seize and "deceive the hearts of the simple-minded"[10] with their apparent sweet-talk. Since, then, it was written about the snake that "it is the most crafty,"[11] always watch its head[12] in case it finds itself a nest and a home inside you, thereby devastating everything. So if you, too, wish to become spiritual, then reject the things of the flesh. For whatever one denies, one also rejects. Listen to the Lord himself, who says: "If any want to become my followers, let them deny themselves and take up their cross and follow me."[13] How else do people deny themselves except by leaving behind their own natural desires and following him? This is precisely why, knowing that he is speaking about natural desires, he advised that one should deny oneself and not what is contrary to one's nature. For if one were to renounce the desires that are contrary to nature, then one has in fact left behind nothing

5. Gn 2.24.
7. 1 Cor 6.16–17.
9. Mt 7.15.
11. Gn 3.1.
13. Mt 16.24.

6. Jn 6.63.
8. Heb 13.4.
10. Rom 16.18.
12. Cf. Gn 3.15.

of one's own for the sake of God, since these are not properly one's own in the first place. If, however, one renounces one's natural desires for God's sake, then such a person always cries out with the holy Apostle: "Behold, we have left everything and followed you; what, then, will remain for us?"[14] Indeed, you shall hear these blessed words like a promise of life. Therefore, what is it that Peter boasted about renouncing, when he was not wealthy, unless he abandoned his own natural desires? Unless a person dies according to the flesh, that person cannot rise to life according to the Spirit. For just as natural desires no longer remain within a person who has died physically, so also they do not remain within a person who has died according to the flesh spiritually. Now, if you have died according to the flesh, how is it that natural desires still live inside you? If you have not reached the spiritual measure, but are still on the fleshly level, then humble your intellect and submit to your teacher, so that he might instruct you with compassion. And "do nothing without counsel,"[15] even if it appears to be good to you; for the light of the demons is later revealed as darkness. If, then, you hear or think or see something, without allowing the slightest turmoil in your heart, then learn that this comes from the demons.

Therefore, accept these things, written briefly, being confident that with sweat you shall make progress in them and that the God who gives to all will also grant to you always to be with his saints, concelebrating and rejoicing with them and inheriting his goods with them, in Christ Jesus our Lord, to whom are due, as to the Father, together with the all-holy and good and life-creating Spirit, glory, honor, and might, now and always and to the ages of ages. Amen.

LETTER 125

Since the [Great] Old Man would meet with no one, except with his own attendant, namely, the abbot (Seridos), the same brother entreated him in a letter to be deemed worthy of seeing him, saying that Abba Moses[16] and the other fathers agreed to meet with those who asked. Therefore, the Old Man responded to

14. Mt 19.27.   15. Cf. Sir 32.19.
16. *Sayings*, Arsenius 38.

him by letter and with a prophecy, whose outcome we came to know through personal experience. For he told him [Theodore] that he would indeed appear to him, revealing also the way and the reason for this appearance: to be "delivered from the unbelievers in Judea."[17] After some time, when the same brother fell into the temptation of disbelief and claimed that there was no one at all in the cell of the [Great] Old Man, but that the abbot only simulated his presence, the Old Man invited this brother together with some others who were there, and washed the feet of them all. I, too, the sinner, was deemed worthy of being washed. Consequently, the brother came to his senses and, recalling this response, confessed to us his own disbelief, as well as the Old Man's prophecy. And we all gave glory to God. Now, the response of Barsanuphius is as follows.

Brother, no one "knows what is truly human, except the human spirit that is within."[18] One knows what is found inside one's home and what is contained in one's purse. And, accordingly, one spends also for the nourishment of others. We also have a command from the Master not to build a tower unless we first consider the expense.[19] You have considered me among the saints, who are wealthy in spirit, and you have given me gladness with your knowledge, and indeed especially with your actions. I am carefully studying their lives, and I find that their excess in good deeds corresponds to the excess of my evil deeds. They were acting boldly, whereas I shrink away from acting but still tremble knowing my actions, fearing the one who says: "You, then, that teach others, will you not teach yourself?"[20] I am struggling to listen to the one who reproaches me and says: "You hypocrite, first take the log out of your own eye,"[21] and so forth. I labor to take out this log but am unable to. I do not despair, however, and I hope to achieve this.

Tell me the truth, brother; if someone should tell a pauper: "Certain people gave a generous donation; you, too, should give the same," can the pauper do this? Or is the pauper prevented by his own poverty? What else can I say? That those who are really thirsty and discover a source of refreshing water are

17. Rom 15.31.
19. Cf. Lk 14.28.
21. Mt 7.5.

18. 1 Cor 2.11.
20. Rom 2.21.

not curious about the source of the well itself, whether it comes from rainwater or river water. Others who are truly enjoying the brightness of the sun will not question whether it is near or far, whether it is material or not. The same applies to the other elements, too. What about the fact that, when questioned on the subject of God, the fathers responded: "Seek the Lord, but do not seek where he dwells"?[22]

What about you now? You abandoned the necessary concern for your own sins, and sought to see me, who am an odorous worm, nothing but "earth and ashes."[23] Nevertheless, I, too, am foolish, and so I gladly sent you this response, being deceived and thinking that I am something, neglecting the words: "If those who are nothing think they are something, they are deceiving themselves."[24] Yes, certainly, I was deceived in this and spoke unworthily. Nevertheless, you should labor like a good and obedient worker, no longer requesting this from me; for I, too, wish to see you, to embrace you and everyone else with the love that is according to God. At the right time, with God's assurance, I shall personally hurry to kiss everyone's feet, for the sake of receiving their intercession and prayer in order to be "delivered from the unbelievers in Judea."[25]

Let us not waste our little time in distractions, brother, but let us acquire mourning filled with tears, so that we may be blessed with those who mourn. Let us visit the poor and the gentle, so that we may become their co-heirs. Let us seek peace with all, so that we may be found to be with the sons of God. Let us endure insult and scorn, so that our reward may be increased in heaven.[26] And let us strive to reach his sight through good deeds, "so that others may see our good works and give glory to our Father, who is in heaven."[27] To him be the glory. Amen.

Brother, I am not writing to you about these things in order to correct you, as though I had myself succeeded in doing them; for I regard myself as being heavily in debt. Rather, I fall down before the kind and loving God with unceasing supplications,

---

22. *Sayings*, Sisoes 40.
23. Gn 18.27; Jb 42.6.
24. Gal 6.3.
25. Rom 15.31.
26. Cf. Mt 5.3–12.
27. Mt 5.16.

that he might grant both to me and to you forgiveness of sins, through the prayers of the saints. Amen.

LETTER 126

Response by the same Great Old Man to the same person, praising the Old Man for his great virtue, and citing scriptural passages, asking whether he should refuse to eat the late-summer fruits [that were offered to him] and instead lead faithfully and decently the life of the fathers; and also about prayer and about the healing of his weak eyes.

Brother, through you the Scripture has been fulfilled in me that says: "My people, those who praise you are deceiving you,"[28] and so on. Such a compliment does not permit us to look upon the shame of our very own countenance. For I believe that it is harmful even for those who have reached some measure, since it removes them from faith in God. For it is said: "How can you believe in me when you accept glory from one another?"[29] Therefore, those who acquire the humility of the Apostle will instead choose foolishness for themselves, in order that afterward they might become wise.[30] For when one shows oneself to be knowledgeable in theory but not in practice, then I would be surprised if such a person will be able to avoid the condemnation that identifies arrogance. It is in regard to the humble that it is written that they will receive grace.[31] If someone confesses the sweetness of the divine words but does not experience it, then that person proves the sweetness to be bitter. Are the following words perhaps bitter: "If any want to become my followers, let them deny themselves and take up their cross and follow me"?[32] If they are indeed sweet, then why do we abandon them, seeking instead to fulfill our own desires?

Someone who obviously knows the way leading to the city will only ask questions in order to humiliate the other, or else in order to test and ridicule that person. Furthermore, if someone knows the way but does not wish to follow it, then the same

---

28. Is 9.15.
30. Cf. 1 Cor 3.18.
32. Mt 16.24.

29. Jn 5.44.
31. Cf. Prv 3.34.

person is proved to be even more negligent. Abba Arsenius also possessed knowledge,[33] although he did not reveal this. For he used to say in a humble manner: "I wish to be saved, but do not know how."[34] Therefore, if one shows the way to another brother but neglects to follow this way oneself, then who is it that is at fault? Think about it. Is it the teacher or the student, who is at fault? In order, then, that you may learn the way, it consists of not allowing those things that we have passed and rejected to attract us backward. Otherwise, we shall again find ourselves in the same place where we began, utterly condemned and worthy of reproach, having labored in vain. Furthermore, learn this, which is necessary for anyone who desires to know the perfect way. Unless one is accompanied along the entire way by one's guide from beginning to end, then one shall never reach the city. Place your will behind you and be humble in all things; then, you shall be saved.

As for the matter of the late-summer fruits, simply examine yourself in the manner that I am telling you, and you will find that you are being mocked by the demons. Do not ask for anything by yourself; if others give you something, then take and eat. If this is not sufficient, do not say anything; if it is too much, then eat what you please and sigh within for your condemnation resulting from this pleasure. If someone should mention the saints to you, try to imitate both the fruit of their renunciation and their faith, mingled also with their works. For without works, faith is clearly dead.[35] And since you speak about leading a decent life, you will not find anything more decent than that which occurs with submission. For submission is obedience, and it is said: "An obedient son will attain to life."[36]

As for praying as much as you can, the commandment is common to all and comes from the Master.[37] As for your eyes, the One who created them is also able to illumine them with

33. *Sayings*, Arsenius 5. Arsenius is explicitly mentioned four times in the *Letters*. See especially *Letter* 256 (*Saying* 40). There are, however, several implicit references to him also in *Letters* 191 (*Saying* 36), 45 (*Saying* 10), 119 (*Saying* 9), 55 (*Saying* 8), and 125 (*Saying* 38).
34. *Sayings*, Antony 1 and Arsenius 1.
35. Cf. Jas 2.26.   36. Cf. Prv 4.3–4.
37. Cf. Lk 18.1.

the eyes of the soul.[38] If, according to the words of the Savior,[39] we understand by means of the inner eyes, then we do not need the [outer] eyes that behold the vanity of the world. Therefore, God is able to place us among the saved, for the glory of his name. To him be the glory to the ages. Amen.

LETTER 127

Response by the same Great Old Man to the same person as well as to some others who were asking: "Who was it that gave power and authority to the devil?"

If you wish to understand something, which nevertheless is not necessary for us to understand, namely, who actually gave power and authority to the devil, this is how you should see things in order, through your ignorance, not to consider God as being responsible for evil. Take yourselves as an example. If one of you, by personal preference, deviates toward evil, then that person chooses to do evil and is judged by God as having done evil by individual free choice. Now, who is it that gave that person the free choice to do so? If it is God, then why does God judge the person? Do not, through the perversion of the devil, try to show God as the one who desires evil. For this is certainly not the case. Far be it from that! In fact, even if some of the saints have spoken in this way, yet you do not fully understand what they meant by this. For what they mean is that God granted authority and power [to the devil] by not preventing or hindering him from the evil result. This is how you should understand the words: "I have hardened the heart of Pharaoh."[40] For if this were truly the case, then why condemn him? Nevertheless, he says this, meaning: "I did not instruct him in advance." One may also learn about this from the Book of Job. For that book informs us that the devil made Job lose all of his belongings and children. Listen to how he says: "The Lord gave, and the Lord has taken away; as the Lord willed, thus it happened; blessed be the name of the Lord."[41] Why, then, does he blame the one who inflicted the damage, but only mentions the one who allowed it

38. Cf. Eph 1.18.
40. Ex 10.1.

39. Cf. Mt 13.13–16.
41. Jb 1.21.

to happen, who could have hindered or prevented the evil, and yet did not do so? Notice also that for no other reason did God say to the devil: "Behold, I am handing him over to you,"[42] except because the devil would have blamed God when the righteous Job offered thanksgiving in return for the benefits that he received.

Children, God is regarded as having given power to him only because he did not prevent the devil. For, in the beginning, God entrusted the devil with a good power; and once he had given this, he never withdrew it. Yet, after receiving this power, the devil rejected it; and instead of this power, he assumed the power of evil. Therefore, inasmuch as God did not prevent him from doing evil, he is said to have given this power to the devil. Nevertheless, it is not written: "He did not accept the blessing, and so God deprived him of it"; but rather: "May he be deprived of the blessing."[43] So you should not think that God is responsible for evil, because this will condemn you. Rather, the devil freely chose the power of evil, and God did not prevent him. Indeed, it also says: "He loved the curse; let it come upon him";[44] it does not say: "God gave this curse to him." Therefore, you should stand firm in the Lord, believing that he is the author of our life and of everything good. And forgive me for being distracted by childish matters and abandoning the perfection that lies before us. Children, may the Lord Jesus Christ bless and increase your fruits to the ages of ages. Amen.

LETTER 128

Question from the same [brother] to the Other Old Man: "Father, what should I do? For I am grieved at leaving behind my children and wife without any protection." Response by John.

It is written in the *Sayings of the Old Men* that, when someone was done injustice by another, that person approached the elder, saying: "I have suffered injustice from someone and wish to take revenge." The elder replied: "Do not do this, my child, but rather let God assume the matter of revenge." Since the elder

42. Cf. Jb 1.12   43. Ps 108.17.
44. Ibid.

was not convincing him, he said: "Let's pray." As they began to pray, the elder began to speak and the brother listened: "God, we no longer have any need for you to care for us; for we shall assume revenge ourselves." The brother was touched by compunction with these words, and said: "Forgive me, Lord; I shall no longer take any revenge myself."[45] This is what I tell you: If we care for our wife and children, then God will no longer care for them. But if we allow him to do so, then God will care about us and about them at the same time. Therefore, do not resolve to care or pray for them; otherwise, you will retain them in your memory, and this thought will become a passion in your soul.

LETTER 129

Question from the same person to the same Old Man: "What, then, should I do? For my sorrow at being separated from my wife persists intensely." Response by John.

It is written about man and woman: "The two shall become one flesh."[46] Therefore, just as if you were to cut off a member of your own flesh, the rest of the body would also be in pain for a while, until the wound is healed and the pain subsides; so also is it necessary for you to be in pain for a while, since your own flesh has been cut away from you.

LETTER 130

Response by the Great Old Man to the same about the same question.

If "all things are possible for the one who believes,"[47] then where is our faith? If you have chosen for yourself to be like a dead person, then ask a dead person whether he desires to see his wife and whether he judges her when she leaves or commits adultery. If you have left the dead to bury the dead, then why are you not proclaiming the kingdom of heaven?[48] Until when shall you be asleep? Wake up and cry out with David: "Do not turn my heart to any words of evil, to busy myself with sinful

---

45. Cf. *Sayings*, Sisoes 1.   46. Gn 2.24.
47. Mk 9.23.   48. Cf. Lk 9.60.

pretexts."[49] If "you have more understanding than all those who instruct you,"[50] then perhaps the wicked demons have entered your heart and further intensified the struggle in regard to your wife. Where have the scriptural words been hidden from you: "God is faithful, and he will not let you be tested beyond your strength,"[51] and so on? And again, do you not hear the voice of the Savior: "Do not be anxious about tomorrow"?[52] If, however, we are suffering in this way on account of our weakness, then no person who is blind should blame the sun for not shining or supporting [this person]. If you believe, according to what is written, that the soul of a person chastised for iniquity will be consumed like the web of a spider,[53] then why are your hands trembling from the outset of the struggle? If the one who is with us is also able to subdue every enemy for our sake, then why do we reveal him to be distant from us through our faithlessness and inaction? If there is none stronger than he, and you boast, saying: "For you are with me,"[54] since you have the powerful one with you, then tell me whom you fear with trembling.

Instead, do me the favor of taking a little of that heavenly fire, which the Master of all came to bring on this earth,[55] in order that when the tares are sown by the enemy,[56] the fire may burn and consume these. Take from this fire and burn incense, so that the Master may smell your fragrance and lead you to his Father, together with the life-creating Spirit, so that he might make a home in your temple, where you have offered yourself as a living sacrifice that is holy and pleasing to him.[57] Then, burning with this fire, you will always desire to be a companion, co-citizen, and co-heir of the saints, who have acquired the things "that no eye has seen, nor ear heard, nor the human heart conceived, what God has prepared for those who love him,"[58] in Christ Jesus our Lord. To him be the glory to the ages. Amen.

49. Ps 140.4.
50. Ps 118.99.
51. 1 Cor 10.13.
52. Mt 6.34.
53. Cf. Ps 38.12.
54. Ps 22.4.
55. Cf. Lk 12.49.
56. Cf. Mt 13.25.
57. Cf. Rom 12.1.
58. 1 Cor 2.9.

Question from the same person to the Other Old Man: "What should I do, father, for I am afraid during the night?" Response by John.

The inhabitants of a city will fear the invasion of barbarians so long as they do not have any assistance from the king. Whereas, if they are informed that a governor or general has reached the city, the inhabitants will not be concerned but rather will be carefree, knowing that these will do battle on their behalf. Indeed, even if they hear that the barbarians are upon them, they will not be concerned, since they have someone doing battle on their behalf. We, too, therefore, should have faith in God and not fear the demons; for he shall send us his assistance.

LETTERS TO A MONK
WHO USED RIDDLES (132–137B)

LETTER 132

A brother, who had three thoughts, wanted to ask the Great Old Man about these. He did not, however, pose his question clearly; instead, he used riddles so that the abbot would not understand. Therefore, he wrote down certain letters of the alphabet, and each time he thought of something he wanted to ask, he would engrave the letters that he thought of at the beginning of each section. These letters were as follows: First, the *iota* (the Greek letter ι),[1] each time that he thought of formulating a question about rigorous stillness and complete silence without meeting anyone at all. Second, the letter *kappa* (the Greek κ),[2] to ask a question about diet; so this letter symbolized whether he should eat dried foods and abstain from wine, meeting only with his own attendant. Third, there was the *lambda* (the Greek letter λ),[3] through which he asked whether he should meet with others and eat some food in order to condescend to his body. To all this, the Old Man responded as follows.

 O NOT SWERVE to the right or to the left"[4] until the two actually meet.

LETTER 133

The same brother addressed another question to the same Great Old Man, but again did not pose the question clearly. This time, he did not even use letters as riddles, in the manner that he for-

---

1. Possibly from the word ἴδιος, meaning "individual" or "aloneness."
2. Possibly from the word κοιλία, meaning "stomach" or "diet."
3. Possibly from the word λαός, meaning "people."
4. Prv 4.27; cf. also Nm 20.17. On the royal or middle way, as well as deviations to the left- or right-hand side, in the early desert tradition, see M. Djuth, "Cassian's use of the figure *via regia* in *Collatio II* 'On Discretion,'" *Studia Patristica* 30 (Louvain: Peeters, 1997), 167–75. Cf. *Letters* 315–316.

mulated the first question, but simply conceived the question in his mind. It had to do with heavy sleep and illness of soul; there was also a question about assistance and prayer for his salvation. Finally, what do the words of the previous response mean, that the two—right and left—will actually meet? To this, the Old Man replied as follows.

The first is harmful, the second beneficial. In fact, as harmful as the first is, so much more beneficial is the second.

LETTER 134

After all this, the brother was again perplexed and asked in order to learn in what way it is harmful and what he should do to remedy this; furthermore, what are "the two" things implied in the earlier response? The Old Man replied to him as follows.

Everything is right for those who understand; nature itself teaches us this. As for what the two are, I was speaking about the two of you, about you that ask the question and about my attendant who conveys the response. As for the matter of sleep, the "two" refers to the soul and the body. For if the physical is not subjected to the spiritual, then one's passions cannot be subdued. This is why I brought the two thoughts closer together.

LETTER 135

The same brother was again perplexed, and asked what bringing the two thoughts closer together meant. He wanted to know about this, and so the Old Man replied as follows.

Forgive me, for the Lord's sake; for I am speaking in utter madness.[5] The Lord said to his disciples: "Are you also still without understanding?"[6] The first and the second points are one and the same.

LETTER 136

When the brother heard this, he declared to the Old Man: "Father, I commend my soul to the mercy of God and into your

5. Cf. 2 Cor 11.17.
6. Mt 15.16.

hands.[7] Therefore, pray for the salvation of my humble soul." In response to this, the Old Man sent him the following answer in the form of a letter.

Brother, let us pay very close attention to ourselves. For it is not possible to deal properly with these matters all at once. If, indeed, the Apostle who had reached such heights declared himself as hardly having reached them,[8] how much more so should we, who are good for nothing, think with a humble mind. Therefore, since I decided through God to receive your thoughts in the form of riddles, I have given you the response similarly in riddles, knowing that this creates spiritual rumination for the rational soul, and especially to those who have some understanding. For when we explore riddles, we discover the benefit that derives from them. Therefore, we have the Apostle goading us and saying: "Do not be haughty, but give yourselves to humble tasks."[9] So do not express your thoughts through riddles any longer. For my own unintelligible response means that you do not understand what I am saying, only leading both of us to further confusion. Truly, then, it is not at all beneficial for us to speak or write to one another in the form of riddles, even if we see that this has been given to us from God. We should do so only when the need arises. Since, according to God, "we are members one of another,"[10] and we know that "a brother assisted by a brother is like a fortified city,"[11] state your thoughts clearly through your brother or else write them down, and you shall hear the response in the same [clear] manner. For this is the way of humility for both of us. Why is it necessary, tell me, to speak in lofty ways, which can cause humility to pass us by? Do this only rarely. For contrition that accompanies thoughts is beneficial to the heart. It makes one say: "I submit my soul and my body." If one decides to submit oneself to one's own brother for the sake of God, one should imagine that one is being submitted to God himself. Therefore, he is able to awaken us from the slumber of spiritual drunkenness. Just as you asked me to

7. Cf. Ps 30.6.
8. Cf. Phil 3.12.
9. Rom 12.16.
10. Eph 4.25.
11. Prv 18.19.

pray for you, I entreat you to do the same for me. For this commandment is scriptural; and it is also said to be healing.[12]

Since you had difficulty in finding the meaning of the term "two" [in the previous letters] I shall explain them both clearly for you now. The first letter concerns you and my son, who is my attendant, namely, Seridos. The second letter concerns the soul and body, referring also to the bodily and spiritual levels. For it is said: "If two of you agree about anything that you ask in prayer, it will be received."[13] This applies also to all of us. For if we do not agree, then we shall never lead a life that is pure. Pray, then, brother, that we may peacefully live our few days [that remain]; for it was not by chance that it was said: "Anyone united to the Lord becomes one spirit with him."[14] May God grant us all to pass in his name through the crossings of the ocean without being harmed. To him be the glory to the ages. Amen. Acquire humility, patience, hope, and that which is greater than all, namely, love for God.

LETTER 137

Question from the same person to the same Great Old Man, [this time] sent in the form of a letter: "Forgive me, father. 'Let the righteous strike and correct me with mercy,'[15] says the Scripture. As a doctor who cuts and cauterizes knows that the patient will also reap the fruit of healing, so also the person who is ill knows that he is in pain as a result of the incision and awaits the healing. As I have already told you, I repeat now: 'Only on the evidence of two or three witnesses shall a charge be sustained,'[16] as Scripture says. Therefore, I commend myself to God and to your holiness. Indeed, I recognize that it is not of my own that I have come here. Since, then, you yourself know everything about me, holy father, reveal it to me because, in the confusion of my many passions and thoughts, my heart has been deserted. Indeed, I am ready to accept eagerly and joyfully everything that comes from you, God willing, with the help of your prayers. As for me, I am writing and communicating, as you ordered, through [the inter-

12. Cf. Jas 5.16.
13. Mt 18.19.
14. 1 Cor 6.17.
15. Ps 140.5.
16. Dt 19.15.

mediary of] my lord, the abbot." Response by the same Old Man
to the same in the form of a letter.

Brother, behold, I am sending you a letter for the second
time, with God's permission, and I entreat your godly love to
awaken your spiritual eye—which is drowsy from despondency[17]— in order that it does not sleep unto death.[18] Therefore,
your intellect should be vigilant in order to understand how to
"traverse the land"[19] that is spiritual, lest any thorns shoot up
and stifle the seed, in accordance with the words: "For the impi-
ous move about in circles."[20] The one, however, who is able to
crush the yoke and their horns at once is powerful. Amen.

LETTER 137B[21]

One of the fathers, who had three thoughts, sent a question to
the Great Old Man about these, although not in a clear manner
but through riddles, desiring to conceal these from Abbot Seridos, who conveyed the response. So he wrote down three letters
of the alphabet and sent these to the Old Man, while in his heart
he had engraved a particular question for each of the letters.
The Old Man responded in similar fashion, using riddles, clever-
ly answering each of his questions. He prevented him, however,
from asking again in this way by means of riddles, saying that this
is not the way of humility inasmuch as it creates turmoil within
both of them, namely, in the person asking the question as well
as in the person receiving the question, leading both of them
similarly to questions and answers without reason or clarity, and
casting both into turbulence. The same Great Old Man wrote to
the same person and to certain other elders who had asked questions, expressing some opinions and theological doctrines in alphabetical order, applying and referring to God their questions

17. Despondency, or *accidie*, is paralleled with the sense of despair in several
Letters, such as 137B, 144, 153, 167, 196, 201, 205, 240, 257, 269, 436, 442,
443, 452, 453, 514, 532, 562, 564, 613, 621.
    18. Cf. Ps 12.4.
    19. Jos 18.9.
    20. Ps 11.9.
    21. On this meditation, cf. P. Noah, "La méditation," in *Byzantion* 53. This
question and its corresponding answer comprise a meditation on the letter *eta*,
found in three manuscripts: Vatopedi 2, Sinai 410, and Panteleimon 192. The
meditation is the continuation and partial clarification of *Letters* 132–135.

and answers under the heading of a letter. All of the words started with the same letter and grouped together certain ideas with
others, according to the letter being explained. Then they profusely developed their various speculations on the detailed interpretation of each word. Therefore, we have selected one part
of the Old Man's dissertation on the theories around the letter
"eta" (η), recording it here as an example of the entire alphabet,
which the saint offered as an interpretation in response.

Eta stands for "abbot."[22] The abbot is a guide. He guides you
toward the light; do not, therefore, seek the darkness. He guides
you in the straight way; do not seek the way of falsehood. He
guides you to the truth; do not deviate toward deceit. He guides
you to peace; do not seek combat. He guides you to joy; do not
run toward sorrow. He guides you to humility; do not come to
pride. He guides you to righteousness; do not seek injustice. He
guides you to bear insults and injuries that come your way; do
not seek praise and vainglory. He guides you to mortification;
do not seek rest. He guides you to the right; do not stand on
the left.[23] He guides you to eternal life; do not seek eternal punishment in the Gehenna of the unquenchable fire.[24] Now, the
sign that one is rejecting that which needs to be rejected is the
choice of good things while not overlooking any of the daily or
evening prayers. May the one who has attained to these, the one
who will attain to these, and the one who expects to attain to
these, rejoice in the Lord.

Eta stands for "the" (ἡ)[25] right hand of the Father. If, then,
you are on the right, do not flee to the left, because you will lose
the strength that is about you. "For the right hand of the Lord
has exalted me; the right hand of the Lord exerts strength."[26]
God will provide strength for those who struggle, and especially
for those who remain beneath the protection of his right hand.
There are some who are vigilant, always paying careful attention
to themselves in order not to fall away from such protection.

---

22. Greek, ἡγούμενος. 23. Cf. Mt 25.33.

24. Cf. Mk 9.43.

25. The emphasis on the letter *eta* stresses the uniqueness of the right hand,
the incorruptible sacrifice, and the joy of the Father.

26. Cf. Ps 117.16.

One falls away from this through gluttony, fornication, avarice, sorrow, despondency, anger, wrath, gossip, hatred, vainglory, pride, or simply by leaving something of the seed of Amalek in the spiritual land of promise.[27] Therefore, the sign of someone who is saved is purification from all these and chanting with the angels of God. May the one who has attained to these, the one who will attain to these, and the one who expects to attain to these, rejoice in the Lord.

Eta stands for "the" (ἡ) incorruptible sacrifice, offered for the life of the world. The one who truly eats thereof is also sacrificed and not dominated by spiritual corruption. For all the works of the devil, both his passions and his thoughts, fill us with corruption, lurking inside us like some worms. About such a person, the Lord said: "The foxes have holes," referring to the demons; "and the birds of the air have nests," namely, the powers of the air; "but the Son of Man has nowhere to lay his head."[28] One who believes, then, that one has already been sacrificed should examine carefully to see whether such worms are lurking within. And if they are not discovered, then it is clear that such a person has died with Jesus and now lives with him, being seated in glory with him. The sign that a person is seated with him is the word of the Savior, that those who believe in him are one, as he and the Father are also one.[29] Therefore, one will find there the faithful who have been purified from the passions, united in the Son and in the same Father. May the one who has attained to these, the one who will attain to these, and the one who expects to attain to these, rejoice in the Lord.

Eta is "the" (ἡ) joy of the Father. The joy of the Father is the Son. The choirs of angels rejoice in him. It is in his name that the martyrs were triumphant. It is through their confidence in him that the saints struggle. It is in him that the curse was lifted from the earth. It is in him that the indictment that stood against us was erased through his cross[30] and we are no longer slaves of the enemy. Therefore, having been liberated by him,

---

27. The list of passions corresponds to that of Evagrius. Cf. *Praktikos* in *SC* 72.

28. Mt 8.20.   29. Cf. Jn 17.20–21.

30. Cf. Col 2.14.

we are servants "of the one who has called us with a holy calling,"[31] "in the new life of the Spirit and not the old written record [of the law],"[32] and we have become saints. For he says: "You shall be holy; for I am holy."[33] Freed thus from this curse, let us not again be enslaved to it, but let us remain in freedom. Listen: "Behold, you have been made well; do not sin any more, so that nothing worse happens to you."[34] The sign that one has attained this measure is keeping—to one's last breath—the freedom that one has received. May the one who has attained to these, the one who will attain to these, and the one who expects to attain to these, rejoice in the Lord.

Eta stands for *El.* And *El* is God. For the prophet Isaiah said: "Emmanuel."[35] The divine Matthew, that holy evangelist of the ineffable joy, interpreted this by saying: "*Emman*, namely, 'with us'; and *el*, namely, 'God.'"[36] Therefore, let us carefully examine ourselves to see whether God is truly with us. If we have been estranged from our evil deeds, becoming as foreigners to the author of these deeds, namely, the devil, then truly God is with us. If the devil has been embittered by us, and our desire to perform good deeds has been strengthened, while we always consider our citizenship to be in heaven,[37] then truly God is with us. If we regard all people as one, and all days as equal, then God is truly with us. If we love those who hate us, insult us, abuse us, despise us, bring harm upon us, and cause us grief, in the same way as we love those who love us, praise us, benefit us, and refresh us, then truly God is with us. The sign of a person who has reached this measure is always to have God within—for God is indeed always with that person—and to recognize all these things. May the one who has attained to these, the one who will attain to these, and the one who expects to attain to these, rejoice in the Lord.

---

31. 2 Tm 1.9.
32. Rom 7.6.
33. Lv 19.2.
34. Jn 5.14.
35. Is 7.14.
36. Cf. Mt 1.23.
37. Cf. Phil 3.20.

LETTERS TO VARIOUS HERMITS
(138–210)

LETTER 138

Response by the same Great Old Man to some solitary, who asked about his attendant, as well as about accepting thoughts and about his relatives according to the flesh.

ROTHER, I AM SPEAKING TO you as if to my own soul. It is written: "Take care that your knowledge does not somehow become a stumbling block to the weak brothers."[1] The brother who attends to you is naïve; do not try to teach him prudence; otherwise, you shall rouse him to anger. Instead, be satisfied when he does whatever you need. Do not offer him some thought, especially in regard to manifesting thoughts. Leave him as he is; do not trouble his heart.

In regard to accepting thoughts, it belongs only to the perfect to allow a thought to enter and then cast it out again. Therefore, do not bring in the spark that will burn the thicket. Do not let your garments be taken, lest you need to recover them by fighting. Do not tempt yourself to become troubled; for you will not withstand such a temptation. So pay attention to yourself, and pray for me.

As for your brothers, I do not know that I have any other brother but Jesus. Do you have brothers? Do as you wish with them; this has nothing to do with me. If Christ himself said: "Who is my mother and who are my brothers?"[2] can I tell you to transgress the commandment of God and retain friendship with your brothers according to the flesh? Now, if they require clothes, why did you not remember the poor? "I was naked and you gave me clothing."[3] Instead, fooled by the demons, you

1. Cf. 1 Cor 8.9.   2. Mt 12.48.
3. Mt 25.36.

162

again remember those whom you left for the sake of God, preferring to become a transgressor. Woe to us, brother, how they work with us. Do you desire the love for them that you owe to every person? Then, pray for them in order that they, too, may be saved by the grace of Christ. Amen.

Therefore, pay attention to yourself in order no longer to be deceived. For we have left behind the syllables and returned to the alphabet. Wrestle in order to die. What is it that you want? Do you want to be saved? Then, steadfastly avoid reckoning yourself as anything, and run toward that which is set before you. Do not allow the devil to bring you untimely care on the pretext of [your] rights. Be free of all cares. Whether they are living or dead, do not send anything there. Remember the Lord, who said: "Let the dead bury their own dead."[4] Pay attention only to yourself; for they will not deliver you in that fearful hour. I tell you so many times to awaken from your deep slumber; for you do not know at what hour the Lord will come.[5] He should come and find you ready.

In regard to the pollutions, these are a fall of the soul. Love Jesus with all your heart, and you shall not fall unto the ages. Peace be to you in the Lord; peace be to you in God's love; peace be to you in a holy kiss.

LETTER 139

One of the fathers living in stillness asked the Great Old Man to pray for him. Response by Barsanuphius.

When someone sends a lawyer to advocate for him before the king, that person always prays for the advocate, so that he may be heard. Then, if he should be heard, it is not the lawyer that was responsible but the prayer that did it. In the same way, then, you, too, should pray that I may be heard. In order to show obedience, I am praying in short for the health and salvation of your soul and body. So if I am heard—and God surely hears everyone—then I attribute this to your prayers. For neither have I become a lawyer, that is to say, a righteous man,

4. Lk 9.60.
5. Cf. Mt 24.42.

in order to plead; nor have I acquired boldness. Rather, I regard myself as a servant on a mission. Therefore, may the Lord hear your prayers and grant you your requests. Pray also for my wretchedness.

LETTER 140

Question from the same person to the same Great Old Man: "Father, how should I pray? In the way shown by the Lord, namely, with the 'Our Father'?[6] Or in the way suggested by Abba Macarius of Scetis: 'Lord, as you wish, have mercy on me'; and if the warfare grows more fierce: 'Lord, as you please, help me'?[7] Could it be that the 'Our Father,' including what follows, was only given for the perfect to say?"[8] Response by Barsanuphius.

The "Our Father"[9] was prescribed both for the perfect and for sinners; for the first, in order that being perfect they might know whose sons they have become and therefore strive not to fall from him; and for sinners in order that, being ashamed to address him as Father, when they so frequently insult him, they might also be embarrassed and turn to repentance. As I consider it further, however, this prayer is more appropriate for sinners. For to say: "Forgive us our debts"[10] belongs to sinners. What debts do the perfect have, when they have become sons of the heavenly Father? And to say: "Do not lead us into temptation, but deliver us from the evil one"[11] is equivalent to the words of Abba Macarius, who said: "Have mercy on me and help me."

LETTER 141

Response by the same Great Old Man to the same person, who asked for his blessing as well as about dispassion.

Brother, God knows what is beneficial. You asked to receive some bread from my weakness. Indeed, there are never more

---

6. Mt 6.9.
7. *Sayings*, Macarius 19. See A. Guillaumont, "Le problème des deux Macaires dans les *Apophthegmata Patrum*," *Irénikon* 48 (1975): 41–59.
8. Cf. Mt 6.9. 9. Cf. ibid.
10. Mt 6.12. 11. Mt 6.13.

than the appointed three loaves a week that arrive in my cemetery.[12] Nevertheless, perhaps it was also a dispensation of God—for one never does anything alone—that even before hearing from you, the sweeter-than-honey son of my sorrows, who regards everyone as being of one soul and reckons their profit as his own, came here with a loaf of bread. And I could not turn him away, saying: "It is best to cut off my own will in this, too." Therefore, I have broken it and sent it to your love, condemning myself as being unworthy of what I have done. May the Lord do unto you according to your faith. May he also not judge me. If there is any talk about this, you may tell the two brothers who visit you.

As for dispassion, this is a gift of God, given by him to whoever longs for it. May God grant you his hand in those things, which you are reaching for in fear and according to his will. Amen. Pray for me, brother.

LETTER 142

Question from the same person to the Other Old Man: "Father, why did the good Old Man[13] call his cell a cemetery?" Response by John.

This is because he has found rest from all the passions there. For he has died completely to sin, and his cell, wherein he is enclosed as if in a tomb for the sake of Jesus' name, is the place of rest, where neither demon nor the devil, the chief of demons, treads. Indeed, it has become a sanctuary inasmuch as it contains the dwelling-place of God. Therefore, in all things, let us all glorify God with one mind.

LETTER 143

Question from the same brother to the same Old Man: "Since in the *Lives of the Old Men*[14] it is written that one of them used

---

12. The "cemetery" implies the cell of the hermit, which is a symbol of the tomb that holds death as well as of the womb that gives life, as explained in the letter that follows.

13. The Greek word is καλόγηρος, which literally means "good old man."

14. *Lausiac History* 20.3.

to offer one hundred prayers and another would offer so many prayers, should we, too, have a particular number in mind when we pray, or not? In addition, how should we offer our prayers? Should we offer prolonged prayers, or simply say the 'Our Father in the heavens,' and then sit down to do our manual work? Again, while working, what should we do? Likewise, in regard to Vespers and the evening services, what should someone do who lives alone? Should we also perform the Hours or sing Odes and hymns?" Response by John.

The Hours and the Odes are ecclesiastical traditions, and they are good for establishing harmony among everyone. So, in monastic communities, they serve to unite a large number of people. Those who live in the scetes,[15] however, neither observe the Hours nor chant the Odes, but rather do their manual labor and study and some prayer, each on one's own.[16] Now when you stand for prayer, you should entreat God to deliver and liberate you from your old self, or else say the "Our Father in the heavens,"[17] or even both of these, before sitting down to perform your manual labor.

In regard to the length of prayers when one stands for prayer, one who prays without ceasing, according to the Apostle,[18] does not need to prolong one's prayers when standing up. For that person's intellect is on prayer throughout the day. Now, when one sits down for manual labor, one ought to recite [verses] by heart or say the Psalms; and, at the end of each Psalm, one should pray while seated: "God, have mercy on me, the wretched one." If one is troubled by thoughts, one should add: "God, you see my affliction; help me." Then, when you have completed three rows of your weaving, stand up for prayer; and, bending your knee and afterward rising in this way, say the above prayer.

15. A scete is a family—or a cluster of families—of monastics living together under the spiritual direction of an elder. Usually distinguished from monastic communities (κοινόβια), scetes are not always distinguished from hermits residing in the desert (ἔρημος). Together, these three ways comprise the traditional expressions of monastic life.

16. This passage is an indication of the fluid arrangement and existence of the three basic monastic ways within the Seridos community spiritually directed by Barsanuphius and John.

17. Mt 6.9.

18. Cf. 1 Thes 5.17.

As for Vespers, the Scetiotes recite twelve Psalms, at the end of each Psalm saying Alleluia instead of the doxology, and simply repeating one prayer.[19] The same also happens at night: they say twelve Psalms, but after these Psalms they sit down to their handiwork. If any so wish, they may recite the Psalms by heart; otherwise, one may search one's thoughts or else read the *Lives of the Fathers*. When one reads, however, one should read five to eight pages and then continue the manual labor. When one sings Psalms or recites them by heart, one should sing with one's lips, at least if there is no other person nearby, in order to ensure that no one knows what one is doing.

LETTER 144

The same person was troubled by despondency and approached the Great Old Man, begging him to pray for him. Response by Barsanuphius.

I know that I am nothing; and if I neglect myself, I am also neglecting you. I know that, bearing in mind the words of Scripture, "we are all members one of another";[20] therefore, when I care for myself with fear of God, I am also caring for you. If it is true that one should strive [to love] "one's neighbor as oneself,"[21] then you, too, should do the same. For it is said: "A brother assisted by a brother is like a city fortified with ramparts."[22] Even before your love asked me to pray for you, I was told and commanded: "Pray for one another, so that you may be healed."[23] You, too, have been told and commanded to do the same. If, however, you are afflicted by despondency, then remember what discomfort Abba Euthymius endured before departing gloriously to the Lord. Expect that day of your departure and you will be relieved of your despondency. He was our fellow traveler and preceded us. What joy it was that received him! Let us strive for that. Let us "run in such a way that we, too, may win."[24] In any case, it is written: "The measure that

---

19. Cf. M. Van Parys, "La lettre de Saint Arsène," *Irénikon* 54 (1981): 76–77.
20. Eph 4.25. 21. Lv 19.18.
22. Prv 18.19. 23. Jas 5.16.
24. 1 Cor 9.24.

you measure out will be the measure you shall yourself receive in turn."[25] Furthermore, the fathers have said: "Obedience for obedience."[26] So offer a hand to your brother, who is beside you and is troubled; you will find that he shall in turn give you a hand in the time of your own affliction. Moreover, "reprove, rebuke, and encourage."[27] For these, too, bring spiritual fruit.

LETTER 145

Question from the same person to the Other Old Man: "I entreat you, my abba, pray for me because I am weak in both soul and body. Pray that God may grant me perfect patience in this holy place. For the enemy and the passions trouble my heart day by day, seeking to drag me backward. It is not that I have done anything good here, but he sees me protected by the prayers of the elders. For the sake of Jesus, then, have mercy on me and pray continually for me, the sinner." Response by John.

May God accept your prayer as sweet fragrance,[28] in the same way as you have gladdened my soul by your godly humility; indeed, this is a burden neither on me, the least, nor on your love. For this is the way of God. If we hold on to this, we shall be saved in the name of our God. Now, as for what you wrote, dearest one, when we contemplate the zeal of the demons and how they are not neglectful in their work, we should also strive to do what is appropriate for us. We should especially know that the power that accompanies us, namely, the power of our Master Jesus Christ, is greater; for he gives us "authority to tread on snakes and scorpions, as well as over all the power of the enemy."[29] Just as an adversary provokes battles and obliges one to appeal to the magistrate so as to obtain justice against his adversary, so it is when we are attacked by the one who from the beginning has hated humanity; he causes us to approach our Ruler and King, Christ, so as to obtain justice against him. Therefore, by fighting against us, he brings benefit rather than harm upon us. Wherever, then, Christ is present, there the attack of the enemy counts as nothing.

25. Lk 6.38.
27. 2 Tm 4.2.
29. Lk 10.19.

26. *Sayings*, Mios 1.
28. Cf. Eph 5.2.

LETTER 146

The same person asked the same Old Man about sleep: "How much should one sleep and how long must one stay awake for prayer? Furthermore, with how many [material things] should one be satisfied?" Response by John.

As for sleeping at night, pray for two hours, starting from the setting of the sun, give glory to God, and then sleep for a further six hours. Afterward, rise for your vigil, and continue this for the remaining four hours. Do the same during the summer, but do so more briefly and with fewer Psalms, since the summer nights are short.

As for clothes, for the weakness of the body, a sick person should have winter and summer clothes in his possession. One who can endure the word of the Apostle about being hungry, thirsty, and naked,[30] however, is satisfied with just one garment. Therefore, brother, let us not have haughty thoughts, but rather let us be occupied with humble ones;[31] and let us not grumble if we happen to possess two or three garments each.

LETTER 147

Question from the same one to the same Old Man: "Father, you told me to pray for six hours. How can I know that I have been awake for six hours?" Response by John.

If you would like to know your hours with accuracy, sleep a little during the day, so as not to deprive your body altogether of sleep, and stay up in prayer for the entire night, from dark to dawn, recording how many lines you recite and then dividing the lines by the hours. Then, you will be able to tell the time by the number of lines. Do the same in the summer. In this way, the hours will become clear to you.

LETTER 148

Question from the same brother to the Great Old Man: "Father, pray for me, the sinner; for I am sick and cannot bear my illness

30. Cf. 2 Cor 11.27.   31. Cf. Rom 12.16.

with joy. Tell me also how I may wash away the pollution." Response by Barsanuphius.

My dearest brother, you make me rejoice with your words, because you appear to be like me, not paying any attention to what you say. In your questions, you call yourself a sinner; and a sinner is a bad servant. Now, you have said that you have an illness; and illness is a confessed correction. Therefore, the correction has been sent to a bad servant. If you grow despondent in accepting your correction, then cease from being bad. For if you rejoice at being corrected, you are not bad. Moreover, one who is not bad is beloved. Indeed, "the Lord reproves the one he loves."[32] So, look at what you truly are and choose for yourself one of those things that I have spoken to you. God knows that, even if I neglect my own salvation, nevertheless I do all that I can for you, fearing the commandment.

As for the pollutions, wash them away, if you like; but wash them away with tears. For tears wash away every stain. Why are you sleeping? Cry out to Jesus until your throat becomes hoarse: "Master, save us; for we are perishing."[33] Remove the ashes from your heart and kindle therein the fire, which the Lord came to cast upon the earth.[34] It will consume everything, bringing out your gold, which is sterling and has been proven in the fire. There is need of much soberness. I shall simply keep silent. Forgive me.

LETTER 149

Question from the same person to the same Great Old Man: "I entreat you that I may know whence this relaxing of the body and melting of the heart come. Further, why can I not keep to a single diet?" Response by Barsanuphius.

Brother, I am astonished and surprised at how those in the world, who desire to make some profit or else be conscripted, show contempt for wild beasts, robbers' plots, and dangers of the sea, indeed death itself. They are not careless in their soul

---

32. Prv 3.12.   33. Lk 8.24.
34. Cf. Lk 12.49.

toward the wealth that they desire, in spite of the fact that they are not even certain about acquiring it. On the other hand, we poor and weak ones have received the "authority to tread on snakes and scorpions, and on all the power of the enemy,"[35] and have heard the words: "It is I; do not be afraid."[36] We know very well that we are not fighting with our own strength but through the power of God, who arms and strengthens us, and yet we fall into carelessness and despondency. How does this occur? It is because our flesh has not been pierced by the fear of God;[37] we have never forgotten to eat our bread as a result of the groaning of our voice.[38] Therefore, we turn from one to the other and from one diet to another, because we have not perfectly accepted the fire, which our Master came to cast upon this earth;[39] otherwise, this would have eaten up and consumed the thorns of our spiritual field. Our weakness and negligence, as well as our love for the body, do not allow us to look upward.

"The Son of the living God"[40] is my witness that I know a man—and he is here in this blessed monastic community, in case anyone should say that I am speaking about myself, or believe that I am something when I am actually nothing—who, if he remains the same as he is now, neither eating nor drinking or wearing any clothes until the Lord visits him, then he shall not require these things ever again. For his nourishment, drink, and clothing are the Holy Spirit. Therefore, if you wish, strive [to become like him]; desire it, struggle for it, hasten toward it; fear God, and he shall fulfill your desires. For it is said: "He fulfills the desire of all who fear him."[41] As for me, although I am nothing, I, too, shall do my best for the sake of the commandment. It is up to God, however, to support and strengthen you, to free you, to lead you toward every good deed, to guard you from every evil, and to save you in his kingdom. To him be the glory. Amen.

Pray for me and entreat the Old Man, who is with you, to do the same and pray for you.

35. Lk 10.19.   36. Jn 6.20.
37. Cf. Ps 118.120.   38. Cf. Ps 101.5–6.
39. Cf. Lk 12.49.   40. Mt 16.16.
41. Ps 144.19.

Question from the same person to the same Great Old Man: "Father, I entreat you to tell me how one acquires perfect humility and prayer. How does a person appear not to be distracted? And, what is best for one to read?" Response by Barsanuphius.

Brother, the Lord taught us how to acquire perfect humility, when he said: "Learn from me, for I am gentle and humble in heart, and you shall find rest for your souls."[42] Therefore, if you wish to acquire perfect humility, learn what he endured and endure it, and cut off your will in everything. For he said: "I have come down from heaven, not to do my own will but the will of my Father who is in heaven."[43] This is perfect humility: to endure insults, rebukes, and everything else that our teacher Jesus suffered.

Perfect prayer is speaking with God without distraction by gathering up all one's thoughts with the senses. What leads one to this is dying unto every person, as well as dying unto the world and all that is in it. Such a person needs to say no more to God in prayer than this: "Deliver me from the evil one"[44] and "Your will be done in me."[45] That person holds the intellect as if present before God and speaking to God. One is then evidently praying when one is delivered from distraction and sees that the intellect rejoices in being illumined by the Lord. The sign that one has reached this point is that one is no longer troubled, even if the whole world should bring temptation. One who prays perfectly is also dead unto the world and its comforts. Those who perform their task carefully for God's sake are not distracted but continue striving for God. It is also beneficial to read the *Lives of the Fathers;* for in this way, the intellect is illumined in the Lord.

Question from the same brother to the Other Old Man: "Since the Great Old Man said that dying unto all people as well as unto the world and its bodily comfort leads to perfect prayer, what

---

42. Mt 11.29.   43. Jn 6.38.
44. Mt 6.13.   45. Cf. Mt 6.10.

should I do, since I am living among people? For it is necessary for me to give orders to my brother. Moreover, because of my bodily weakness, I am unable to eat anything except vegetables; but once I have eaten these, my thought seeks other things. In addition to this, if the vegetables are not well done, because of my weakness, my thought is troubled against my brother. For I have often suffered bad nights as a result of this. In any case, since I live among people, how can I die unto them? And another thing: if the food is well done, in a manner appropriate for my illness, then the temptation of pleasure slips in. How, then, can I die unto fleshly comfort and the world? And what should I do during Holy Week? I entreat you to tell me about these things, and forgive me." Response by John.

What does one do when one is with people and wants to die unto them? One neither judges nor despises anyone, while also not holding onto one's own will; this is what it means to die unto people even as one is living among them. Now, if something happens which, because of some need, provokes you, then react with gentleness to your neighbor who did this, saying: "God knows what is best. Perhaps God wants me not to find comfort in the flesh but only affliction." Therefore, do not be troubled when your food is spoiled. For it may so happen that this arises from demonic influence in order to trouble us. If you receive a second meal on account of your bodily weakness, then give thanks to God, judging yourself as being unworthy, and this will be to your benefit. Moreover, always remember the words: "Give thanks in all circumstances,"[46] and you shall find rest. For such a person is dominated neither by the spoiling of cooked food nor by its sweetness, but rather is protected by God through this thanksgiving.

As for Holy Week, because of your illness, always eat some vegetables at the eleventh hour; and if you cannot do without wine, then take whatever you see that you require, even if it is as much as two cups. Do not hesitate at all, but do everything for the glory of God, according to the Apostle.[47] Pray for me and forgive me for the sake of your love.

46. 1 Thes 5.18.
47. Cf. 1 Cor 10.31.

LETTER 152

Question from the same person to the same Old Man: "How is it that I want to control my stomach and start to eat little, but then am unable to stop there? Instead, even if I eat a little less, nevertheless, after a while, again I return to my first measure, [eating and] drinking the same amount." Response by John.

My brother, your love should remember that all the passions that you speak to me about, I, too, share; for I, too, suffer from the same ones. No one is delivered from these except the person who comes to the measure of him who says: "I have forgotten to eat my bread; because of my loud groaning, my bones cling to my skin."[48] Such a person quickly reaches the point of eating and drinking only a little; for that person's tears themselves become like bread, and so one begins to be fed by the Spirit.

Believe me, brother, that I know a man, whom the Lord knows, who has attained such a measure; this person is taken captive once or twice a week, or more, into the spiritual nurture and, from its sweetness, forgets about material nourishment. When this person is about to eat, he [turns away] like someone who is already filled or disgusted, and so he does not want to eat. When again he does eat, he condemns himself, saying: "Why am I not always like this?" And he longs to attain it again. Where are we, still, brother? Let us depart; let us die. Forgive me, for I do not find anything in myself of which to boast, and so I boast in the labors of others; and this again I do to my own condemnation.

LETTER 153

Question from the same person to the same Old Man: "Father, I entreat you to clarify for me the meaning of all this. How does one reach what you said? For I am ignorant about this. Whenever I have tried to eat only a little, my weakness and despondency did not permit me, and so I returned again to the original measure. Now, how is it that you said that someone who comes to the measure of the one that said: 'From my loud groaning, my bones cling to my skin'[49] also comes to require little food? Explain to me, fa-

---

48. Ps 101.5–6.   49. Ibid.

ther, how 'my bones can cling to my skin'[50] before eating only a little. I do not know anyone who eats so little." Response by John.

Brother, you are forcing me to speak about things beyond my measure, and I fear that I may be condemned when I speak about the achievements of others. For it is written: "My bones cling to my skin,"[51] namely, that all of a person's bones become one; this refers to all human thoughts that become one according to God. Afterward, the bones cleave to the flesh; that is to say, the flesh becomes spiritual and follows godly thoughts. Then, the joy of the Spirit comes to the heart, feeding the soul and fattening the body, while strengthening both alike.[52] So the person is neither weak nor despondent. For Jesus becomes the Mediator, presenting that person before the entrance gates, where "grief and sorrow and sighing are no more."[53] Then, the scriptural words are fulfilled in that person: "Where your treasure is, there also your intellect[54] will be."[55] What brings a person to this measure is perfect humility, in Christ Jesus our Lord. To him be the glory to the ages.

LETTER 154

Question from the same person to the Great Old Man: "Please teach me how to reach abstinence and how to distinguish between natural weakness and demonic weakness. Moreover, how much should I eat?" Response by Barsanuphius.

Brother, you are scraping little by little to reveal things that are actually hidden. Yet, being a fool, I think that no one except someone who has reached this measure can discern what you ask me. For a living human being has a perception of warmth and coldness when something approaches. However, a dead person has no such perception at all; for a dead person has lost every perception. Likewise, one who learns comes to the measure of the knowledge of letters, and is able to distinguish be-

---

50. Ibid.   51. Ibid.
52. For the connection between heart and body, cf. *Macarian Homilies* 15.20.
53. Is 51.11.   54. Matthew actually says "heart."
55. Mt 6.21.

tween them; but one who neither has learned nor is learning will be unable to grasp their meaning, even if such a person asks and is told tens of thousands of times what the letters are. The same applies here as well. No matter how much you ask some-one, one needs to have the experience itself.

As for your illness, if your body can accept daily food and is still slack, then this comes from the demons; otherwise, it is from the illness itself. Abstinence means getting up from the table with a little less [in terms of food and drink], as the elders ordained for those who have not yet made progress.[56] When a person reaches the measure of the Apostle, who says: "Indeed, we are not ignorant of his designs,"[57] then one cannot fail to know how much to eat; for that person is trained. You have com-pelled me, then, to speak about matters that are beyond me; and there is really no need for this. Perhaps, however, those who are able to accept and understand these things are only few and far between. The God of our Fathers will lead you to this joy. For this is an ineffable light, which is both brilliant and sweet. It does not remember bodily food and "has forgotten to eat its bread."[58] Its intellect lies elsewhere; it seeks, ponders, and med-itates on the things above, where Christ is seated at the right hand of the Father.[59] To him be the glory to the ages. Amen.

LETTER 155

Question from the same person to the Other Old Man in order to clarify for him the measure of abstinence. Response by John.

The fathers say about the measure of abstinence that it is always [to consume] a little less, whether in regard to food or drink; namely, one should not fill the stomach with one or the other. Furthermore, one ought to calculate the food cooked and the wine [consumed]. In winter, one does not drink as much; and so the "little less" should be calculated accordingly. And in summer, one drinks more; and so the "little less" should be calculated accordingly. The same applies to food. Neverthe-

56. See Abba Isaiah, *Ascetic Discourse* 4.
57. 2 Cor 2.11.   58. Ps 101.5.
59. Cf. Col 3.1–2.

less, the measure of abstinence applies not only to these matters, but also to speech, sleep, dress, and all the senses. Each of these likewise has its own proper measure of abstinence.

LETTER 156

Question from the same [brother] to the same Old Man: "Father, tell me how much is this 'little less' in terms of actual food, drink, basket [of vegetables], or fruit?" Response by John.

From the entire weight of the bread, the food, or the basket [of vegetables], or fruit, I mean eating as much as one ounce less; from both the wine and water, half a cup less. Indeed, if you are able to endure it without becoming exhausted, then it is good to drink only once; if that is impossible, then drink twice, but only a little[60] each time. Moreover, in regard to your movements and warring thoughts, we should cut down a little from our normal habit, namely, another ounce of food and half a cup of whatever we drink, so that together we eat two ounces less and drink one cup less. Pray for me, brother.

LETTER 157

Question from the same person to the same Old Man: "How does one know how much one should eat or drink?" Response by John.

From daily experience, it is possible to observe what the body can accept in terms of food or drink. For example, if someone drinks three cups a day and eats one pound of bread a day, but sees that his body demands more than three cups, without having labored more or eaten salty foods, then this comes from temptation and must be resisted by abstinence in this case.[61] If, however, there is a good reason for this, then it is not temptation. Therefore, from the three cups, one should try to hold back half of one of the cups, except during times of temptation.[62] Likewise, in regard to the food, one should hold back

60. Or, "a little less than one would like."
61. See Abba Isaiah, *Ascetic Discourse* 9.
62. See *Letter* 160.

one ounce from the pound. Nevertheless, one must first test, as we have said, whether one is able to drink only once a day or else needs to do so twice. For not all human dispositions are the same. If, then, one requires drink twice, one ought each time to consume a little less [than satiety].

LETTER 158

Question from the same person to the Great Old Man: "We entreat you to tell us, if God asks us to act according to our strength, then what happens if this is mixed with one's own weakness and one always thinks this is all that one can actually do? How, then, shall we know what is truly our capacity?" Response by Barsanuphius.

God has given us the prudence to be discerning in all things. If a person is unable to maintain the same measure as on other days because one is weary from travel or from other heavy duties, then one should condescend a little to the body. For instance, one will eat, let us say, half a pound of bread a day. If, for the sake of weariness, this person eats another ounce, then one is doing one's best not to eat more. If a person keeps daily vigil from midnight, and then rests a further hour because of weariness, then that person has acted according to his capacity. Therefore, one's weariness becomes a sign for that person to relax a little, as we have said. And the sign that this person is obliged to keep the regular vigil is the consumption of the customary food. Acting according to capacity, then, again means consuming a little less,[63] whether in terms of food or sleep. If you are asking about the measure of sleep, the fathers ordained half of the night. The measure of food is observing that one desires a little more and always consuming only a little.

LETTER 159

Question from the same brother to the Other Old Man: "What should be the appropriate daily measure of wine and cooked food for someone living in solitude? How is it that the fathers adopted a very strict diet?" Response by John.

63. Or, "a little less than one would like."

For a healthy person who wishes to exercise abstinence, one cup of wine each day is sufficient, and no more. If, however, one is frequently ill, then one should take two full cups. The same applies to cooked food: one should eat one bowl and not worry about anything else.

As for how the fathers adopted a very strict diet, they found that their bodies were obedient. Therefore, those who control themselves well and with discernment conform their routine to their body. Pray for me.

LETTER 160

Question from the same person to the same Old Man: "Should everyone have the same rule about which you told me, or do the elders respond according to the condition of the person asking?" Response by John.

Brother, what I told your love about abstinence, I spoke in regard to people like us and according to my own measure. So, if we achieve the intermediate stage, we shall progressively reach the greater measures. We should not desire at once to set our foot on the highest rung of all before we have placed it on the first rung of the ladder. For all those who come to the measure of which the Apostle spoke are able "to be well-fed and go hungry at the same time,"[64] and so on; "for they have learned the secret in all things."[65] Therefore, you know your measures, brother. When temptation comes, I told you to cut down another ounce and, likewise, to drink less.

LETTER 161

A brother asked the same Old Man: "Father, what is the difference between taking food according to one's desire, and taking it according to one's [natural] condition?" Response by John.

Taking food according to one's desire is longing to take food, not for the body's need but for gluttony's sake. If, however, you see that your condition takes to herbs rather than to pulse, for example, not for the sake of desire but for their lightness, this is

---

64. Phil 4.12.   65. Ibid.

where the difference lies. There are conditions that tolerate sweet things, others that tolerate salty things, others bitter things; and this is neither passion nor desire nor gluttony. To long for and desire something, however, in spite of its heavy nature, is called desire, which is the servant of gluttony. Be careful of this, when the passion of gluttony has overcome you and has mastered your thought. Nevertheless, if you resist this, making moderate use of your food for the sake of your need, then this is not considered as gluttony.

LETTER 162

Question from the same person to the same Old Man: "Father, what happens when the passion is not there from beforehand but is suggested during the time of partaking? What should I do then? Shall I abstain from the food or not?" Response by John.

Do not abstain from it altogether, but act against your thought, remembering that the food becomes a foul smell and is of no profit, as well as that we are condemned when we eat while others entirely abstain. If the thought leaves you, then partake of the food while at the same time condemning yourself. If it persists, then invoke the name of God to help you, and you shall have rest. If it masters you, so that you are unable to eat in an orderly manner, then cut off the food. Nevertheless, if others are seated beside you, so as to prevent them from noticing, eat a little at a time. Now, if you should happen to be hungry, fulfill your need with bread or some other food by which you are not tempted.

LETTER 163

Question from the same brother to the same Old Man: "Clarify for me what the sign of gluttony is." Response by John.

When you see your thought taking pleasure in a particular food and driving you to take your food before others do, or else taking pleasure in pulling this food toward yourself, this is gluttony. Therefore, pay attention to yourself in order not to perform its will, and do your best to restrain yourself not to partake of it eagerly but in an orderly manner. Rather, try to push the food before those who are seated with you. It is not necessary, as I have told you, to refuse altogether to partake of the food on the grounds of gluttony. Instead, one should be very careful not to partake of it in disorderly fashion.

Even apart from gluttony, the fathers write that we should not stretch our hands before others at the table;[66] for this is improper and foreign to common orderliness. When, however, the food set before us is such that it is unclear what the portion of each should be, but everyone is supposed to eat of it in common, then it is not improper to take some food along with all the others, although again we should do this in orderly fashion so as not to fall into gluttony and condemnation. Another sign of gluttony is when one desires food before the appropriate time, which must not be done, unless there is good reason to do so. In all things, however, we should invoke the help of God, and he will come to our assistance.

LETTER 164

Question from the same person to the same Old Man: "Whence comes the movement of the body?" Response by John.

The movement of the body comes from negligence. For negligence seizes you without your noticing it, leading you to judge and condemn others; in this way, it betrays you. When Israel served God genuinely, God guarded Israel from its enemies. Nevertheless, when Israel neglected its genuine service, God allowed its enemies to trample it.

LETTER 165

Question from the same brother to the same Old Man: "Should one ask the elders about all the thoughts that arise in the heart? Moreover, when one prays or chants the Psalms, should one do this with one's voice? In addition, about memories of what one has done, heard, or spoken. Finally, should one enter into discussions with the fathers?" Response by John.

---

66. Abba Isaiah, *Ascetic Discourse* 3.

Brother, it is not necessary to ask about all of the thoughts that may arise; for [many of] these are fleeting. One should ask about those which abide and tempt us. For a person who is insulted many times will take no notice of these insults and become carefree in regard to them; however, if someone should attack or assault that person, then the latter will accuse the culprit before the magistrate. That is how we, too, should act.

As for prayer and chanting the Psalms, it should be done not only with the intellect but also with one's lips. For the prophet David says: "Lord, you shall open my lips, and my mouth shall declare your praise."[67] Furthermore, the Apostle reveals that the lips are required, when he speaks of "the fruit of the lips,"[68] and so on.

As for those things which you have seen or heard or practiced or thought, nothing else can put an end to these except humble prayer, namely, a prayer that has no will of its own at all and is accompanied by tears. Those fathers who achieved this did not do so without toil, tears, and the excision of the will. Now, entering into discussions [with the fathers] means counting yourself as being something and regarding yourself as their equal. Asking questions and trusting their answers, however, is humility and progress in the Lord. Pray for me, brother.

LETTER 166

Another one of the fathers asked the same Old Man: "How does one guard the heart? And in what way does the warfare come from the enemy? Should one contradict temptation? And concerning the thought of fornication, should one block its entrance? If it does enter, what should one do? And about food, what should one do: weigh the exact measure of ounces or simply guess and exercise caution?" Response by John.

Guarding the heart means having the intellect vigilant and pure of the one against whom one is at war. Initially, perhaps, we treat the thought with contempt; but when the enemy sees this contempt, he struggles to engage us in warfare. Indeed, if

67. Ps 50.17.
68. Heb 13.15.

you wish to learn whether you are dealing with friend or foe, say a prayer and ask: "Are you with us or against us?"[69] And he will respond with the truth. Therefore, betrayal comes through negligence. Do not contradict temptation; for that is what the demons want, and then they will never stop. Rather, resist it by taking refuge in God, casting your weakness before him; for he is able not only to shut their mouths but also to abolish them.

As for the demon of fornication, it is good—in fact, it is very good—to block his entrance. If, however, he seizes the entrance and comes in, then wrestle with him and cast your weakness before God, praying to him, and he shall cast him out.

As for the question about food, regulate your life by guessing and guarding. And pray for me for the sake of love.

LETTER 167

Question from the same person to the same Old Man: "Father, how does it happen that my heart is burdened so that I sleep excessively and have no compunction?" Response by John.

These things always happen to the person living in stillness, so that one may come to despondency and leave the arena in despair. We should, however, cast our weakness before the one "who is able to accomplish far more than we can ask or imagine,"[70] until he crushes the camps of the Amorites from before us, not allowing Midian and Amalek and the sons of the east to spoil our fruits.[71] Let us, therefore, endure with the help of God our Master. For he is mightier than they; and we shall be saved.

LETTER 168

Question from the same [brother] to the same Old Man: "How is it that during the night I fantasize about other faces, while during the day I am actually tempted by them? Sometimes, this also happens without any face. Moreover, I fantasize at times with pleasure and at other times without pleasure." Response by John.

---

69. *Sayings*, Nau 99.   70. Eph 3.20.
71. Cf. Jgs 6.3–4.

The ones that besiege you by day are the same ones that besiege you by night. They are showing you that you are still in their hands. Yet, they are transformed into both the one and the other. The fact that sometimes it occurs with pleasure while at other times without pleasure is part of this transformation, of which I have told you, in order that a person may come to confusion and trouble. Now, the warfare of the night is twofold. It may occur as a result of pleasures, and this comes from the temptation of the devil[72] in order to bring a person to despair and to make one think that one no longer can be saved. So, when the temptation of such a warfare occurs to you, do seven sets of seven prostrations, that is, forty-nine prostrations, saying with each: "Lord, I have sinned; forgive me for the sake of your holy name." If you also happen to be ill, or else if it is Sunday, when it is not appropriate to perform prostrations, then pray this phrase seventy times instead of the forty-nine prostrations. Moreover, the difference between the temptations is as follows. To be tempted by the temptation of the devil results from arrogance; to be tempted by the experience of pleasures results from gluttony.

LETTER 169

Question from the same brother to the same Old Man: "You told me in your response, father, that those things that occur to someone during the night arise either through the temptation of arrogance caused by the devil or else through the experience of pleasures caused by gluttony. Is it, then, possible for the devil to stir this up in someone out of envy alone, while one is neither arrogant nor indulging in pleasure? In addition, how should one know whether a movement occurs naturally during the night? I am entreating you to teach me. Do the perfect endure any natural movement? Finally, should one kneel before the day of Pentecost or not?" Response by John.

The devil can certainly cause a movement out of envy. When, however, neither arrogance nor pleasure is present, he can do

---

72. Cf. *Letter of Antony* 1.37–41, and Cassian, *Conferences* 22.3.

no more than that. For just as someone who wishes to build a house but does not find the necessary materials will labor in vain, so, too, the devil is found to be such. The sign of a natural movement, however, is when someone notices that this occurs neither through arrogance nor through pleasure or even again through envy of the devil. One may learn that this is not through envy but from natural causes, when one is able to sleep confidently and recite many prayers, naming the holy and consubstantial Trinity, while also performing the sign of the cross, and yet still experiences this.

The perfect do not even experience this. For they have quenched every natural movement, having rendered themselves spiritual eunuchs for the heavenly kingdom.[73] That is to say, they have mortified their own earthly members.[74]

As for kneeling before the day of Pentecost, you have already been told on another occasion that you should continue to kneel in your cell. Pray for me, brother.

LETTER 170

Question from the same person to the same Old Man: "If a fantasy occurs to me by night and, on the next day, there is holy Communion, what should I do?" Response by John.

Let us approach with all our wounds and without any contempt, as people who are needful of a doctor;[75] then, he who healed the woman with the issue of blood[76] will also heal us. Let us love much, that he may also say to us: "Your many sins have been forgiven; for you have shown great love."[77] When you are about to take Communion, say: "Master, do not allow these holy things to be unto my condemnation but unto purification of soul and body and spirit." Then, you may approach with fear, and our Master, who is kind and loving, will work his mercy with us. Amen.

73. Cf. Mt 19.12.   74. Cf. Col 3.5.
75. Cf. *Historia monachorum* 20.2–3.
76. Cf. Mt 9.22.
77. Lk 7.47.

LETTER 171

Question from the same person to the same Old Man: "Is it good, Abba, to confess this fantasy to one of the brothers and to perform a prostration before that person, asking him to pray for me?" Response by John.

About the nocturnal fantasy, it is a good thing to admit it to someone who is able to hear it, but not to younger brothers. Once one has performed a prostration [before that person], then one should ask for his prayers. For the word of the Scripture is: "Confess your sins to one another, and pray for one another, so that you may be healed."[78]

LETTER 172

Another one of the fathers, who was living in stillness, asked the same Old Man: "Abba, tell me how one should sit in the cell." Response by John.

To sit in one's cell means to remember one's own sins and to weep and mourn for these, as well as to remain vigilant so that the intellect is not taken captive but rather struggles, and, if it is taken captive, to return it to its place.

LETTER 173

Question from the same person to the same Old Man: "Father, how do I know whether I am cutting off my own will when I am in my cell? Likewise, how do I know that I am doing this when I am with other brothers? Moreover, what is the difference between the will of the flesh, the will that is from demons but concealed as good, and the will of God?" Response by John.

To cut off one's own will while sitting in the cell is to despise fleshly comfort in all things. The will of the flesh seeks to produce fleshly comfort in any matter. If you do not work toward such comfort, then be sure that you are cutting off your will while sitting in the cell. Cutting off the will, however, when one

78. Jas 5.16.

is with others, is dying unto them and being with them as if not being with them. The will that is according to God leads us to cut off the fleshly will, according to the Apostle.[79] Nevertheless, the will that is from the demons leads to self-justification and self-confidence; then one is ensnared. Pray for me, brother, and forgive me.

LETTER 174

Question from the same person to the same Old Man: "What food should I prepare for myself each day?" Response by John.

Preparing your daily food in the cell, as you have asked, entangles you in matters of concern and warfare. Instead, live as God opens the way for you. "For one who walks in integrity walks securely."[80]

LETTER 175

Question from the same [brother] to the same Old Man: "Is it good for me to be occupied with the prayer 'Lord Jesus Christ, have mercy on me,'[81] or should I declaim by heart certain passages from the sacred Scriptures and recite the Psalms?" Response by John.

You should do both: a little of one and a little of the other. For it is written: "These you ought to have practiced without neglecting the others."[82]

LETTER 176

Question from the same person to the same Old Man: "When I chant the Psalms, should I say the 'Our Father' with each Psalm, or should I simply say the 'Our Father' occasionally, spending the rest of the time in supplications?" Response by John.

Reciting the "Our Father" once or supplications once is really one and the same thing.

79. Cf. Eph 2.3.
81. Lk 18.38.
80. Prv 10.9.
82. Mt 23.23.

LETTER 177

Question from the same person to the same Old Man: "My thought tells me that meditation makes pure prayer. Is it true?" Response by John.

Brother, do not be ridiculed by the demons and say that meditation is the preparation for pure prayer. Otherwise, how is it that the passions still remain in someone who prays purely?

LETTER 178

Question from the same brother to the same Old Man: "Should one at the end of Vespers or else after nocturnal fantasies also say a prayer in memory of the peace of the holy churches, the king, the governors, the people, the poor, widows, and the like? And if someone asks another to pray for him, even if the one asked knows himself to be full of passions, should that person still pray?" Response by John.

It is good to remember to pray for the peace of the holy churches and the rest, but one should do so as someone who is unworthy and unable in fact to do so. For this is an apostolic commandment.[83] It is also good to pray for those who ask. For the word is clear in the Gospel and the Apostle: "Give to everyone who asks from you."[84] Also: "Pray for one another, so that you may be healed."[85] Again: "Do to others as you would have them do to you."[86] Some people even used to pray for the apostles themselves.[87] Those who neglect prayer condemn themselves. Therefore, whether I am able to or not, I force myself to do so for the sake of the commandment.

LETTER 179

Question from the same person to the same Old Man: "How does the intellect become the prey of wild beasts?" Response by John.

83. Cf. 1 Tm 2.1–2.
84. Mt 5.42.
85. Jas 5.16.
86. Mt 7.12.
87. Cf. Acts 12.5.

The intellect becomes the prey of wild beasts if one does not anticipate them by blaming oneself. If one delays in blaming oneself, then one endures the mark of their teeth and the wound of their claws. Therefore, one will need plaster, namely, repentance.

LETTER 180

Question from the same [brother] to the same Old Man: "Should I shut my eyes before the fantasies of the enemy? And when the body rises up against me, what should I do?" Response by John.

The devil reveals things to a person both with and without perception. Therefore, one who is weaker shuts one's eyes in order not to see. One who is stronger both sees and ignores them. "For the righteous are as bold as a lion."[88] As for the rebellion of the body, hasten to flee toward Jesus through prayer, and you will find rest.

LETTER 181

Question from the same brother to the same Old Man: "Whence does it occur to me that, even after I address a question to you, I continue to condemn others?" Response by John.

You continue to condemn others even after asking me a question because the pretense to rights has not died within you. Therefore, you are not at any great pain in regard to this passion or about how to escape it. Condemn yourself, and the condemnation of others will depart from you.

LETTER 182

The same person was troubled by thieves and was greatly frightened. By the grace of God, however, he was protected from coming to any harm from them. He expressed his fear to the same Old Man, at the same time asking for his prayer for protection in the future. Response by John.

88. Prv 28.1.

God does not betray anyone; for he says: "I will never leave you or forsake you."[89] Rather, our lack of faith is what betrays us. Nevertheless, with God's permission, temptations come in order to prove the faith of those who place their hope entirely in God. Do thieves come in greater numbers than the chariots and forces of Pharaoh? And yet, it became clear that, with one word and one nod of the Lord, they were all drowned together.[90] Do you not remember how he blinded those who went against Elisha? Who was it that blinded them, and for whose sake did this occur?[91] Let us learn that he who knows how to deliver the godly from temptation did so then and continually does all these things. Where have we cast aside and in what corner have we abandoned the Scripture that says: "The Lord will keep you from all evil; he will keep your life"?[92] How have we delivered to oblivion the words: "Even the hairs on your head are all counted. Not one sparrow will fall into a snare apart from your Father. Are you not of more value than a sparrow"?[93]

O fright, the daughter of faithlessness! How it has brought us down! It is altogether most terrible. It blinds the intellect, slackens the heart, and tears people away from God. It is the sister of hopelessness, exiling people from the fear of God to the land of destruction. Brother, let us flee this fear and awaken the Jesus that lies asleep within us, saying: "Master, save us; for we are perishing."[94] He shall rise and rebuke the assault of the wind; and it will be still. To us, he shall say: "It is I; do not be afraid."[95] Let us leave behind the rod of reed and assume the rod of the cross, through which the sea was divided and the spiritual Pharaoh was drowned,[96] the lame were supported, the dead arose,[97] the Apostle boasted,[98] and we have been delivered from betrayal, committing ourselves to him who was crucified for us. For he knows how it is through this rod that he shepherds us, his sheep, and drives away from us the bloodthirsty wolves. To him be the glory to the ages. Amen.

89. Heb 13.5.
90. Cf. Ex 14.26–28.
91. Cf. 2 Kgs 6.18.
92. Ps 120.7.
93. Cf. Mt 10.29–31.
94. Lk 8.24.
95. Mt 14.27.
96. Cf. Ex 14.16–28.
97. Cf. Lk 7.22.
98. Cf. Gal 6.14.

LETTER 183

The Great Old Man was likewise asked about the same matter. [He replied as follows.]

Sleeping brother, examine your slackened [heart]; for I wonder how it fears the slaves that stand outside and cannot see their masters that stay inside. The visible thieves are slaves of the intellectual thieves, namely, of the demons that work within them. You ought to be grateful to the thieves who have assaulted you; for in coming, they have also awakened their masters, the thieves who lie asleep within you. Has Jesus gone so far away that you cannot run to him and entreat him to come to your assistance? Does your ear not hear the Psalm that your lips recite? "The Lord is near to all who call on him in truth. He will fulfill the desire of all who fear him; and he will hear their cry and save them."[99] Cleave to him and he will abolish from you both the inner masters and their outer slaves. To him be the glory.

LETTER 184

The same person asked the Other Old Man, saying: "Two thoughts have troubled me in regard to the thieves. One of these condemns me, saying: 'Whatever you have belongs to the monastic community, and it is a sin that you allowed them to take them [from you]. You should have made some noise or shouted out.' The other thought condemns me, telling me that the Lord said: 'If anyone wants to take your coat, give your cloak as well.'[100] What do you order me to do, master, since I am torn between these two thoughts? Furthermore, forgive me for allowing the intellectual thieves to enter and exit in order to plunder my heart; yet I am also asking about the visible thieves. Therefore, pray that God may first abolish those." Response by John.

If you have no authority over any matter, then do not show contempt toward any charity that you receive from the monastic community. Otherwise, you will be condemned for this.

99. Ps 144.18–19.
100. Mt 5.40.

For someone under authority is not under the commandment. Therefore, make noise or cry out without turmoil, saying: "Bless whatever he demands," and God will assist and protect you. As for the intellectual and the visible thieves, the Lord will abolish both of them. "Be strong and bold,"[101] and pray for me.

LETTER 185

The same person read in the *Sayings of the Elders* that someone who truly wants to be saved must first endure insults from other people, as well as contempt, dishonor, and loss,[102] and must have the senses liberated and thus come to perfect stillness, even as our Lord Jesus Christ also did. For having borne all of this, he afterward ascended the holy cross, namely, the mortification of flesh and passions, as well as perfect and holy rest.[103] Then, [the same person] said to himself: "I, the wretched one, have neither known nor practiced any of these things. From the weakness of my passions, however, I have caused scandal to everyone and withdrawn from people. Perhaps, then, I should return to live among people and, with the assistance of God, do whatever the elders have told us; then, I can come to stillness, in order that my labor may not be in vain."[104] So he reported this to the same Old Man. Response by John.

The fathers spoke well; there is no other way. Since, however, there are many reasons why one thinks one is doing well and is then found to be hurt for some other reason, one should protect oneself. For you are already settled [in stillness]; and if you return to live among people, this may give rise to vainglory in you. Perhaps, too, it is not easy for you to be among others, and so two wrongs will result. Nevertheless, if you blame yourself for not doing what is required in regard to the ascent of the cross, saying: "I have settled in ignorance," then blame knows how to insult and dishonor itself, thereby bringing one who truly accepts it to the measure of the cross, in Christ Jesus our Lord.

101. Dt 31.6.
102. *Sayings*, Nau 325.
103. Abba Isaiah, *Ascetic Discourses* 8 and 13.
104. Cf. 1 Thes 3.5.

LETTER 186

Question from the same person to the Great Old Man: "Father, pray for me; for I am greatly afflicted." Response by Barsanuphius.

May the God of heaven and earth give you, through the prayers of his saints, the requests that I ask him to grant you. Therefore, since you wish to hear and rejoice, it is you that are obliging me to speak, in order that the words may be fulfilled in me: "I have been a fool! You forced me to it."[105] Even before you asked me, for the sake of Christ's love that burns within me like a flame of the fiercest fire—for Christ said: "You shall love your neighbor as yourself"[106]—and from the burning and warming of my spirit, I have not ceased praying to God [for you] night and day. I pray that he might make you God-bearing, that he might dwell in you and walk inside you,[107] that he might send you the Holy Spirit, "the Spirit of truth,"[108] so that when it comes it may teach you all things, remind you of all things,[109] and "guide you into the whole truth,"[110] making you fellow-heirs with the great saints of that which "no eye has seen, nor ear heard, nor the human heart conceived."[111] Indeed, I became toward you as a father striving zealously to enroll his children with the king in glorious campaigns, while they were carefree as children. May God give you the burning of this love. For the Lord will assure you that it raises those who possess it to the seventh heaven, as some already now are ascending confidently and being blessed, "whether in the body or out of the body, I do not know; God knows."[112]

Now, in order that you may learn the beginning of the road toward such joy, listen. First, the Holy Spirit comes to a person. Then, that Spirit teaches one everything, as well as how one must set one's mind on things above, on those things on which you are not yet able to set your minds. After this, guided by that first burning, one ascends to the first heaven, and after this

---

105. 2 Cor 12.11.
107. Cf. 2 Cor 6.16.
109. Cf. Jn 14.26.
111. 1 Cor 2.9.

106. Lv 19.18; Mt 22.39.
108. Jn 14.17.
110. Jn 16.13.
112. 2 Cor 12.2.

to the second, and proceeds by progression until the seventh. There, one contemplates ineffable and fearful things, which no one can hear except those who reach this measure, of which may the Lord make you worthy.

Those who die perfectly unto the world through endurance of many afflictions are able to enter therein. O beloved brother, the Lord endured the cross, and yet you are unable to rejoice in tribulations, the endurance of which leads you to the kingdom of heaven. You rightly said that you are in distress. Do you not know, however, that, when someone asks the fathers for their prayers, or asks God to grant one assistance, then the afflictions and temptations sent in order to test one are in fact multiplied? Therefore, do not seek bodily comfort, unless the Lord gives it to you, just as you have already heard from my fellow-slave. For "every comfort of the flesh is an abomination before the Lord."[113] The Lord himself said: "In the world, you shall have tribulation."[114] The Lord will assist you in everything. Forgive me for what I have said; for I have spoken as someone out of his mind. Pray for me; for I have spoken about those things which I heard from others, namely, the saints.

LETTER 187

The same person suspected that the death of the Great Old Man was impending and grieved for his own salvation as well as that of the entire monastic community. So he made this known to the same [Great] Old Man.

Most desired brother, you were moved according to God's love and have spoken words of humility, drawing even the unmerciful ones to compassion toward someone who is sinful and the least of all. What do I have to say to you, when I am a person without compassion or mercy? I am constrained by your words, and yet have nothing to give you. If I had anything, I would have the following to say to you: "I shall not leave you for now as orphans, during these years or at this time. Behold, I shall remain

113. *Sayings*, Poemen 38.
114. Jn 16.33.

with you by the command of God, who does all things for the benefit of us, his servants, and for the salvation of our souls." Nonetheless, even if this were to happen, it would not be for my own sake but for you that have asked this. I am glad, however, although I am nothing, that you shall bear fruit to God while we still have time with one another. In this way, I shall be deemed worthy to lead you to my God, who always loves the salvation of us all, and I shall say: "Here am I and my children, whom you have given me,"[115] "keep them in your name,"[116] protect them with your right hand. "Lead them into your desired haven,"[117] "inscribe their names in your book,"[118] and grant to them the pledge of life. I would tell them, in order to make them rejoice: "Do not be afraid, little flock, for it is your Father's good pleasure to give you the kingdom."[119]

Pray, moreover, that he might grant me to say: "Father, grant me that, where I shall be, my children also will be,"[120] in the life that is ineffable. Believe me, brother, the spirit is eager to say to my Master, who rejoices at the requests of his servants: "Master, either bring me with my children into your kingdom, or else blot me out of your book."[121] My weakness and negligence, however, prevent me from having such boldness.

Yet his mercy is great. Therefore, since we have such a Master, let us take comfort, believing that he shall certainly work his mercy with us. God will not overlook the labor, the ascetic discipline, the mourning, and the constraint of our fathers, both those who have fallen asleep and those who are now living. Instead, he will say: "I shall spare this place for my own sake and for the sake of those who have served and still serve me genuinely." I certainly believe without hesitation that there are some people here, in this very place, who are able to entreat God for myriads of people; and these are not rejected. For he fulfills their will. They shall ask that the Lord's eyes may look upon this place day and night.[122] For indeed, already prayers have been offered to him for their sake, flashing as lightning and rising

---

115. Is 8.18; Heb 2.13.
116. Jn 17.11.
117. Ps 106.30.
118. Rv 21.27.
119. Lk 12.32.
120. Cf. Jn 17.24.
121. Cf. Ex 32.32.
122. Cf. 1 Kgs 8.29.

upward like the sun's rays, wherein the Father is gladdened, the Son rejoices, and the Holy Spirit exults.

Let us, then, only pay attention to ourselves, brother; for God is taking care of this place. In fact, it has become the resting place of his servants, in whom is fulfilled: "There are glad songs of salvation in the tents of the righteous."[123] So, it is up to the right hand of the Lord to exercise power, to give us strength, to grant us to follow in the steps of our Fathers—their teaching, conduct, steadfastness, love, patience, persecutions, and sufferings,[124] and whatever else was experienced by them as a result of the enemy, things pertaining both to the senses and to the intellect. For unless we possess something of their life, then how can we be their children? The Lord says: "If you were children of Abraham, then you would be doing what Abraham did."[125] Unless we suffer with them according to the capacity of our weakness, then how shall we be glorified with them at that hour? Unless we die with them by cutting off our own will, even if a little, then how shall we be raised with them in the right-hand portion, expecting to hear with great joy and gladness that blessed voice: "Come, you that are blessed by my Father, inherit the kingdom prepared for you from the foundation of the world,"[126] and so on?

Brother, if God has granted our requests in order that we might have our fathers lead us and in order that we might be with them inseparably, both here and there, then let us be careful not to be separated from them by our laziness, our slackness, our indolence, or our faithlessness. For it is said: "If the unbeliever separates, then let it be so."[127] Let us remember him who said: "The one who endures to the end will be saved."[128] Let us pray to the Lord day and night in order that we may not be separated from our holy fathers either in this age or in the age to come. Where would we go? What more could we find? Where else might we be received? Let us not abandon the light and seek the darkness; let us not leave the sweetness of honey and accept the bitterness of the serpent. Let us not be envious

---

123. Ps 117.15.
125. Jn 8.39.
127. 1 Cor 7.15.

124. Cf. 2 Tm 3.10–11.
126. Mt 25.34.
128. Mt 10.22.

of one another and love death; let us not hate life; let us not receive curses instead of blessings; let us not anger Christ or serve the enemy. Let us become vigilant, alert, swift, and prepared. Let us awaken from our deep sleep; let us understand what God has bestowed upon us in order that we should be under the feet of his holy servants. Why do I even say "under their feet"? We are actually their children and fellow heirs.

Blessed is the soul that has tasted these things! Blessed is the soul that is illumined in order to understand these! Blessed is the soul that has been wounded with such love! Blessed is the soul that is taken captive by such things! Blessed is the soul that meditates on these! Blessed is the soul that cleaves unto these things! Blessed is the soul that has been counted worthy of these! Blessed is the soul that believes in these things! Blessed is the soul that has been perfected in these! For the joy, gladness, and reward of the kingdom of heaven await such a soul, in the eternal light, before the angels and archangels and all the heavenly powers, to the glory of the blessed Son, to the glory of the blessed Holy Spirit. Amen. Brother, fare well.

LETTER 188

Response by the same Great Old Man to the same person and to the brothers with him, who asked for his assistance against the enemies through prayer, as well as to tell them about the life of the Other Old Man, Abba John.

Rejoice in the Lord, dearest and most beloved children. May the Lord fulfill your requests in many good things and weaken through you the bow of the mighty; may you also be girded with power.[129] I wonder whether you desire the benefit of your soul as much as I do, I who entreat God day and night about your salvation. I did not say: "You do not desire," but: "You do not know." For it is from here that are revealed the orders, ranks, and measures, as well as where their inheritance shall be. Just as a person who is famous in the world and experienced in life's affairs, who knows the grandeur, eminence, and dignities of the soldiers, struggles to enroll his children in this grandeur; yet,

129. Cf. 1 Sm 2.4.

since they remain carefree as a result of their inexperience, and perhaps their ignorance in regard to the glory of great soldiers, they long to become craftsmen of handicrafts. So it is also with me in regard to you.

Forgive me, however, for I have spoken as someone out of his mind. Nevertheless, coming to myself, I remembered that I am "earth and ashes,"[130] and a sack filled with every evil. I have mourned over what I have told you, saying: "What is it that earth and ashes have boasted about?" Yet, since I have already said that I long for your salvation and wish to become the cause of every good thing for you, if I could, I would do my very best.

As for the life of my soul-mate and child, that blessed and humble disciple, who has denied all of his desires, even unto death, what can I say? The Lord said: "Whoever has seen me has seen the Father";[131] while about the disciple he said that he can be "like his teacher."[132] "Let anyone with ears listen."[133]

LETTER 189

Request from the same [brother] to the same Old Man about the health of the Abba, who had long been ill, as well as about the passions of the soul. Also, whether he should visit an elder who lived nearby. Further, whence has the body been badly commingled? Response by Barsanuphius.

Rejoice in the Lord, brother. As for the health of my son, some of the saints here were able to pray to God, as I have assured him, too, in order that he might not be ill for even a day; and it would have been so. Would he then, however, have received the fruits of patience? He himself does not know what I endured: illnesses, fevers, and afflictions, until I entered this harbor of clear weather. The illness has benefited him greatly in terms of endurance and gratitude.

As for the passions, one should subject the body to want and affliction as much as possible.

Visiting the brother is a good thing; however, idle talk with him is a bad thing. Therefore, the matter brings you to test-

---

130. Gn 18.27; Jb 42.6.
132. Lk 6.40.
131. Jn 14.9.
133. Mt 11.15.

ing. Visit the neighbor; but guard yourself in order not to talk idly, instead imitating the encounters of the holy fathers, namely: "How are you, Abba?" After this, say: "Tell us a word of life, about how we may find the way of God. Pray for me; for I have many sins," and other such things, as well as a prayer. Then depart from him in peace.

The weight of your body is badly commingled because of your slackness and the weight of the demons. May God strengthen you against them in order to strive lawfully, conquer, and be crowned[134] in Christ Jesus our Lord. To him be the glory and the might to the ages. Amen. Pray for me, brother.

LETTER 190

Response by the same Great Old Man to the same person.

O brother, you said that you are ill in soul and body. Yet why did you not admit that you are healthy in your will? In regard to soul and body, you do not know what is beneficial to you. In regard to your will, however, there are not even ten thousand specialists that know things as you do. Do you not know that I am continually biting you again and again? If you are able to endure it, then do so. For I speak as a fool, since I am a fool, and you yourself are saying this. Indeed, to say that I do not know what is beneficial, is precisely this. May the Lord grant you prudence in all things. Forgive me and pray for me.

LETTER 191

Question from the same person to the same Great Old Man, as well as a request for prayer: "I entreat you, honorable father, explain to me about good will and evil will, in order that I may not overlook your holy words. Forgive me, too, and pray for me, that I may be delivered from the devil and his turmoil." Response by Barsanuphius.

Brother, "every comfort of the flesh is an abomination before our God."[135] For [Christ] said: "The road is narrow and hard that

134. Cf. 2 Tm 2.5.
135. *Sayings*, Poemen 38.

leads to life."[136] Therefore, one who chooses this way is following the good will. One who holds onto this way chooses voluntary affliction in all things, as much as one can. Do you not know what the Apostle says: "I punish my body and enslave it"?[137] You see that, although the body did not want it, yet that divine man voluntarily subjected it. One who has this good will of salvation mingles a little affliction with every personal need. Here is what I mean. I find a feather bed on which to sleep; yet I afflict myself a little, if indeed it is affliction, and sleep upon woolen blankets for the mortification of my body. I should be ashamed, however, that some are sleeping on the ground, others on straw pillows, such as Arsenius[138] among the saints and so many others. Others even placed thorns on their heads, preferring affliction. [Or, take another example.] I find that I am near the water-fountains and the kitchens for my comfort; as an ascetic worker, I should choose a place farther away, in order that I might afflict my body a little. Or, I find good food and pure bread; I should choose that which is of inferior quality in order to be afflicted a little, remembering those who did not even taste a cooked meal at all, and especially our Master Jesus, who tasted bitterness and vinegar for my sake.[139] This is God's will. The flesh's will wants a little comfort in all that I mentioned. Do you not understand what we are saying? "Shut the door quickly in order that I may not feel the draft or get wet." "Look, brother, you have burned the meal, and I am unable to eat it," and so on. . . . This is the evil will. Cut this off, and you will be saved. If, however, you are overcome, then blame yourself entirely and justify your neighbor.

Reluctant brother, be assured in the Lord that "my soul is consumed like a spider's web."[140] It is a labor to be saved; so, then, how can one be deceived thinking that one shall be saved when taking comfort in all things? If you labor with me a little, I pray that God will grant you your request; and, when you remember him and his saints, the devil and his turmoil will depart from you. Yet if I say I shall not pray that the Lord will strengthen and empower you in every good deed, I am lying. Neverthe-

---

136. Mt 7.14.
137. 1 Cor 9.27.
138. *Sayings*, Arsenius 36.
139. Cf. Mt 27.34, 48.
140. Ps 38.12.

less, the kingdom of heaven is for those who do violence.[141] Unless we do violence unto ourselves a little, then how can we be saved? Or else, how can the prayer of the righteous be powerful unless it is also effective?[142] Pray for me, brother.

LETTER 192

Response by the Other Old Man to the same brother and those living with him.

May the Lord Jesus Christ our God bless you "with every spiritual blessing"[143] and every gift of righteousness. He himself bears witness how I desire the comfort of everyone, especially you. Indeed, I am speaking to you as to my soul-mates, who desire to travel the way that we have walked with constraint and affliction for the sake of his name. Brothers, I do not remember any time that we found complete comfort and seized it; instead, we mingled this in every way with a little constraint and affliction, fearing him who says: "You have received your good reward during your lifetime";[144] and: "It is through many trials that we must enter the kingdom of God."[145] I say this because much money has passed through our hands. Yet he himself knows how we have lived with poverty for the sake of the one who became poor for our sake.[146] It is not a good thing to enjoy comfort in all things. For one who desires this lives unto oneself and not unto God. Such a person is unable to cut off the individual will. Pray for me, most honorable brothers.

LETTER 193

Question from the same brother to the other Old Man, namely, the Great One: "Tell me, my Abba. Around morning, and up until about the second hour, I perceive certain thoughts but do not know why I suffer this. Again, tell me how it is that the demon is able to depict the face of my wife or some other person in my mind. For the face appears together with the thought itself; the face and the thought do not appear separately but simultane-

---

141. Cf. Mt 11.12.
143. Eph 1.3.
145. Acts 14.22.

142. Cf. Jas 5.16.
144. Lk 16.25.
146. Cf. 2 Cor 8.9.

ously. What can I do to be liberated? Pray for me." Response by
Barsanuphius.

Brother, when one is idle, then one has the leisure for any
thoughts that approach. When, however, one is working, there
is no leisure in order to receive these. Therefore, rise up at dawn
and hold onto your hand-mill in order to grind your corn for
nourishing loaves. Nevertheless, if the adversary arrives there
before you, then you will grind tares instead of corn.[147]

As for the other matter, brother, artists usually paint faces in
color; however, if the tablet has already been previously paint-
ed, it no longer takes either color or faces, both accomplished
together. If you wish to be liberated, then you must previously
paint your tablet. Let us struggle to do our best, and God will
come to our support. To him be the glory. Amen. Pray for me,
brother, and forgive me for the Lord's sake.

LETTER 194

Request from the same person to the same Great Old Man in
regard to prayer for his own sake and for the sake of those with
him. Response by Barsanuphius.

Beloved little children, I embrace you in the Lord, praying
that he might protect you from every evil, granting you endurance like Job, grace like Joseph, gentleness like Moses, military
campaigns like Joshua son of Nun,[148] leadership over thoughts
like the judges, submission of enemies like David and Solomon
the kings, as well as the stillness of the land like the Israelites in
his reconciliation with them. May he also grant you remission of
sins and health of body like the paralytic,[149] and save you from
the tempest like Peter.[150] May he deliver you from affliction like
Paul[151] and the other apostles. Finally, may he cover you from
every evil, as his genuine children, granting you the requests of
your heart for the benefit of soul and body in his name. Amen.
Pray for me.

---

147. Cf. *Sayings*, Nau 592.   148. Cf. Sir 46.1.
149. Cf. Mt 9.2–6.   150. Cf. Mt 14.31.
151. Cf. 2 Tm 3.11.

LETTER 195

Likewise, prayer and supplication from the same person to the same Great Old Man about the good things appropriate for the soul. Response by Barsanuphius.

I rejoice in the Lord and the Lord rejoices in me, when good requests are addressed to me by my children, namely, about the salvation of the soul and about life eternal. Therefore, let your spirit also be gladdened, brother; for I have enlisted you in a service of eminence, so that you may unceasingly be in the treasure house of ineffable blessings. Indeed, you are already in that service. Therefore, see that you acquire bright garments to dignify this service, so that you may not be expelled from it; also acquire a wise and humble heart and a stable countenance, removed from every movement of anger and turmoil. For this place needs such ministers, who abstain from passions and are dressed in wedding garments, in order not to be expelled with great shame.[152]

Behold, then, you have been enlisted; do not cast it away. Indeed, it is up to you. I have led you inside; do not depart from there. I have separated you from those on the left; do not mingle with them again. I have blessed you; do not seek the curse. Furthermore, I also sought to enlist you in other ineffable and pure treasure houses of the Spirit; but it told me that it was not yet time. Rather, when one makes an effort to make of the left as the right, and to render the old self new, ready to receive the worshipful and Holy Spirit, then one receives the Spirit, which teaches one everything, guiding and leading one into such tabernacles, into which few enter as a result of their humility, obedience, gentleness, and patience. Do not be idle, then, but work "not for the food that perishes, but for the food that endures for eternal life,"[153] in Christ Jesus our Lord, in whom may you always fare well, blessed one.

152. Cf. Mt 22.11–13.
153. Jn 6.27.

LETTER 196

The same person entreated the same Great Old Man to pray for him and to declare to him how one is deemed worthy of the pure and spiritual life. Response by Barsanuphius.

Beloved brother in the Lord, God has given us to walk easily in the way of his will, which leads to eternal life. Let me tell you what this is and how we are able to achieve this in order thus to acquire all of the eternal goods. Since our Lord Jesus Christ has said: "Ask and you shall receive; seek and you shall find; knock and [the door] shall be opened for you,"[154] then pray to this good God in order that he might send the Holy Spirit, the Comforter, to us. When this [Spirit] comes, it shall teach us about everything[155] and reveal all of the mysteries to us. Seek to be guided by this Spirit. It will not allow deceit or distraction in the heart. It will not permit despondency or melancholy in the mind. It illumines the eyes, supports the heart, and uplifts the intellect. Cleave to it, trust it, and love it. For it renders the foolish wise, sweetens the mind, and bestows, teaches, and grants strength and modesty, joy and righteousness, long-suffering and gentleness, love and peace.

Therefore, you possess a sure rock. Do not be negligent; for the winds, rains, and rivers are unable to prevail over the structure that is built upon it.[156] You have the great Helmsman, who rebukes the winds and the sea, and they are calmed, so that the ship is protected from sinking.[157] You have the good Teacher, who legislates that we should "forget what lies behind and strain forward to what lies ahead."[158] Behold an inviolable treasure; behold an impregnable tower. Therefore, why do you reckon me as being someone? Even I cannot reach these things unless I conquer wrath and stifle anger in order to acquire a condition of calmness, wherein the divine rests.

Therefore, let us leave behind craftiness and assume integrity. Let us cultivate deep in order to plant a fruitful vine in our field, so that we may reap grapes and create wine of gladness,

154. Mt 7.7.   155. Cf. Jn 14.26.
156. Cf. Mt 7.24–25.   157. Cf. Mt 8.26.
158. Phil 3.13.

and so that we may become drunk and forget the afflictions and pains that control us unto the destruction of our soul. Brother, it is the will of our Master that we may be saved. Why is it that we do not want this? Always, then, pray fervently that the joy of the Spirit may come to us. For when the Fathers were filled with this Spirit, they cleaved to it in perfect love, crying: "Who will separate us from the love of God?"[159] Furthermore, they replied: "Nothing." Therefore, let us love in order that we may be loved. Let us approach with all our heart in order that we may be received. Let us be greatly humbled in order that he might exalt us.[160] Let us weep in order that we may laugh.[161] Let us be sorrowful in order that we may rejoice. Let us mourn in order that we may be comforted.[162] Let us implore the Holy Spirit to come to us and "guide us into the whole truth."[163] For he does not lie, who says: "Ask and you shall receive."[164] May the Lord accompany us in all things according to his mercy, in order that we may learn who we are, what we need, and what we want. To him be the glory to the ages. Amen.

LETTER 197

The same person entreated the same Great Old Man to pray for him that God may grant him progress. Response by Barsanuphius.

Brother, entreat the goodness of the one who "desires that all may be saved and come to the knowledge of the truth"[165] to grant you spiritual alertness, which kindles the spiritual fire that the Master of heaven and earth came to cast upon the earth.[166] I, too, shall entreat him with you, according to my ability, in order that God may grant you this; for he gladly bestows it upon all those who ask with pain and longing. If it comes, it will "guide you into the whole truth."[167] It illumines the eyes, restores the intellect, and expels the sleep of slackness and negligence. It also polishes the weapons that have been rusted by the crust of

159. Rom 8.35.
161. Cf. Lk 6.21.
163. Jn 16.13.
165. 1 Tm 2.4.
167. Jn 16.13.

160. Cf. Mt 23.12.
162. Cf. Mt 5.5.
164. Jn 16.24.
166. Cf. Lk 12.49.

indolence and brightens the garments that have been soiled in
the captivity of barbarians. It makes one hate the abominations
of their carcasses and desire to be filled with the spiritual sacrifice offered by our great High Priest, about which the prophet
heard that it cleanses sins and removes iniquities;[168] it is granted
to those mourning, given to the humble, and reserved for the
worthy. Through this, they inherit eternal life, in the name of
the Father and of the Son and of the Holy Spirit. Amen.

LETTER 198

The same person fervently requested the same Great Old Man to
pray for him, that he might be deemed worthy of "the death of
Jesus."[169] Response by Barsanuphius.

I rejoice in asking God to grant you every good request; and I
believe that he will grant them all. For he does not lie, who says:
"Ask and it shall be given you."[170] So may God grant your requests. Amen. Do not, however, be negligent in your obligation
to labor a little yourself. For those who desire imperial grants,[171]
though they may have many patrons, yet they must also endure
afflictions, dangers at sea or on journeys, and labors, until they
achieve these. Therefore, you, too, should likewise contribute a
little labor in order to find great mercy. "For the prayer of the
righteous is powerful and effective."[172] Tell the brother who is
with you, my beloved in the Lord: "Be a little patient, and give
thanks to the Lord, who always reproves the one he loves,"[173]
and he shall grant you his great mercy there, where you are only
seeking a drop of water. Nevertheless, here too, God is not chastening you and us with anger. I greet you all in the Lord and implore you to pray for me for the sake of love.

---

168. Cf. Ps 50.4.
169. 2 Cor 4.10.
170. Mt 7.7.
171. The term used derives from the Latin term *sacra,* meaning an imperial
script or rescript.
172. Jas 5.16.
173. Prv 3.12; Heb 12.6.

LETTER 199

Request from the same brother to the same Great Old Man for prayer in order that he might leave behind the old self. Response by Barsanuphius.

Listen, beloved brother, and give your heart over to keeping the divine words spoken to you not from mortals but from the Holy Spirit. Jesus is the Physician of souls and bodies. If you have a wound, I shall lead you toward him and pray to him to heal you in both, that is, if you also desire this. Our Lord, the Son of God, is the Giver of all good gifts; and I am asking him to grant you not only your requests but exceedingly more than you request or imagine; and he tells me: "If he, too, desires this, then I shall grant it." Jesus is the Son of God, the Light and Strength, who was incarnate of the holy Virgin Mary. "He also appeared on this earth and lived among people,"[174] offering himself as "a living sacrifice, acceptable to God"[175] the Father for our sake, in order that he might prepare us "for himself as a chosen people, who are zealous for good deeds,"[176] "a royal priesthood and holy nation."[177]

He who endured these things for our sake also left for us an example of patience; and he rejoices when we ask him. I am asking him to illumine your heart in order to understand how he desires to make you prudent as well, through my nothingness. I am asking for you to receive strength; you, too, should request this. I am asking for you to be a son of God; you, too, should labor with me and sweat. For the Son of God says: "Come to me, all you that are weary and carrying heavy burdens, and I will give you rest."[178] Therefore, I approach him for your sake without shame; however, unless you also approach, the shame is great. I am also bearing his yoke and burden for your sake. Indeed, how you will hear this at the proper time! Jesus rejects no one. In fact, he hired laborers for his vineyard even at the eleventh hour.[179] Cleave to him and make a little effort in order that you may receive the

---

174. Bar 3.38.   175. Rom 12.1.
176. Ti 2.14.   177. 1 Pt 2.9.
178. Mt 11.28.   179. Cf. Mt 20.6.

full reward equally like all the rest, as I, too, pray that you may.

The Son of God became human for your sake; you, too, should become god through him.[180] For he wants this, especially when you also want it. Moreover, I pray that you may be liberated from the old self. You are found, however, in this place. Therefore, if you struggle, the Son of God has given you an intellect; give him this in return for the sake of heaven, "by seeking the things that are above and setting your mind on the things that are above,"[181] where he is found, "at the right hand of God,"[182] where I claim that you may reach, together with all those "who love his name."[183] For in this way, one is liberated from the old self. Jesus said to the apostles: "You are the salt of the earth."[184] The earth is your body; for it is said: "You are dust, and you shall return to dust."[185] Therefore, become as salt unto yourself, salting and drying up the festering wounds and worms, namely, the evil thoughts. If you do this, I, too, shall labor and apply salt with you, in order that they may not stink and disgust one another.

God our Savior wants us to be saved. It is up to us, however, to cry out without ceasing: "Save me, Lord, and I shall be saved."[186] For some people have cried out: "Behold, I have entered your desired haven,"[187] into which I hope that you, too, will enter, if you give me a hand as best you can. Understand what has been said here, and adhere to it, and you shall attain it, according to him who says: "Run, therefore, that you may win."[188] Pray for me, brother, so that I may not be condemned for speaking but not acting.

LETTER 200

Question from the same brother to the same Great Old Man about various thoughts and about the strictness of God's way. Response by Barsanuphius.

All that you have written to me, asking God through my nothingness, my lethargic brother, converges into one thing, name-

---

180. Cf. Athanasius of Alexandria, *On the Divine Incarnation* 54.
181. Cf. Col 3.1–2.   182. Col 3.1.
183. Ps 68.37.   184. Mt 5.13.
185. Gn 3.19.   186. Jer 17.14.
187. Ps 106.30.   188. 1 Cor 9.24.

ly, your liberation from the old self and your salvation in the kingdom of God and in the ineffable joy of the saints. This is precisely the place of which I spoke to you, namely, the measure of being released and cleansed from the old self and being found in sanctification of soul and body. Constrained by love, I am in fact asking God to grant you "abundantly far more than all you can ask or imagine."[189] If you do not prevent him from doing so, through your slackness and negligence, then you will be surprised and will glorify God as to how he transforms you from non-being to being. Understand what I am telling you. God will forgive you your former sins and will prepare forgiveness for your later sins.

As for the nocturnal fantasies, the devil is tempting you out of envy because you are repenting before God; and, in order to discourage you from repenting, he wishes to ridicule you, by saying that the repentance that is very powerful is in fact of no benefit. But do not surrender. For in this way, you shall receive much assistance through the prayers of the saints, should you also desire this. Yet if you are seized in some word or deed, remembering that you have sinned against someone, you must strive immediately to go out and make a prostration before that person; and, when God sees this, he shall protect you from your enemies.

As for the matter of food, let us not take too much care of the body; for it happens that this constitutes war deriving from the demons, who try to cast us into concern in order that, being preoccupied with foods, we may leave the goods that lie before us.

As for the strictness of God's way, let us not speak about this now in order that I may not bring you to despair. Nevertheless, believe that God will save you gratuitously through the prayers of the saints. For these are able to entreat him. Pray for me, brother.

LETTER 201

Question from the same person to the same Great Old Man about despondency and certain other thoughts. Response by Barsanuphius.

189. Eph 3.20.

May God, who alone is sinless, "who saves those who hope in him,"[190] also strengthen your love "to worship him in holiness and righteousness all the days of your life"[191] until your last breath, in the temple of the altar of the inner self, where spiritual sacrifices are offered to God, where tested gold and incense and myrrh are offered, where the fatted calf is sacrificed and the precious blood of the blameless lamb is sprinkled, where the cries of the holy angels are heard in harmony. "Then bulls will be offered on your altar."[192] But when will this be? When the great High Priest arrives, who offers and receives the bloodless sacrifice; when in his name the paralytic who is seated at the beautiful gate of the Temple hears with his own ears the voice of joy: "Stand up and walk,"[193] when he enters "into the temple, walking and leaping and praising God."[194] Then, the sleep of despondency and ignorance ceases; then, the drowsiness of sloth is abolished from our eyelids; then, the five wise virgins kindle their lamps and dance with the bridegroom in the holy nuptial chamber,[195] together singing noiselessly to one another: "Taste and see that the Lord is good. Blessed is the man who hopes in him."[196] And then, wars and pollutions and turbulence are abolished, and the holy peace of the Holy Trinity reigns. Then, the treasure is sealed and remains inviolable. Pray that you will understand and reach this point in order to rejoice in Christ Jesus our Lord. To him be the glory.

LETTER 202

Question from the same person to the Great Old Man about a secret temptation and about [spiritual] progress. Response by Barsanuphius.

Brother, I am amazed that your love is ignorant of the wiles of the demons. For as God witnesses to Job, they have grown intense against him. And, as they learned that the child was very close to being cleansed, they tore him apart.[197] So then, when

---

190. Dn 13.60.
192. Ps 50.19.
194. Acts 3.8.
196. Ps 33.9.

191. Lk 1.75.
193. Acts 3.6.
195. Cf. Mt 25.7–10.
197. Cf. Mk 9.26.

they also see someone progressing, they tempt that person with envy. They do not, however, tempt the one who has made progress by means of his own actions; for this person has already conquered them. Instead, they tempt the one who has made progress, thanks to the prayers of the saints, and God permits it so that this person may know his own weakness and be humbled in order not to become proud over the grace received. Just as there are many armies that surpass each other, so are there also many mansions in the house of the Father of lights, mansions that surpass each other. For if this were not the case, then why are these said to be many?[198] Therefore, since I have assigned you, or rather God has done so through me his servant, wherever I asked him to do so, this is why I told you that I have conscripted you. For this military service is truly spiritual. May God strengthen you in his fear. Pray for me.

LETTER 203

Question from the same person to the same Great Old Man about the progress of the soul, about advising a brother, and about faith in the same shared Father. Response by Barsanuphius.

Believe me, much-desired one, that, with God, you are not standing outside the gates of the heavenly kingdom. However, stand well and pay attention to yourself with precision so as not to be cast out from there. For it is God's role to lead a person inside, through the prayers of his saints; and it is that person's role either to remain there or to be cast out from there. Indeed, I am leading you progressively, with the will of God, to great heights. So take courage in the Lord and walk eagerly on his way, and you will receive assistance from him according to his will.

As for the brother, receive him with humble heart and tell him whatever God posits in your heart to say, bearing in mind that, when it was necessary, he even opened the mouth of the ass.[199] And if everything depends on him, then attribute the

198. Cf. Jn 14.2.
199. Cf. Nm 22.28.

benefit of everything to him, even the benefit that your brother receives through you. And if God sees your humility, he will attribute to you the reward of the advice, since you gave the word through your mouth. And then, what is written will be fulfilled in both of you: "A brother assisted by another brother is like a city fortified with ramparts."[200] May the Lord Jesus work with you to bring about all good.

As for me, the least servant, if God granted you his faith, then he is the one who increases and preserves it. It is not possible to reveal great mysteries to great people through the least of persons. For he becomes "all in all."[201] Forgive me, father, and pray for me.

LETTER 204

Question from the same person to the Other Old Man: "What should a person do when he wants to live in stillness, when he also happens to be developing a reputation for this, so that this may not cause him damage? For the fathers have said: 'Woe to that person whose reputation is greater than his deeds.'[202] And whether he should be in the company of certain people, or avoid everyone altogether." Response by John.

Bearing a reputation or glory greater than one's deeds is not harmful to the person who does not take pleasure in or give consent to whatever happens to be said. Just as in the case of the one who has been falsely accused of murder but has actually done nothing of the sort, such a person should be thinking in regard to whatever other people think of him: "What am I, anyway, that they do not know me?"

As for being in the company of some people and not with others, rejecting some people and welcoming others, this makes one come to the point of discriminating among people. So in what way is it that one can say: "Bring me this person and not another"? Therefore, one who is able to show no favoritism whatsoever to any person—and I am speaking here from my foolishness—

---

200. Prv 18.19.
201. 1 Cor 15.28.
202. Cf. *Sayings*, Silvanus 10.

that person does well, in as much as he is aware of his own weakness.

LETTER 205

Question from the same person to the same Old Man: "I entreat you, venerable father, to condescend to my weakness and allow me to accept, should one of the fathers wish to come to my cell in order to pray for me, to receive him. For I have seen myself burdened by despondency, until God fortifies my soul through your prayers." Response by John.

I beg of your love, my brother, do not regard me as being superior. For I am foolish and flatter myself. Rather, I must know that I am much inferior. For to tell me that I must condescend signifies that I am sitting higher, at some great height. Do you not know that it is demanded of me that I should be below every person? Indeed, the one who is below everyone else has no place at all to which to descend. You know the advice of the holy Apostle, who says: "Testing all things, hold fast to what is good."[203] Everything that a person does according to godly fear is of benefit to the soul. Therefore, if the company of others is of benefit to you, it is not up to me to prevent you from keeping such company. Otherwise, in so doing, I am also preventing what is beneficial to you. So then, it is not only that I will not prevent you, but I even regard myself as being the most miserable of all those who come to pray for you in order to benefit you. Therefore, whether or not you are in the company of others, may the Lord strengthen your genuine love in Christ. For why do I count myself as being among people, except in order that I may demand this of myself as well? Your gain is my joy. What I think is the following. Being in the company of others for the sake of God is a good thing; and not being in the company of others for the sake of God is also a good thing.[204] When you are in the company, then, of those holy people who come to you for your benefit, ask them to pray for me as well, that I

203. 1 Thes 5.21.
204. Cf. *Sayings*, Poemen 147.

may not be put to shame. In this way, you also will be doing the same thing for me, for the sake of love.

LETTER 206

The same brother cut off the company of many people, and sought the company of only one person. He asked the same Old Man, saying: "Since I have a relationship of love with a certain brother, who wants to keep me company, should I see him or not?" Response by John.

If you in any way have a relationship of love with one of the brothers, then why do you have thoughts about the other brothers? Is it because you are not among their company? Or why else is it? Learn where it is that you now stand; and if you so wish, [continue to] see that brother, while at the same time blaming yourself. And pray for me.

LETTER 207

Request for prayer by the same person to the Great Old Man; and a question about perfect stillness. Response by Barsanuphius.

May the Lord Jesus, the Son of the blessed and supreme God, strengthen and fortify you to receive his Holy Spirit; and may this Spirit come to you and, through its good presence, teach you about all things, enlighten your hearts, and lead you into the whole truth,[205] so that I may see you as a tree flourishing in the paradise of my Father and God,[206] and so that you may be found to be like "a fruitful olive tree"[207] in the midst of the saints, as well as like "a fruitful vine that is completely authentic, on holy ground."[208] May the Lord render you worthy to drink "of the fountain of wisdom."[209] For all those who have drunk of this fountain have already forgotten themselves; and all of them have moved outside of the old self. Moreover, from this fountain of wisdom, they have been led to another fountain, namely, that of love that never fails.[210]

---

205. Cf. Jn 16.13.
207. Ps 51.10.
209. Prv 18.4.

206. Cf. Rv 2.7.
208. Jer 2.21.
210. Cf. 1 Cor 13.8.

And having arrived at this point, they attained to that measure where there is no agitation or distraction, becoming all intellect, all eye,[211] all living, all light, all perfect, all gods. They toiled; they were magnified; they were glorified; they shined; they were perfected; they lived, because first they died. They rejoice, and they make others also rejoice. They rejoice in the inseparable Trinity, and they make the heavenly powers rejoice. Aspire to their measure, run their way, be envious of their faith, acquire their humility and their patience in all things, that you may receive their heritage.

Keep their unfailing love, so that you may be found to be with them in the ineffable goods, which "no eye has seen, nor ear heard, nor the human heart conceived, which God has prepared for those who love him."[212] As for the stillness, discipline yourself a little longer now, and God will show his mercy on you [later]. May God enlighten your hearts to the understanding of the concepts that lie herein; for they are difficult to understand for the person who has not reached their measure. Forgive me, and pray for me, that I may not be lacking in this holy measure, even though I am unworthy of these things.

LETTER 208

Question, once again, from the same person to the same Great Old Man, asking whether he is permitted to practice complete stillness. Response by Barsanuphius.[213]

I have already spoken to your love, beloved brother, about stillness, telling you that you should wait for the time being, not because I do not want you to reach the state of such a measure. Certainly not! I wish and pray, however, that the Lord will grant you this state, and even more than this. For my joy is great whenever all of you show progress. Yet these are spiritual gifts, given by God in their proper time, and it is he who calls and supports and protects. Indeed, it is said: "It is not those who commend themselves that are approved, but those whom the Lord commends."[214]

211. Cf. *Sayings*, Bessarion 11. 212. 1 Cor 2.9.
213. Cf. *Letters* 6 and 185. 214. 2 Cor 10.18.

Therefore, if you wish to construct your home, first prepare the material and all other necessary things. And then, it is up to the professional builder to come and build the house.[215] The necessary building materials for such a construction include firm faith for the building of walls, luminous wooden windows that allow in the light of the sun to brighten the house, so that there may be no darkness inside. These wooden windows are the five senses, affirmed in the precious cross of Christ, which allow in the light of the spiritual Sun of righteousness,[216] and do not permit any darkness to appear inside the house; and I am referring to the darkness of the enemy, the one who hates good. Furthermore, you need the house to be covered by a roof, "so that the sun does not strike you by day, nor the moon by night."[217] The roof is symbolical of love for God, "which never ends,"[218] which covers the house and does not allow the sun to set upon our anger,[219] so that we may not find the sun accusing us on the day of judgment, consuming us in the fire of Gehenna, nor again the moon bearing witness to our slackness and laziness by night, consuming us in eternal hell. Furthermore, the house needs a door, which allows the person dwelling there to enter inside and to be protected. When I speak of a door, brother, you should understand the spiritual door, namely, the Son of God, who says: "I am the door."[220]

Now, if you prepare your house in this way, so that you do not have any of those things which are hated by the Son of God, he will come with the blessed Father and the Holy Spirit, and will make a home with you,[221] teaching you what stillness is and enlightening your heart with ineffable joy.

LETTER 209

Question from the same person to the same Great Old Man on prayer, and instruction on the virtuous life. Response by Barsanuphius.

215. Cf. Dorotheus, *Teaching* 14.149–52. In the patristic tradition silence is often compared to the construction of a house, for example, in Origen of Alexandria, the Desert Fathers, Evagrius of Pontus, and others.

216. Cf. Mal 4.2.   217. Ps 120.6.

218. 1 Cor 13.8.   219. Cf. Eph 4.26.

220. Jn 10.9.   221. Cf. Jn 14.23.

May our Lord Jesus Christ, God, enlighten the eyes of your heart, dearest and beloved son, in order to shine in them the light of the holy, sovereign, eternal, consubstantial, and life-creating Trinity, in order to guide you to understand his ineffable mysteries and to enjoy these eternally, in order to depart from Egypt and divide the sea with a rod and escape from the hands of the barbarian Pharaoh,[222] in order to rejoice in God with a sacrifice and feast in the sacred Passover, and to redden your lips through his sacred and precious blood, girding your loins and holding your rod with pure hands, while wearing sandals on your innocent feet.[223] May you be nurtured by the manna from heaven through the service of the clouds, may your garment never grow old,[224] and may the hair of your head not grow long. May your heart be purified to receive the law of the Master, may you smash the golden calf in the midst of your people,[225] may the earth swallow the enemies that oppose you, and may you reign over the kings of the Amorites. May God wipe off the seven nations from your face, and may you inherit their land forever.[226] May you cross the Jordan by the power of the holy miracle.[227] May you seize the city of the palms[228] and save Rahab the harlot, who believed in your God.[229] May you sow, plant, eat, be filled, and give glory to the God who gives you everything. May there be no other God found in you, that henceforth you may be holy unto God, and that foreigners may no longer pillage your country because you have become terrifying for them. May you kill Goliath,[230] in order that you may reign with David and leave that which is old in order to find that which is new. May you believe in Christ in order to be crucified with him and die with him, to be buried with him, to be raised in glory with him,[231] and to ascend with him from this earth in honor and live with him eternally.

Therefore, melt the wax and it will soften. For to the degree that you melt these, you will discover the meanings that they contain for life eternal in Christ Jesus our Lord. Amen. As for

---

222. Cf. Ex 14.16–28.
224. Cf. Dt 8.3–4.
226. Cf. Dt 7.1–2.
228. Cf. Dt 34.3.
230. Cf. 1 Sm 17.50.

223. Cf. Ex 12.11.
225. Cf. Ex 32.20.
227. Cf. Dt 11.31.
229. Cf. Jos 6.23–25.
231. Cf. Rom 6.6–8; Col 2.12.

the brother who is [eating] with you, bear with him as much as you can. For the one who is in good health should bear the one who is ill, until God accomplishes for him what is beneficial. "Rejoice in the Lord."[232]

Question from the same person to the same Great Old Man: "Holy father, give me a spiritual blessing, and bless for me the cowl and the *analabos*[233] which I sent to you, so that I may have these as protection in Christ from every temptation." Response by Barsanuphius.

Beloved brother, if Christ the Master, the Lord of heaven and earth—for through him everything is possible—said to the person who approached him: "Let it be done to you according to your faith,"[234] then what is it that I, who am completely impoverished, could have to say to you? Yet, may the God of all blessings bless you with every spiritual blessing[235] and with every grace of righteousness. And may he render you a participant in the splendor of the saints, an heir of the kingdom, freed from the passions of dishonor, through the prayers and intercessions of all the saints. As for what you have asked, since you are bold enough to do so, I am wearing these [items of clothing] for three days; and I shall send them to you when they are blessed through the company of the saints' prayers to God. Through this company, I ask that you also pray for me.

232. Phil 3.1.
233. See p. 96, n. 134, in *Letter* 71.
234. Mt 9.29.
235. Cf. Eph 1.3.

LETTERS TO A MONK,
WHO WAS A PRIEST (211–213)

Once, one of the fathers, a priest, who had toiled a great deal in the desert and now sought to live in stillness in the monastery, asked the Other Old Man how he should begin to live in stillness. Response by John.

OHN THE BAPTIST said to our Master Christ, God: "I need to be baptized by you, and yet you come to me?"[1] Your love, however, has done the right thing and given us a lesson in humility, in order that we may in this way be ashamed and speak of our passions. "For it is beyond all dispute that the inferior is blessed by the superior."[2] Therefore, you ought to take care of me. For you are also a priest, a priest of God and a spiritual physician who has been called to anoint with oil those who have been afflicted, and to heal them from bodily illness; indeed, you also mix the anointing with the forgiveness of sins.[3]

Therefore, I, who have not been counted among the clergy because of my unworthiness, and because the luster of my white hair has not prevented me from having immature thoughts, am surely unable to give advice to one who is my superior. If the person asking me were someone on my level, my babbling would not allow me to keep silent without replying to him; for I have an uncontrolled tongue. And I would have said to him that a child progresses from the stage of a beginner to the stage of the more advanced. And he surely would have said to me that of course this is the case. Since, however, I have considered what I would have responded to him, I would also have said the fol-

1. Mt 3.14.   2. Heb 7.7.
3. Cf. Jas 5.14–15.

lowing: "Therefore, you also should live in stillness five days of the week and be in the company of your brothers for the other two days.[4] And if your sitting in the cell is indeed according to God, that is to say, if you come to know what you want from sitting in your cell, you will not fall into the hands of the demon of vainglory. For people who know what they came to do in a city desire that alone and do not divert their hearts toward anything else; otherwise, they would fail in that which they seek." Forgive me, Abba; for I have nothing else to say to you. But pray for me to the Lord; for I have neither any good deed to show nor any good word to say.

LETTER 212

Question from the same [brother] to the same Old Man: "When I give to my body more than is necessary, it does not help me during the liturgy; and if I give it less, I am afraid it will collapse completely. What should I do about this? And in regard to holy Communion, since I want to partake of this every day, is it a burden to me that I approach holy Communion as a sinner, or should I continue to partake of it? And, again, how can I protect myself in stillness?" Response by John.

I have previously mentioned to your love, Abba, the words of John [the Baptist] to the Savior; and yet you have written once again to me, the foolish and ignorant one. Therefore, if John did not refuse to respond, why should I, who am contemptible, refuse? For I am speaking the truth when I say that I am nothing and that I know nothing. Yet, for the sake of obedience, I speak that which I have in my heart. I will not say, however, that it is exactly like this, but I am speaking according to what I have.

God does not demand from the one who is ill any physical liturgical function, but only a spiritual function, namely, prayer. For it is said: "Pray without ceasing."[5] As for bodily diet, if the body cannot perform the liturgy when it receives sufficient food, and if you are afraid of illness when it receives insufficient food, then retain the middle way. Give it neither too much nor too lit-

4. This was the customary lifestyle for early Palestinian monastics.
5. 1 Thes 5.17.

tle. Then the Scripture is fulfilled that says: "Deviate neither to the right hand nor to the left."[6] But give the body just a little less than it requires. Indeed, this is the way of the fathers: neither to be extravagant nor to be crushed in one's discipline. As for approaching holy Communion, when this happens to you, not out of scorn but as a result of illness, then there is no condemnation. For the greatest physician personally visits those who suffer greatly and are ill, just as our Lord Jesus himself came to us sinful and sick people. Forgive me, father, but I the unworthy one have only spoken out of obedience.

LETTER 213

Question from the same person to the same Old Man: "A widow who suffered injustice sent for me, requesting comfort, and asking me to write to her housemaid in order that she may help her. And I have two thoughts on this matter: one thought tells me that I have come here in order to die, and that if I write to her, I am transgressing the regulation of this mortification. Another thought tells me that if I do not write to her, I am transgressing the commandment that tells me to help those who are in need. Please, father, be so kind as to tell me what to do." Response by John.

If you were dead and the widow who had suffered injustice came to you, would you be able to help her? And if you help her, and another woman later comes to you asking the same, could you overlook her and transgress the commandment at that time? A dead person does not worry about such matters. And if they complain against you, this, too, should not affect you.

6. Nm 20.17.

LETTERS TO MONKS ABOUT ILLNESS
AND DEATH (214–223)

A brother who lived in the monastery, serving an elderly monk
who was ill, asked the Great Old Man about his own thoughts.
Response by Barsanuphius.

OU ARE SILLY, and this is why your thoughts rule over
you, especially the pretense to rights. The Lord wants
you to consider every person as being superior to you,
and your hardheartedness does not allow you at this time to see
even the elderly monk, who is advanced in age, as being superior to you. Therefore, show obedience to him in all things and
do whatever he tells you, submitting yourself to him, whether in
matters of eating or drinking or any other such thing. And if you
are asked to do something that is burdensome, seek the advice
of the abbot, and do whatever he tells you. In regard to psalmody and vigil, do what he tells you and everything will be for the
salvation of your soul. If he speaks falsely against you, rejoice; for
this is especially beneficial to you. And if he brings you grief, be
patient. "For the one who endures to the end will be saved."[1]

In all circumstances, give thanks to God;[2] for thanksgiving intercedes with God for our weakness.[3] In all things, always blame
yourself as being sinful and erring, and God will not condemn
you. Be humble in everything, and you will find grace from God.
If you learn all these things, God will help you to find strength.
For this is his will, namely, that "everyone may be saved and
come to the knowledge of the truth."[4]

1. Mt 10.22.
2. Cf. 1 Thes 5.18.
3. Cf. *Sayings*, Nau 637.
4. 1 Tm 2.4.

Response from the same Old Man to the same person.

Brother, do not try to discern the thoughts that come upon you; for this, too, is not something within your limits. They trouble you in whatever way they wish; for you do not know their method. If they trouble you, however, say to them: "I do not know who you are, but God knows and he will not allow you to deceive me." So cast your weakness before God, saying: "Lord, I am in your hands; help me and free me from their hands." And if any thought persists and wars against you, declare this to your abbot, and he will heal you through God. As for your manual labor, do whatever you are told, and you will be saved in the name of God. As for the Psalms, do not stop studying these; for they are a great strength. Force yourself to learn them by heart; for this will benefit you greatly. And as for listening to those things that are beyond your capacity, do not seek to do this. For you have enough lessons for now, according to your measure, which can be of benefit to you.

Response from the same Old Man to the same [brother].

Do not naïvely [allow yourself to] be ridiculed. You cannot trust your enemies. For if you are careless and negligent, they will return once more. A soldier prepares for war even in time of peace. Consider how the Lord said to the serpent: "He will watch over your head, and you will watch over his heel."[5] Therefore, a person should not be careless, even until one's last breath. Rather, guard yourself, brother, from anger, vainglory, sleep, and the other passions, knowing that the enemy neither sleeps nor is negligent.

---

5. Gn 3.15.

LETTER 217

Response from the same Old Man to the same person.

Brother, if you wish to be saved, acquire humility, obedience, and voluntary submission; and when you hear anything from the elderly man, no matter what it is, tell him with humility: "Pray for me, father, that God may grant me wisdom and vigilance, so that I may not afflict you." Guard these things, and you will be saved.

LETTER 218

The same brother fell ill and thought that he would die. He asked the same Great Old Man, with much humility, about forgiveness of sins and about endurance of this illness to the end. And he responded to him in this way.

Do not be saddened, brother; for death which is without sin is no death at all, but only a transferal from affliction to repose, and from darkness to the ineffable light and eternal life. God, our great King, is saying to you: "All your many sins have been forgiven you,"[6] especially through the prayers and supplications of the saints and through your own faith in him. May he grant you patience to the end.

LETTER 219

From the same [brother] to the same Great Old Man: "My master and father, I am in your hands, in the hands of God and in your own hands. Therefore, show your mercy on me to the end; and hasten to release me, presenting me to your Master Christ, guiding me with your holy prayers, and accompanying me in the air and along this way, which I do not know." Response by Barsanuphius.

I commit you, brother, to Christ, who deigned to die for our sake, to the Master of heaven and earth, and of our every breath, that he may calm you before your fear of death, and that he may render the ascent of your soul free from obstacle, so that you may venerate the Holy Trinity with boldness, namely, with free-

6. Lk 7.47–48.

dom, fearing and trembling like the angels, and that he may give you repose among the saints. Go, then, and pray for me.

LETTER 220

Another brother[7] fell ill from typhoid, and was in great danger. He entreated the same Great Old Man to pray for him and to ask for the forgiveness of his sins. Response.

Do not be afraid, brother, but rather let your soul rejoice and be glad in the Lord. And truly believe that, behold, God has forgiven all your sins in accordance with your request, from your childhood to this time. May God be blessed, who desired to forgive all your sins. Therefore, do not grieve, for there is nothing wrong with you. It is pain, and it will cease.

LETTER 221

When the same person was again crushed even more, some other brothers entreated the Other Old Man to interpret for them the previous response, as to whether the Old Man was speaking about life or about death. Response by John.

He spoke about death. [The Old Man] can ask for life, however, if he receives assurance from God.

LETTER 222

Having heard this, they entreated the Great Old Man to ask for life in the case of the ill brother. Response by Barsanuphius.

May my God, who is good and merciful, fill you again and again with the joy of the Holy Spirit. Amen. As for the brother, it is enough for him to receive that which is deemed worthy; for he has suddenly become rich and free from slavery. Yet, blessed is our God, who approved and accepted this supplication. Therefore, do not say anything to the brother, that he may not be grieved, but keep this secret to yourselves. For he will not die, but only be transferred from death to life eternal and from affliction to repose. Rejoice in the Lord, beloved children.

7. *Letters* 220–223 are addressed to Dositheus, the disciple of Dorotheus.

LETTER 223

When the brother was again crushed and was in great suffering, they asked the same Great Old Man to pray that God may render his mercy on him more swiftly. Response by Barsanuphius.

This is why his labor has been prolonged, in order that the supplication made for his sake may not remain in vain. And God has rendered and is continually rendering that which is beneficial to him, through the prayers of the saints. Amen.

And after this response, the brother died[8] in peace.

8. Lit., "was completed" or "perfected" (ἐτελειώθη).

LETTERS TO
VARIOUS MONKS (224–251)

LETTER 224

Someone asked Abba John about a certain matter. And after receiving a response, he addressed a question about the same matter to Abba Barsanuphius, without telling him that he had already asked the Other Old Man about this matter.

The Old Man responded in this way: "Do as you were told by brother John."

And again, sometime afterwards, it happened that the same brother asked Abba John about something and, having heard the response, conveyed the same question to Abba Barsanuphius. The Old Man, however, stated the following to him: "From now on, one response is enough for you. For the God of Barsanuphius and John is but one." And that brother never again approached the two Old Men with the same question, being content with the response of just the one.

LETTER 225

A brother asked the same Great Old Man: "Tell me, father, what should I do when thoughts trouble my heart? And should I entirely cut out wine? Moreover, should I sleep while sitting? Pray for the weakness in my eye, and tell me whether I should show myself to a doctor. I entreat you to pray that God may grant me a little progress so that I may not be separated from your holy steps." Response by Barsanuphius.

ROTHER, SINCE YOU have asked to hear from me who am worthless on the matter of your thoughts, could it be that you were not satisfied with what you heard from brother John? Nevertheless, you are tolerating this turmoil because you have a light heart. If, according to the word of the

Savior, "all things can be done for the one who believes,"[1] then where is your faith? Now then, about the wine, it is not necessary to cut it out entirely, but you should only consume a little. As for sleeping on your seat, even if this ultimately brings you to humility, nevertheless submit yourself to God according to your fear of him. And as for your eye, do not be afraid, because you have God as the one who illumines you. If, however, you happen to come across some skilled physician and show yourself to him, you are not sinning because this, too, is a cause for your humility.

These things have been dictated by me for you, and written down by means of my son [Seridos]. So then, unless you happen to face some spiritual warfare that tries to render vain the words which I have spoken to you for the sake of God, I pray that God may lead you to greater progress and that you may not be estranged or separated from us, whether in this age or in the age to come.[2] Therefore be wise, even beyond all those demons that instruct you in scandals, and you will always attract your soul and your thoughts towards what is good. But do not establish any covenant with them;[3] for they are extremely powerful and foreign. Then you will inherit the land of the Israelites, in Christ Jesus our Lord. To him be the glory to the ages. Amen.

LETTER 226

Question from the same person to the same Old Man: "I entreat you, father, tell me whether the first response is from you. Because my thought tells me: 'Could it be that it is not from the [Great] Old Man, but perhaps only written in his name?' Moreover, tell me how my passions will be healed, grant me a commandment for the salvation of my soul, and ask for the forgiveness of my sins. Tell me also if it is good, as my thought tells me, to consent to continue working in the kitchen." Response by Barsanuphius.

Listen, child, for every passion there is a medicine, and for every sin there is proper repentance. If you are entirely faithless, as you said, and wish to be healed of this faithlessness, then the medicine for this is faith, namely, believing without hesita-

---

1. Mk 9.23. 2. Cf. Mt 12.32.
3. Cf. Dt 7.2.

tion in that which is good.[4] If, however, you continue to be faithless, see to it that you are not excluded from that beatitude:[5] "Three times blessed are those who have not seen and yet have come to believe";[6] for it is written: "Believe in the light, so that you may become sons of light."[7]

So then, look, I have sent you a second response since you did not trust the first. Had you received a prophet in the name of a prophet,[8] you would have received the reward of a prophet. That is to say, if the first response was not from me, but you had received it as if it were from me, you would still have received a reward according to your faith. For faithful is the one who has said: "May the Lord grant to you according to your heart."[9] In the first response, I told you that I wish to be strengthened by you rather than by the abbot. How can you compare yourself with those who tempted the Lord and said: "Show us a sign"? The Lord turned them away as tempting him, saying: "No sign will be given to them."[10] And yet you did not compare yourself to Ahaz, who, upon being ordered to ask for a sign, nevertheless refused, saying: "I will not ask, nor will I put the Lord God to the test."[11] If, having heard, you had simply believed, you would have received much benefit. Since once again, however, you did not struggle for faith, behold, I have ordered the abbot to stand at my door and to cry out with a loud voice, reading[12] the words that I wrote to you in order to shame the devil. For if you read these things aloud, how can the devil attack you, saying: "I cannot hear"?

Moreover, if I hear what you are saying, and if another person has written to you that which he has wished, why do I not reproach that person? If you held me to be a discerning person, and someone who knows according to God that which occurs, then you would trust that no one would dare to change my word without my knowledge. The enemy, however, has also secretly made me look small in your eyes, making me appear to you as if I could not foresee anything. So if you desire to receive

4. Cf. Jas 1.6.   5. Cf. Gal 5.4.
6. Cf. Jn 20.29.   7. Jn 12.36.
8. Cf. Mt 10.41.   9. Ps 19.5.
10. Cf. Mt 12.38–39.   11. Is 7.12.
12. Using the variant reading, ἀναγινώσκοντι, instead of ἀναγινώσκων.

from me a commandment for the salvation of your life, first acquire profound humility and obedience in all things. For these uproot all of the passions and plant all of the goods. And do not be discontent when you hear lessons from your abbot; for this seed is sown by the enemies. And if you do everything that is in your power "to serve and to preserve,"[13] then I hope in the incarnate and crucified Christ, who has saved sinners,[14] that you will not be long in producing good and beautiful fruits.

With regard to those things you say have been done, if you keep my commandment in Christ Jesus, then believe without any hesitation[15] that the Lord has forgiven you these sins and that you have just now been born of God in repentance. As far as each one of the passions is concerned, it is not necessary for me to write to you; for in a word, I have indicated to you the [prescribed] medicine for these. The Lord said: "I will dwell in the humble."[16] What then? Do you think that it is at all possible for anything of the enemy's evil to dwell there where it sees the Lord dwelling? Understand this; a criminal cannot appear in the courtyard of the magistrate.

As far as the kitchen goes, you are not able to endure this to the end; for this matter involves a great deal of envy. If, however, you are ordered to do so, then do not be reluctant or dispute the matter, but respond with eagerness; for this will be a source of grace for you.

As for the two passions, namely, forgetfulness and negligence, ask with eagerness, brother, and work with greater zeal. Do not do as with your earlier questions, which you conveyed with forgetfulness and its sister negligence, but renew your spiritual questions through the grace of the Holy Trinity; and become fervent in godly fear, awakening this grace from the spiritual sleep brought about by the two above-mentioned terrible passions. For when it is warmed, it acquires a desire for the future goods.[17] And henceforth, let your attention focus on these things, and your sensory sleep will be far from that concern. Then you will say, with David:

---

13. Gn 2.15.   14. Cf. 1 Tm 1.15.
15. Cf. Jas 1.6.   16. Cf. 2 Cor 6.16.
17. Cf. Heb 10.1 and 9.11.

"And in my attention, a fire will burn."[18] Therefore, having asked about the two passions, you have briefly heard about all the passions; for these are like charcoal and are burned by the spiritual fire. Indeed, if I speak to you about spiritual behavior, when there is an absence of vigilance in the master thought, then the thought is in vain for that person. Therefore, apply yourself to your labor and [apply yourself] to these matters, and you will discover the royal way[19] of the person who fearlessly walks in the Lord. I have written this to you, and believe me when I say that, if I see your zeal in God, I will pray for you to the Lord without ceasing,[20] that he may save you from death unto life eternal, in Christ Jesus our Lord, to whom be the glory to the ages. Amen.

LETTER 227

Question from the same [brother] to the same Great Old Man: "Abba, my thought frightens me, saying that I ask questions but do not produce actions, and perhaps the Old Man will curse me. But pray for me, that God will grant me to understand what you have written to me and to practice this." Response by Barsanuphius.

Child, one who hears and practices does so for one's own interest and benefit. Since, however, you said that your thoughts frighten you with the possibility that I may curse you, how is it possible for someone who fears God to curse someone else, when the Lord says: "Bless, and do not curse"?[21] So be careful, brother, that your thoughts do not try to deceive you in those things which are of very little benefit, such as sleeping while you sit, or not placing a headrest, which resemble the mint and the dill[22] and the cummin, enticing you to leave the more significant matters of the law, such as quenching your anger, drying your irritation, and submitting in all things. They sow these seeds within you in order to weaken your body, so that you may come to the point of passion and may desire soft mattresses and diverse foods.[23] But be content with one headrest and lay yourself down with fear of God.

---

18. Ps 38.4.
20. Cf. 1 Thes 5.17.
22. Cf. Mt 23.23.
19. Cf. Nm 20.17.
21. Rom 12.14.
23. Cf. Song 19.11.

As for understanding whatever I say to you, pray to God, and he will bestow on you sound intelligence, for he is the Giver of every good gift.[24] And believe firmly that, if you do your best in what you have heard, I will also do ten times more than you are able, so that you may receive assistance from the loving God. Therefore, fill your stove-pot with spiritual foods, such as humility, obedience, faith, hope, and love. For whoever possesses these feeds on the heavenly King, Christ, to whom be the glory to the ages. Amen.

LETTER 228

Question from the same person to the same Great Old Man: "I entreat you, father, since I am reading the Greek but do not understand what it says, pray that the Lord will grant me to understand my reading, and tell me whether I should learn the Psalms in the Greek." Response by Barsanuphius.

With regard to reading in Greek, if we ask according to God and in humility for those things that are beneficial to our soul, God is there to offer understanding. And if it is a gift from God, it is clear that this occurs for the salvation of our soul. For most of the books are written in the Greek language. And if you also toil to learn the Psalms in this language, it will prove helpful to you in reading other books in the same language. So whether you read or understand the Psalms, unceasingly remember God, who says: "Learn from me that I am gentle and humble in heart, and you will find rest for your souls."[25] Understand what I am saying to you; and if you toil, your labor will find grace[26] unto life eternal, in Christ Jesus our Lord, to whom be the glory to the ages. Amen.

LETTER 229

Question from the same person to the same Great Old Man: "I pray you, Master, since the thought of blasphemy has overtaken me, forgive me for the sake of the Lord, and pray for me that I might be corrected." Response.

24. Cf. Jas 1.17.   25. Mt 11.29.
26. Cf. Heb 4.16.

If I could fill these letters with tears and send them to you, since you have afflicted yourself, it would have been of greater benefit to you. For what can I do for a person who has not cultivated well the earth of his own heart in order to receive these words, which were previously sown[27] by me through written responses, in order to restore his soul from oldness to newness of life eternal?[28] Indeed, if you had eagerly received my words, then you would have tasted their sweetness, which sweetens the soul and chases away any terrible bitterness sown by the demons in you. It is some time now since the demon of blasphemy has attacked you, namely, the one that destroys the souls who receive it. Search, and you will discover that, even without finding any excuse worthy of mention, this demon has trapped you by the ankle in order to put you to death. May my God not grant this demon the opportunity to fulfill its own desire within you.

If we do not despair, the God who receives our repentance always stands firm. Yet, if we do despair in ourselves, then we are found to be self-condemned, each of us bearing our own blood over our heads. So awaken from the captivity of error; and recall your senses, which the enemy has captured from you, and which he has withheld from the teachings of Christ that you have learned through me. First, they order you to quench your anger and irritation, when you know that these bring us to destruction through blasphemy against God. So acquire humility, the incineration of the demons; acquire obedience, which brings the Son of God to dwell in us; acquire faith, which saves us; acquire hope, which does not shame us;[29] acquire love, which does not allow us to fall away from God. Nevertheless, instead of caring about these things, you have chosen for yourself the opposite, namely, anger and irritation and blasphemy, which is the culmination of destruction.

After this, you should also listen to the following: if you do your best to abstain from these passions, as well as to be attached to these goods,[30] then I, too, shall do whatever I can, even ten times more than you are able to do.[31] Perhaps you do not care

27. Cf. Lk 8.15.   28. Cf. Col 3.9–10; Eph 4.22–24.
29. Cf. Rom 5.5.   30. Cf. Rom 12.9.
31. Cf. Dn 1.20.

about putting to shame my gray hair. Yet, for the goodness of God, in order that you may learn how good he is, labor to correct yourself. And since we have received the commandment to forgive,[32] your past is forgiven you; but correct yourself from now on. Repent for forty days before God over your sins of yesterday, by making three prostrations and saying: "Forgive me; for I have blasphemed against you, my God," and confess to him with the same mouth that blasphemed, saying three times each day: "Glory to you, my God, and blessed are you to the ages.[33] Amen." And do not return to the same condition, "so that nothing worse happens to you."[34] For it is as a result of the hardness of your heart that you have come to anger, and from anger to estrangement from holy Communion. Moreover, by being completely dominated, you have fallen into the sewage of blasphemy. Unless the hand of the loving God and the prayers of the saints had prevented you, your soul would have been cast into the destruction of despair. Therefore, God says to you through me, the least person: "You have sinned, but do so no longer."[35] As for your former sins, pray. For God is merciful,[36] and he forgives our sins when we so desire. Further, remember that "the prayer of the righteous is powerful and effective."[37] If it pleases you, labor in these things; otherwise, forgive me for everything.

LETTER 230

When the same brother asked for forgiveness, the Great Old Man immediately responded.

Our death and our life are in our hands.[38] Now, then, if we do not practice our former sins, we already have from God the forgiveness for these sins, so long as we do not continue to doubt. Therefore, my brother, keep yourself good from now on, so that the following words are not also fulfilled about you: "Behold, you have been made well; do not sin any more, so that nothing worse happens to you."[39] Renounce your defiance, remove

32. Cf. Lk 6.37.
34. Jn 5.14.
36. Cf. Ps 102.8.
38. Cf. Dt 30.19.

33. Cf. Dn 3.26, 52.
35. Cf. Sir 21.1.
37. Jas 5.16.
39. Jn 5.14.

far from you your faithlessness, estrange yourself from hopelessness, and cling to God, loving, trusting, and hoping, and you will have life eternal in him. Amen.

LETTER 231

Question from the same person to the same Great Old Man: "Father, pray for me that I may be protected from nocturnal fantasies, and if possible make me worthy of prostrating myself before you and of hearing your holy voice. For I believe that, if this happens to me, I shall find great protection in this." Response.

Scripture says: "Whoever is faithful in little is also faithful in much."[40] If you believed me in my absence, you would also believe me in my presence; for the Lord blessed "those who have not seen, and yet have come to believe."[41] Indeed, I have written to you many times about defiance, anger, and hardness, and I see that you consider my words to be of consolation. Therefore, since I am obliged to offer you whatever I have, according to the Scripture that says: "Give to everyone who asks from you,"[42] then I say to you: acquire humility, obedience, love, faith, and hope, and I will respond on your behalf to the loving God in regard to all your sins.

Moreover, know this, that if you are not humbled, then you will not be obedient; and if you are not obedient, then you will not love; and if you do not love, then you will not believe; and if you do not believe, you cannot hope. If, then, you labor to acquire these, I will count upon myself all of your sins. And if you regard yourself as a leper, I believe that you too will hear from the Savior: "I do choose; be made clean."[43] If you consider yourself a sinner, you will hear: "Your many sins are forgiven you."[44] And if you regard yourself as being blind, you will receive "according to your faith."[45] I have already written these things to you in the past, and you were able to rest. Guard your mouth so that it does not again fall into the most terrible sin of blasphemy; for if your soul reaches this point, it will sweat a great deal

---

40. Lk 16.10.
42. Mt 5.42.
44. Lk 7.47–48.

41. Jn 20.29.
43. Mt 8.3.
45. Mt 9.29.

in offering supplication to God for this. So if you guard what I have said with all your soul, these things will protect you not only from nocturnal fantasies, but also from all the machinations of the enemy with the help of Christ. Amen.

LETTER 232

Question from the same person to the same Great Old Man: "Be merciful to me, master, and tell me how I can be saved at this time; for a thought of fear has arisen in my heart.[46] What, then, do you order me to do?" Response.

At every moment, if a person is able to cut off the individual will in all things, and possesses a humble heart, holding death at all times before one's eyes, that person can be saved by the grace of God. And wherever that person may be, fear cannot dominate him. For such a person has forgotten those things which have passed and is turned towards those things that lie before us.[47] Do these things, and you will be saved for the sake of God without having any concern.

LETTER 233

A younger brother, who confided in the same brother, would frequently visit him, supposedly for the benefit of his soul. And every now and again, the latter would take care of his needs, as if attending to him. The younger brother did not understand what he ought to do, and so did not ask anything about this. The Old Man, however, knew this from God, since he had the gift of insight,[48] and wrote to him the following of his own accord.

Brother, your first sins which occurred with God's tolerance[49] have been forgiven by God through the intercession of the saints and of your abbot, in order that you may display the fruits of righteousness,[50] so that the Scripture might be fulfilled in your

46. Cf. Lk 24.38.
47. Cf. Phil 3.13.
48. Lit., "being clairvoyant" (διορατικός).
49. Cf. Rom 3.26.
50. Cf. Phil 1.11.

case: "Where sin increased, grace abounded all the more."[51] Why then do you again encourage the fire to enter your forest? For the demons do not let you become aware until they have taken you into their hands, and then they fulfill in you their will. So then, this matter is not profitable but dangerous. Pay attention to how they offer you the right to teach, in order that you may receive the reprimand of the Apostle, who says: "You, then, that teach others, will you not teach yourself?"[52] Listen, brother, I am speaking to you as my child; have you become so paralyzed, that you desire to be attended to by another? Do you not know that it is a matter of condemnation, especially for a younger brother capable of serving others? Believe me, I, the least one, would attend to my own needs even before God assured me in regard to living alone in stillness. And in my illness, too, I would cook for myself a little warm meal. Do not do this, because you will suffer an evil death; instead, when need arises, do not say anything to anyone beyond what is required at the time.

For how can one who does not construct his own cell construct that of another person? Do you not know that the Lord said: "The Son of Man came not to be served, but to serve"?[53] Do not be led astray by deviating from this; otherwise, your blood will be on your head.[54] But speak the truth with humility to those who ask you about anything. Forgive me, I have strayed; for I asked and heard that a young man does not benefit another young man, even if he nourishes him with the powerful drink of the entire Scripture. If you do your best, I, too, give you my word before God that you will not be wiped out from my heart. I am doing, however, what I can in praying to God that he might see you through this terrible darkness and bring you to the ineffable light,[55] and from the deceit of the demons to the knowledge of Christ,[56] from the second death of sin to life eternal.[57] If you desire to be saved, do not despise these words. Let me see you bearing fruit in the vineyard[58] of our Lord Jesus Christ, thir-

51. Rom 5.20.   52. Rom 2.21.
53. Mt 20.28.   54. Cf. 1 Kgs 2.37.
55. Cf. 1 Pt 2.9.   56. Cf. 2 Pt 2.20.
57. Cf. Rv 1.11.   58. Cf. Jn 15.5.

ty times and sixty times and one hundred times,[59] to the glory of
the Father and the Son and the Holy Spirit. Amen.

LETTER 234

Request from the same brother to the same Great Old Man: "For
the Lord's sake, forgive me, father, that in my ignorance I have
been ridiculed by the demons; and pray that I might 'make a
new beginning.'"[60] Response by Barsanuphius.

We find, brother, that when some people came to the Master
Christ in true repentance, they received forgiveness of sins, just
as he said to that sinful woman: "Your many sins have been forgiven you."[61] And I tell you that, if you do your best to keep my
words, you will receive mercy from him who was merciful to David; and you will receive forgiveness from him who forgave both
him[62] and the sinful woman. Yet, since you said that you wish to
make a new beginning, you give me joy as well. For the beginning is [found in] humility and fear of God. "The fear of God is
the beginning of wisdom."[63] The beginning of wisdom is abstention from evil deeds. And abstention from evil deeds is to refrain
from all those things hated by God. Now, how else does one refrain from these except by doing nothing without either questioning or consulting [one's elders] and except by saying nothing unnecessary? And together with these things, one should
always consider oneself foolish, unseasoned, despised, and literally as being nothing at all. God knows that it is not as a righteous man that I am saying what I am about to tell you, brother.
If you believe, however, the Lord will grant to you "according
to your faith."[64] For it is written: "The prayer of the righteous
is powerful and effective."[65] Therefore, do your best to place in
your purse the hundred denarii, and I shall add to it my ten

---

59. Cf. Mk 4.8.
60. This copticism (βάλλειν ἀρχήν) is henceforth established as a phrase in
Greek monastic terminology. See also *Letters* 55, 266, 276, 493, 497, 500, 562,
614, and 788.
61. Lk 7.47–48.   62. Cf. 2 Sm 12.13.
63. Ps 110.10.   64. Mt 9.29.
65. Jas 5.16.

thousand talents.[66] Do not neglect these things; otherwise, your grief will be great. Rather, always remember and keep them, and I believe that your labor will not be in vain;[67] nor will my labor for you be in vain. If you guard the pearl,[68] you will find wealth in him, in Christ Jesus our Lord, to whom be the glory to the ages. Amen.

LETTER 235

Letter from the same person to the same Great Old Man: "Master, I am afflicted in my relationship with my abbot, thinking that he is discriminating between me and the other brothers; indeed, I am so scandalized by him in this regard that I am even tempted to hate him. Pray for me, and declare to me what I should do." Response by Barsanuphius.

Brother, you are tempting yourself. Do you not know that "one is tempted by one's own desire, being enticed by it"?[69] Pay attention to yourself; for the devil has hurriedly sought to disturb you from the advice you have received. May God not grant him room to do so. The Lord said to Peter: "Listen! Satan has demanded you, to sift you all like wheat, but I have prayed to my Father that your own faith may not fail."[70] Brother, do not pay attention to anyone else but yourself. And do not be curious; for it will be of no benefit to you at all. It is for nothing that Satan has so troubled your heart. See that you do not render vain my prayer for you to God. Had you not even come at this time, I would still declare these things to you.

You have sinned; stay calm, and do not think of evil things but only of good things. For a good person thinks about good things, while an evil person thinks about evil things. The Lord will forgive you. Get back up again, supported by the hand of God, and do not trust your thoughts. The demons present matters to you as they want. Guard yourself from them; for they are fearful and rage against you. The Lord will abolish them from you swiftly,[71] brother. Amen.

66. Cf. Mt 18.24–28.
67. Cf. 1 Thes 3.5.
68. Cf. Mt 13.46.
69. Jas 1.14.
70. Lk 22.31.
71. Cf. 2 Thes 2.8.

LETTER 236

The same brother was still afflicted by the same thoughts, and again wrote to the same Great Old Man, imploring him to convey to him a word of life. And the latter responded to him with the following.

Brother, your thoughts and the demons wrongly trouble you against your abbot, according to their evil strategy, so that you may hate the one who loves you and distress him who wants to protect you with his soul. They do this in order to fulfill against you what has been said: "In return for my love, they accuse me, rewarding me with evil for good, and with hatred for my love."[72] For he often assures you that he loves you, and you do not believe him. Yet the envy of the devil blinds your heart, so that it reckons good things as being evil and sweet things as being bitter, that you may hear the words: "Ah, you who call evil good and bitter sweet, putting darkness for light and light for darkness."[73] They rob you, because you are senseless and slow of heart. So you do not understand that they want to lead you to the destruction of your soul. And you hide inside yourself and overlook my words, refusing to cultivate them. These things are of no benefit to you; they do not benefit you at all. If, however, your heart is not assured, then you are not a human being but a devil. For it is the devil who is established in disbelief and disobedience; and those who do not obey [their abbot] become devils like the devil himself.

Do you not understand what you are doing, my brother? For you often lead your elder to the point of frustration, and yet he bears your awkwardness. And often he implores you as a genuine and beloved son—which, indeed, he considers you to be—and for a while your heart is softened. Nevertheless, again you do not stay with the good, but change once more like the moon.[74] I stand before my Master Christ, that I am not telling you anything without God for the salvation of your soul. And often I have sought to send you a word about the movements [of

72. Ps 108.4–5.   73. Is 5.20.
74. Cf. Sir 27.11.

your body] and the meditations of your heart; yet I have been long-suffering until now, waiting for you to understand what is of benefit to you. Yes, child, bear with me, the least of all people; abstain from your evil thoughts and assume good ones such as guilelessness, love, long-suffering, and humility, which entirely empties the quiver of the devil[75] and refreshes the head of those who acquire it, drawing on itself the grace of God.

Wake up, stay alert, be of good cheer, take comfort in this, and long to be saved. Hate envy, jealousy, discord, slander, and the like. And become an innocent sheep of Christ's flock,[76] an honorable member of your monastic community, a consecrated vessel,[77] a son of the kingdom,[78] an heir of the glory,[79] so that by living according to the commandments of Christ himself you may obtain eternal life and the glorious resurrection. For God is my witness how I pray for the salvation of your soul. May he grant me according to my desire that you be saved and come to the knowledge of truth.[80] Had you meditated continually on my words, you would not have fallen into error or strayed, but you would have walked the narrow way according to God, which leads to life eternal that is in Christ Jesus our Lord. May God grant you to understand his will, brother.

LETTER 237

Question from the same person to the same Great Old Man: "Forgive me, lord Abba, for the sake of the Lord; and I recall that the fathers say we should enter into the cell and remember our sins.[81] And when I remember them, I feel no pain about them; indeed, often I even desire compunction and it does not come. Tell me what it is that prevents it from coming." Response.

Brother, you are fooling yourself when you say that you desire this, because you do not truly desire it. For entering into the cell is a matter of the soul, of searching it out and of gathering our thought from every person. It is then that we feel pain and com-

---

75. Cf. Eph 6.16.
77. Cf. 2 Tm 2.21.
79. Cf. Eph 1.18.
81. *Sayings*, Poemen 162.

76. Cf. Is 53.7–8.
78. Cf. Mt 13.38.
80. Cf. 1 Tm 2.4.

punction. So what prevents compunction from coming to you is your own will; indeed, if a person does not cut off the individual will, the heart does not feel pain. Unbelief, however, does not allow you to cut off your own will, and unbelief develops out of desire for human glory. The Lord said: "How can you believe, when you accept glory from one another and do not seek the glory that comes from the one who alone is God?"[82] Often I prevent water from descending through your mouth to your stomach, and yet you absorb it through your nostril. This is precisely the terrible [sin of] pretense to rights, which drags a person down to hell. So this is why the bitterest demons deceive you, making simple things appear difficult. Therefore, either ask me questions and reject your own will, your pretense to rights, and the desire to please others; or else I shall stay away from you. If, then, you do not feel pain when you cut off your own will, and if your heart does not truly so desire, then of what use is your question?

I have already told you: "You give the hundred denarii, and I shall add my ten thousand talents."[83] Behold, your former sins have been forgiven, and you are competing to fall into worse sins through the window of your pretense to rights. Cease, brother, for this is not a good way. Amma Sarah said: "If I want to please everyone, I find myself at their doors repenting."[84] And the Apostle says: "If I were still pleasing people, I would not be a slave[85] of Christ."[86] If you truly wish to weep for your sins, then pay attention to yourself and die to all people. For it is a real labor, brother, for a person to be saved. Cut out these three things: your own will, the pretense to rights, and the desire to please people. Then compunction will truly come to you, and God will protect you from all evil. Brother, I bear witness that you should pay attention to yourself; rejoice when you are beaten, rebuked, insulted, and disciplined.

Reject the craftiness of the serpent, but not its prudence; and

82. Jn 5.44.
83. Cf. Mt 18.24–28. See above, pp. 238–39.
84. *Saying* 5.
85. Cf. Barsanuphius's self-characterization elsewhere as "a slave on a mission" in *Letter* 139.
86. Gal 1.10.

retain the innocence of the dove[87] with prudence, and the Lord will help you. Behold, this is the way of salvation. If it pleases you, walk it; and God will offer you a hand of assistance. If it does not please you, then it is up to you. For one who wills also has authority over oneself. If, however, you release this authority to another person, then you are carefree, and the other person bears your care. Choose what you want.

LETTER 238

Question from the same person to the same Great Old Man: "What are craftiness, prudence, and integrity with prudence?" Response.

I have spoken to you of the craftiness of the serpent in consideration of your prudence. For the craftiness of the devil brings a person every evil thought against other people. Understand what I am saying. Indeed, if a person persists in these, then the devil extends this craftiness against God; everything that relates to craftiness brings destruction of the soul. "Every bad tree bears bad fruit."[88] On the other hand, prudence leads a person to discernment. I told you, brother, retain the innocence of a dove[89] with prudence; for all of its thoughts are good and beneficial. "Every good tree bears good fruit."[90] Craftiness implants harm to a person's soul and body, whereas integrity through prudence leads a person to calmness of thoughts, stillness of soul and body, as well as life eternal. Strive to achieve these, and the Lord will help you. For this is his will, namely, the salvation of us all.[91]

LETTER 239

Question from the same person to the same Great Old Man: "I pray you, master; my thought tells me that, without stillness, there is no repentance. So if it is possible, allow me to practice stillness for a few days, and give me also a commandment for salvation, and pray that I may keep it." Response.

---

87. Cf. Mt 10.16.
89. Cf. Mt 10.16.
91. Cf. 1 Tm 2.4.

88. Cf. Mt 7.17 and 12.33.
90. Cf. Mt 7.17 and 12.33.

Brother, I have received your intention, or rather God, too, has received it. For he is the one able to cooperate in the good for your benefit, according to his will and not according to your own will. This is how he taught us to live, not according to our own will but according to his, just as he himself lives according to the will of his Father.[92] And, after him, to this day I have extended my wings over you; I bear your burdens[93] and transgressions, as well as the contempt for my words to you and your negligence. Indeed, beholding them, I have covered them, just as God beholds and covers our sins, awaiting your repentance. As for you, you have become like a person sitting under a shady tree, who came out from it into the sun until he was scorched to complete destruction. Yet, in spite of all this, as surely as the Lord lives, I did not give in. Do not be surprised, for indeed even God swore to himself that he did "not desire the death of sinners but rather that they should turn from their ways and live."[94] And when someone does not return, that person remains in destruction.

You, however, my child, asked for things that are bittersweet. For I call your own will vinegar, and your repentance honey. When you say: "Allow me to practice stillness for a few days," as if you supposedly know what is beneficial to you, this, too, is arrogance. Instead, you should say: "Guide me in the way of God." It is God who will illumine "the eyes of your heart"[95] to know how I labor for you in my concern that you not be lost. But I need a little cooperation from you. In the name of God, behold, I am giving you a commandment for salvation. If you keep this, I shall bear the indictment[96] against you. And, by the grace of Christ, I shall not abandon you, either in this age or in the age to come.

Do not be deceived by filling your stomach; do not take pleasure in receiving more food or drink than your body requires; and guard yourself against judging anyone. Become obedient, and you will come to humility, while all the passions will be

---

92. Cf. Jn 6.38.   93. Cf. Gal 6.2.
94. Ezek 18.23.   95. Eph 1.18.
96. Greek, χειρόγραφον; cf. Col 2.14.

burned away from you. Do not be discontent thinking that this commandment is heavy. For it is not possible for anyone to be saved without labor and keeping the commandment. So, then, I have taken from you the weight, the charge, and the obligation. Behold, you have become new, free from guilt, and purified. Therefore, stay in this purity. Listen to the Savior, who says: "Behold, you have been made well; do not sin any longer, so that nothing worse happens to you."[97] And do not suppose that salvation comes without labor. Sweat, toil, and violence are needed. Do not relax your body, because it will overcome you. For indeed, even great people are overcome if they do not pay attention. So take courage, my brother, and keep my commandments, or rather the commandments of God; you will give me joy, and the Lord will protect you from evil and grant you joy in his kingdom. "Devote yourself to these things"[98] continually; long to be saved, and God will save you. For his is the glory to the ages. Amen.

LETTER 240

Question from the same brother to the same Great Old Man: "Forgive me, lord Abba, for the sake of the Lord, because your holiness said to me: 'Behold, your faults are forgiven.' Abba Isaiah also says that so long as a person retains the pleasure of these sins, they have not yet been forgiven.[99] Behold, I still retain their pleasure. For the sake of the Lord, then, clarify these things for me. My thought is afflicted, saying that, since I am such a person, I should not have accepted ordination, since this, too, implies a sense of vainglory and the burden of responsibility. So now I hesitate even in my ministry as a deacon. At the same time, I implore you to answer me because my thought tells me that I have been abandoned by God inasmuch as I have been weighed down tremendously this last week by fornication." Response.

97. Jn 5.14.
98. 1 Tm 4.15.
99. Preserved in the Armenian edition of the *Ascetic Discourses*, no. 8. The influence of Abba Isaiah is particularly and profoundly evident in the *Letters*; see *Letters* 252–253, 311–313, 240, and 528. See the translation by John Chryssavgis and R. P. Penkett, *Abba Isaiah of Scetis: Ascetic Discourses* (Kalamazoo, MI: Cistercian Publications, 2002).

Oh, the counsel of the evil demons! Oh, the deceit of their leader, the devil, who hates good and hates people from the beginning to the end! For just as he was separated from God, he desires that all people may perish. Brother, I told you that your former sins have been forgiven, but not that the warfare against them has also disappeared. Nevertheless, a man stands upright in a contest. Even if you had no sins, the devil would still bring you their pleasure; and because you did have them, he does the same, again bringing you their pleasure.

The way in which Abba Isaiah spoke, however, refers to pleasures and to those who cultivate them. For indeed, it is one thing for someone to remember the sweetness of honey, and another to have the taste as well as its memory. So then, it is for the person who remembers the pleasure of sins but who does not enact these pleasures—instead contradicting and opposing them—that former sins are forgiven. Nevertheless, such are the machinations of our enemy and adversary, who always desires to devour all living people,[100] in order to lead to despair, in regard to salvation, and to hopelessness, in regard to eternal life, all those who are not established on the firm rock[101] of faith, according to which measure all will receive [their reward].[102] So guard yourself against these in order that you may not fall entirely into the hands of the devil; and the Lord, who lives to the ages, will have mercy on you.

As for your ordination, who dares to call himself worthy except one who is truly mad and completely ignorant about himself? Therefore, condemn yourself and at the same time minister to God in the lot that has been given you; for to him belong the mercy, support, and strength. During the liturgy, remember the words: "Serve the Lord with fear, and rejoice in him with trembling,"[103] as well as the words: "He makes his angels spirits and his ministers a flame of fire."[104] Do not be afraid; God has not abandoned you. For if we do not abandon him, he does not abandon us. It is his will that we return to him and be saved.[105] As for you being weighed down tremendously by fornication,

---

100. Cf. Ps 123.3.
102. Cf. Prv 24.12; Mt 16.27.
104. Ps 103.4.
101. Cf. Mt 7.24; Lk 6.48.
103. Ps 2.11.
105. Cf. 1 Tm 2.4.

this happens by having thoughts against and judging your neighbor. It also happens from speaking boldly with those with whom I told you not to. If those who want to become wealthy in the world often take risks on journeys by sea and land, and endure these risks, how much more so should we who eagerly await the kingdom of heaven in order to be proclaimed children of God![106]

We hear that "our struggle is not against enemies of blood and flesh, but against the rulers and against the authorities."[107] Until now, you have not struggled against sin to the point of blood. Does the spirit of listlessness, then, already paralyze you? What have you endured? What have you borne? What variety of temptations have you endured rejoicing? Ah, sleepy monk! Show the devil that you live for God, taking refuge in him, moving with hands and feet, swimming in the onslaught of the intellectual waves, which rise to the heavens and drop to the abyss.[108] God is my witness, that my heart has been unfolded with you, as the God who fashioned it knows, he who set within it the covenant of the sacred commandments, which must be preserved within it, in order to lead you out— by the power of God—from darkness to true light and from the death of condemnation to the life of righteousness. Pay attention to yourself, brother; for it is impossible to be saved without labor and humility.

LETTER 241

Question from the same person to the same Great Old Man: "Father, since your holiness ordered me to serve at liturgy, declare to me, I implore you, what I should be pondering or meditating as I stand before the altar with the priest, or when I am cutting up the holy bread or offering people to drink of the holy blood, or again when I am carrying Communion and taking it to someone. And should I have a special vestment for liturgical use or a covering for my legs?" Response by Barsanuphius.

Brother, all of this is a spiritual allegory, but you understand it literally. The deacon serves like the Cherubim, and ought to

106. Cf. Mt 5.9.   107. Eph 6.12.
108. Cf. Ps 106.26.

be all eye, all intellect,[109] with his intellect and thought looking upward, with fear, trembling, and doxology. For he bears the body and blood of the immortal King. He even assumes the face of the Seraphim in proclaiming the doxology and in fanning the hidden mysteries as with their holy wings, recalling through these wings the levitation from this earth and from things material, while crying out ceaselessly with his intellect in the temple of the inner self[110] the victory hymn of the magnificent glory[111] of our God: "Holy, holy, holy, Lord of Sabaoth; heaven and earth are full of your glory."[112] And from the dreadful and fearful voice of this proclamation, the devil falls away trembling from the captive soul, and the demons are made to flee in confusion and shame, leaving it free from their slavery.

So now the soul recognizes that the true light[113] has dawned upon it; and, focusing its attention, it sees the beauty of the immortal Lamb and seeks to be filled with his body and blood. Then, it hears the loud voice of David crying out and saying: "Taste and see that the Lord is good."[114] And approaching with fear, it becomes a partaker of his body and blood, and this taste becomes indelible in the soul, protecting it from every passion. "Devote yourself to these things,"[115] whether you are standing before the holy mysteries, or else dividing or distributing the drink, or while carrying Communion to someone or gathering up the holy things, and generally in every service that you perform at the altar.

As for your vestment, acquire a spiritual cloak in which God is well pleased. The covering for your legs signifies mortification of the members.[116] Tell me, brother, if a person wears a purple, fully silken robe and yet is a fornicator, does the clothing purify that person from fornication or from the other passions? What then shall they do who are worthy of the holy mysteries but who lack garments? The Lord ordered us to have one garment,[117] and that is the garment of virtues, of which may God make all of us worthy to the ages. Amen.

109. Cf. *Sayings*, Bessarion 11. 110. Cf. Rom 7.22.
111. Cf. 2 Pt 1.17. 112. Is 6.3.
113. Cf. Jn 1.9. 114. Ps 33.9.
115. Cf. 1 Tm 4.15. 116. Cf. Col 3.5.
117. Cf. Mt 10.10.

LETTER 242

Question by the same person to the same Great Old Man: "Master, forgive me, and pray for me for the sake of the Lord, that my senses may be sanctified. And although your holiness said that the deacon ought to be like the Cherubim and the Seraphim, yet I am polluted in the senses. What, then, shall I do in order that my ministry as a deacon may not be to my condemnation? For I am wretched and cannot control myself. For God's sake, help me so that I may not lose my soul in every way." Response.

Do your best always to remember this image of how the deacon ought to be and of how you actually are, remembering death and how you are going to encounter God. And in continually condemning yourself, your heart feels compunction in order to receive repentance. For he who said by the prophet: "First confess your sins, so that you may be justified,"[118] this same one justifies you and renders you innocent of every condemnation. Indeed, it is said: "It is God who justifies; who is it then that will condemn you?"[119] So, as I have on other occasions stated to you, acquire humility, obedience, and submission, and you shall be saved. And do not argue at all, saying: "Why this, or why that?" but become obedient, especially to your abbot, who, after God, cares for you and has been entrusted with your soul. And if you have the zeal to keep these things, then I shall do abundantly more than I possibly can, so that God may grant you the strength to make this possible. The Lord shall keep you and protect you from the evil one. Amen.

LETTER 243

Question from the same [brother] to the same Old Man: "Father, tell me what you advise me to do for the little need that I have. For if I am not being ridiculed by the demons as always, yet I am not able to keep simply to one garment gladly. Therefore, whatever you order me to do in order to receive mercy, God knows that I am in great disorder and passions. Pray for me for the Lord's sake, that I may not be separated from your side, at

118. Is 43.26.
119. Rom 8.33–34.

least in this age; for on account of my passions, I am ashamed to talk about the age to come." Response.

Brother, "forcing oneself in all things"[120] and humility bring one to [spiritual] progress. For even the Apostle says this: "We are afflicted in every way, but not crushed."[121] When we, too, then, surrendered our material life to the abbot, keeping nothing at all in our own hands, God knows and bears witness that we did not consider that he owed us gratitude in these things, but we were grateful to him because he bore our burden,[122] rendering us carefree. The apostle Peter also says: "For the Lord's sake, accept the authority of every human institution."[123] And James says: "Whoever keeps the whole law but fails in one point has become accountable for all of it."[124] This is why one should not retain one's own will but in everything blame oneself, and then that person shall receive the mercy of God. If, however, the devil fools one into proudly thinking that one has done well, then everything achieved is lost. Therefore, as you go about doing whatever you do, humbly say: "Lord, forgive me; for I have burdened the abbot, casting on him my burden." The Lord Jesus Christ will save you. Amen.

LETTER 244

Another brother, who was a deacon, excused himself from serving at the altar, recalling his past sins. So he asked the same Great Old Man about this, as well as about his bodily sickness. The latter responded to him in the following way.

Brother, Scripture has taught us that, "indeed, those who want to live a godly life according to Christ will be persecuted."[125] Yet how is it possible to be persecuted even in the present age? It is from the demons who drive them away from the fear of God and his worship. "Repentance from sin," however, "means no longer committing this sin,"[126] while abstaining from evils is riddance of these. Do not let past sins grieve you, and do

---

120. *Sayings*, Nau 102.
121. 2 Cor 4.8.
122. Cf. Gal 6.2.
123. 1 Pt 2.13.
124. Jas 2.10.
125. 2 Tm 3.12.
126. *Sayings*, Poemen 120.

not be hindered from serving as a deacon before God, but do so with fear and trembling;[127] and pay attention to the fact that it sanctifies your soul. And if you believe this, you will always tremble in order not to sin, so that you do not lose this sanctification. Therefore, endure passions and afflictions thankfully; for they are a discipline from God, and he will have mercy on you, and they shall be for the salvation of your soul. Amen.

LETTER 245

Another brother asked the same Great Old Man: "Father, tell me whether anger is natural or against nature. And what is the difference between the two?" Response.

Brother, there is anger that is natural, and there is anger that is against nature.[128] So the natural anger struggles not to give rise to the urges of desire and does not require remedy; for it has already been cured. The unnatural anger, however, struggles not to fulfill the urges of desire, but this requires remedy even more so than desire itself. Indeed, greater than the soldier is the one who bestows strength on him; however, if that strength is cut away, then the soldier is worthless since he finds no strength.

LETTER 246

Question from the same brother to the same Old Man: "From where do people derive passions?" Response.

God created both the soul and the body dispassionate, but through disobedience people fell away to passions.[129]

LETTER 247

Another brother asked the same Great Old Man: "For the Lord's sake, since I am tormented by the passions of my soul, tell me what I must do to be freed from these; and pray for me." Response.

127. Cf. Phil 2.12.
128. See Abba Isaiah of Scetis, *Ascetic Discourse* 2.
129. Ibid.

Brother, the person who desires salvation and longs to become a child of God[130] must acquire great humility, obedience,
and submission, as well as modesty.[131] Notice how you said: "Tell
me what I must do." Behold, I have told you to do these things,
and I give you my assurance that you will not be dominated by
the passions of the enemy; for these will be consumed by humility as if by fire, and the heart will be calmed and illumined in
Christ. To him be the glory to the ages. Amen.

LETTER 248

The same brother received an order from his abbot to dwell with
an elderly man and to serve him. So he asked the Other Old
Man: "Father, how should I know whether I am staying there according to God, or whether I am being hurt by not being with
the brothers in the monastic community but instead being on
my own? Moreover, the passions afflict me. And in regard to the
Psalms, how do you instruct me to recite them? Likewise, speak
to me in regard to sleep; for I fear that it might overcome me.
And what should I do about forgetfulness as well? And since this
shameful passion torments me so much, what is the sign of consent?"[132] Response by John.

If you wish to learn whether you are being hurt or receiving benefit by staying on your own, use this as a sign: if you are
staying there as a result of obedience, then you may know that
you are benefiting. For it is said: "Obedience is greater than sacrifice."[133] But if it is as a result of contradiction, then you are
being hurt. For it is an evil choice. You have not been separated from your brothers; never say that. But God has so provided
that, according to the weakness of your body, you should find a
reward for yourself through the elderly man. As far as the passions go, it is not possible for them not to be moved against

130. Cf. Jn 1.12.
131. This concept (τὸ ἀπαρρησίαστον) is literally the opposite of παρρησία,
namely, boldness.
132. There exists an extensive ascetic literature that refers to the concept of
"consent": cf. Sayings, Isidore the Priest 3; Evagrius, Praktikos 75; Macarian Homilies 15.28; Historia monachorum 1, John of Lycopolis 34–35; Mark the Monk, De
lege spirituali 142; and Cyril of Scythopolis, Life of Euthymios 24.
133. 1 Sm 15.22.

us in order to test us;[134] for "the untempted is also untested."[135] Yet since you said that you are sitting alone, do not believe this because it will be harmful to you. Indeed, you are not alone, if you believe, but you have God, to whom the Great Old Man has entrusted you, and you have his prayer assisting you. Simply do not desire to display anything else but obedience, and you will be saved. So you are not being hurt; do not be afraid.

As for the Psalms, do as the brothers also do, saying with each canticle three Psalms and making a prostration, and sleep will not overcome you. Unless you are unwell, this is what you should do every night. Forgetfulness is the destruction of the soul, and it comes as a result of contempt and negligence. As for the other shameful and spiteful passion, it requires labor of heart and body in order to be uprooted: labor of heart, in order to pray to God without ceasing; labor of body, in order to be tamed and disciplined according to our ability. The sign of consent is when something pleases a person and brings sweetness to the heart, and so one meditates on it with pleasure. If, however, one contradicts this thought and struggles not to receive it, then this is not consent but warfare, and it brings one to the level of proving and progress. The Lord Jesus Christ will purify you of your sins and strengthen you in your weakness by his goodness. Amen.

LETTER 249

Question from the same person to the same Old Man: "What is obedience? And what should I pray? And if someone tells me to pray for them, what must I do? Should I always remember that person?" Response.

Obedience cuts off the will, but without toil no one can acquire obedience. If you are staying there for the sake of obedience and not for bodily comfort, then this is not the result of your will; nor are you staying there passionately, but rather you are pleasing God. If you are staying there in order to receive pleasure in comfort, then you are not pleasing God. In regard

134. Cf. Rom 5.4.
135. *Agraphon*, no. 90.

to prayer, say: "Lord, deliver me from my sins and from the passions of dishonor." And if someone tells you to pray for them,
then say in your heart: "May God have mercy on us,"[136] and it is
sufficient. Nevertheless, remembering that person all the time
is not for you, but rather a matter for the perfect who can pray
for one another.

Question from the same person to the same Old Man: "Father,
I implore you to tell me how I might know that I am in submission and how I might surrender my own will and what I must do
to identify[137] in everything with the brothers? For I hear from
the fathers that one who is in submission and does not carry out
one's own will, but instead is identified with the brothers in everything, quickly comes to [spiritual] progress. Moreover, I am
examining my heart as to whether I am staying in the monastic community like the brothers, but I have no assurance. For
I break the fast before them and receive my meal sooner than
they; and I also eat alone. And I wish to try and see whether I can
eat later, but I am afraid on account of my illness." Response.

From this you can learn whether you are living like the others in the monastic community: by not doing anything of your
own will, eating neither alone nor with the brothers, but doing
whatever you have been ordered without any discussion. Regard
yourself as one of the sick. Are the sick outside of the monastic
community because they eat alone? Surely not! But they are doing this on account of their illness, on the order of the abbot.[138]

Thus God has given to you also the excuse of serving the elderly man in order that the inexperienced may not be scandalized when they see you eating earlier. As for eating later, with
those who are not ill, this is something you cannot endure. For
if you happen to fall ill, then you will again wish to take care of
yourself and will once again find yourself in affliction. So then,
since you have found an excuse not to give rise to thoughts in
anyone, do not worry about eating alone.

136. Cf. Lk 17.13.
137. Lit., "to be equaled" (ἵνα ἐξισωθῶ).
138. The Greek here simply says *abba*.

Therefore, doing everything on the order of the abbot and not according to one's own will is the sign of communality and equality with the brothers in the monastery. Do you not remember the time when you were facing that warfare of temptation to go away with your abbot and yet he did not want to take you [with him]? How did you dare to complain foolishly? Was it a matter of eating then? Was it not rather a matter of your will? If you wish to receive benefit and to remain in the monastic community, then cut off your will in all things and submit yourself in the same way as the brothers. For behold, you are a member of the same community for the benefit of your soul, directed by your fathers, by the Great Old Man, and the others. Follow their counsel, and you will progress by the grace of Christ; for much more so than you, they know what is best for your soul, brother.

LETTER 251

The same brother, who was not a priest, was ordered by the elderly man whom he was serving, who was a priest, to say a prayer or to bless the meal or some other such thing; and feeling burdened by this, he asked the Great Old Man whether he should obey him in this. Response by Barsanuphius.

Be careful not to take joy in counting yourself as being someone; but show obedience, which dispels the contentiousness that is hateful to God and to those who love him. And hold to the obedience that leads up to heaven and renders those who acquire it like the Son of God. To him be the glory to the ages. Amen.

LETTERS TO DOROTHEUS
OF GAZA (252–338)

LETTER 252

Question from another brother[1] to the Other Old Man: "Since I have money and wish to give some of it to the monastic community while distributing some to the poor, tell me, father, whether I should do this through the abbot." Response by John.

ROTHER, I ADDRESSED my first responses to a person who still appeared to require milk.[2] But now that you are talking about complete renunciation, listen to what has been written: "Open your mouth wide, and I shall fill it."[3] Brother, you do not need to learn from me, the least, what you must do; instead, listen to what has been written in the Acts of the Apostles about those who sold their goods and cast their money at the feet of the apostles: "it was distributed to each as any had need."[4] And they did not distribute the money by themselves, but rather through the apostles. Indeed, they were freed of care and money and vainglory. So if you desire to reach that measure and to enjoy being carefree, as well as to find the time to care about God, then you should do the same. Brother, your money is very little compared to what was given by some [brothers] to Abba Isaiah. For they gave him thousands of coins, telling him to dispose of them as he knows best, telling him neither where nor how he should do so. Therefore, these brothers did the perfect thing and were carefree. As for you, if it is the will of God that you reach this joy, you should be grateful and confess this grace to the one who bears your burden. Thus the one who sows evil

---

1. Manuscript 1307 of Iveron Monastery on Mt. Athos indicates that the word "brother" here refers to Dorotheus of Gaza, who begins to ask questions from this point—until and including *Letter* 338—in the correspondence.
2. Cf. Heb 5.12.   3. Ps 80.11.
4. Acts 4.35.

will not sow in you the thought that whoever receives the money owes you any thanks. God will do what is in your interest for the salvation·of your soul.

LETTER 253

The same person asked the Great Old Man whether he ought to distribute the money through his abbot, and how he should distribute it, as well as to whom. Response by Barsanuphius.

May the Lord bless you, child! For you want to become carefree, and yet at the same time you do not want to, being tormented by your own will. Simply say what you wish to donate to the monastic community, and in your will reserve whatever you wish for the poor, and then be carefree. For this is obedience: not having control of oneself. What is more precious than your soul, about which the Lord said that it is more precious than the whole world?[5] And if you have entrusted it to God and to your spiritual fathers, then why do you still hesitate in entrusting these small things to them? Look how stealthily vainglory and faithlessness war against you. And if this is the case, then in truth you have not even entrusted your soul to them. So how do you expect to receive mercy from them? Be carefree if you want to have time for God, and I shall bear the care of dealing with whomever you so order. Just be carefree toward God, and forgive me for the sake of love.

LETTER 254

Question from the same brother to the same Great Old Man: "Father, tell me how one comes to cut off one's own will and to the point of realizing the words: 'Behold, we have left everything and have followed you.'[6] For I have retained a small share of property for my nurture, because I am ill." Response by Barsanuphius.

To renounce one's own will is a sacrifice of blood. It means that one has reached the point of laboring to death and of ig-

5. Cf. Mt 16.26.
6. Mt 19.27.

noring one's own will. The statement "Behold, we have left everything and have followed you" is about perfection; it is not about property and small amounts of money, but about thoughts and desires. You, however, have not yet come to this perfection; when you approach there, you will hear what you have to do. For the time being, simply remain carefree in all matters and concerns. As for your property, keep it for now for your nurture. The Lord Jesus Christ will bring you to that ineffable joy; for he is eternal light. Amen.

LETTER 255

The same person questioned the same Old Man: "I am facing a great battle against fornication, and risk coming to despair, and I cannot even keep abstinence on account of my body's illness. For the Lord's sake, pray for me, and tell me what to do." Response.

Brother, it is out of envy that the devil has aroused within you this warfare. So guard your eyes, and do not eat to the point of satiation. Drink only a little wine, for the sake of the illness that you describe. Acquire humility; for it shatters all the snares of the enemy.[7] And I, the least, shall do whatever I can in prayer to God, that he might protect you from every temptation and guard you from all evil. Neither surrender, brother, nor cast yourself into despair; for this is the great joy of the devil. Pray without ceasing, saying: "Lord Jesus Christ, save me from the passions of dishonor." And you will find mercy from God and thus receive strength through the prayers of the saints. Amen.

LETTER 256

The same brother faced warfare in the same passion of fornication, and implored the same Great Old Man to pray for him and to tell him how one is to understand whether the temptation derives from one's own desire or from the enemy. Response.

Brother, no one can be saved from the passions or please God without labor of heart and contrition. Therefore, when

---

7. Cf. *Sayings*, Antony 7.

people are tempted by their own desires,[8] this means that they have neglected themselves and allowed their hearts to meditate on deeds committed in the past. Then, they actually bring wrath upon themselves from personal desire. So the intellect gradually becomes blinded and begins unconsciously to heed or to speak to people with desire. And the intellect proposes excuses to itself about how to speak or sit with a particular person, and tries to fulfill this desire in every way possible. Now, if one allows the thought free rein in these matters, the warfare is increased to the point of falling into sin, if not in body, then at least in spirit through consent; as a result, one finds oneself adding wood to the fire that burns within. The vigilant and prudent person, however, who wants to be saved will see where the damage comes from and will guard the self with precision from the evil thought in order not to dwell on these passions through some glance or encounter or some other pretext, for fear of igniting the fire that is within. Such is the warfare that derives from one's own desire, namely, through one's own free will.

As for the warfare derived from the devil, it works like this: The heart of the person who wants to be saved relaxes and smiles a little in order not to receive the seed. Yet even then, that person guards himself also with vigilance from the evil thought in order not to dally with the passions, whether by a glance or an encounter or some other pretext. If the need arises to attend to some matter with the person [in regard to whom one is tempted], then it is better to leave aside the entire matter than to lose one's soul. Be vigilant, brother; for you are mortal and ephemeral. Do not consent to lose eternal life in exchange for a fleeting moment. Of what benefit is the stench and impurity of sin except for purposes of shame and reproach and scandal? Abstinence, on the other hand, contains victory and crown and glory. Restrain your horse with the rein of the science of discipline, so that it may not stray in its attention here and there, by looking madly at some woman, or even at some man, and throw you as its rider off its back. Pray to God, that he might "turn

---

8. *Sayings*, Sisoes 44. One of two references to the *Sayings* of Abba Sisoes; see also *Letter* 385.

away your eyes from looking at vanities";[9] for when you acquire a brave heart, then wars will depart from you. Become astringent, like wine when it is beaten, and you will not allow stench and impurity to gather.

Acquire mourning, in order that it may alienate you from boldness, which destroys the souls that acquire it. Do not throw down the tool without which the fruitful earth cannot be tilled. This tool is humility, crafted by our great God, through which all the tares are uprooted from the Master's field and which bestows grace on those who live therein. Humility does not fall; it merely raises those who possess it from their fall. Embrace mourning with all your heart; for it is an associate of this good work. Labor to cut off your will in everything; for this is considered as a sacrifice for a person. This is what it means, when it is said: "For your sake we are being killed all day long, and accounted as sheep for the slaughter."[10] Do not become relaxed in conversations, because they will not allow you to progress according to God; torment your senses severely and with violence: your sight, hearing, taste, smell, and touch. Then you will progress through Christ's grace. For without torment, there is no martyr, as the Lord said: "By your patience you shall gain your souls."[11] And the Apostle says: "In great patience, in afflictions,"[12] and so forth.

Be careful not to show the treasures of your house to the Chaldaeans,[13] because they will take you as a captive to Babylon and there subject you to Nebuchadnezzar, king of the Babylonians.[14] Trample upon the passions, always meditating on this response, so that they may not trample upon you; subdue them with strength, so that they may not subdue you powerfully. Flee from them, as a deer runs from traps, so that they may not slaughter you like a lamb. Therefore, do not fear them; for they have no power. Our Lord Jesus Christ cut off their nerves and rendered them powerless. So do not fall asleep; for even if they are half-dead, yet they are certainly not sleeping. And do not be neglectful; for they are certainly not neglectful. Stretch out your hand a little to your fathers, who wish to raise you up from

9. Ps 118.37.
10. Ps 43.23.
11. Lk 21.19.
12. 2 Cor 6.4.
13. Cf. 2 Kgs 24.13.
14. Cf. 2 Kgs 25.

the filth of the stench. Remember that "the prayer of the righteous is powerful and effective."[15]

Do not judge anyone; do not scorn or scandalize anyone. Do not imagine something you have not seen about someone. For these things bring destruction to the soul. Pay attention to yourself, and expect your impending death. Say to yourself the words of the blessed Arsenius: "Arsenius, why did you leave the world?"[16] Learn what you have come here seeking. Run to Jesus, that you may win him.[17] If you want to be saved, run swiftly so that you may be found to be in the good company of the holy elders. If you want to progress, work hard. Seek earnestly to be with the saints, glorified in the ineffable glory, and not with the filthy demons in the indescribable punishment. Long to be in the kingdom of heaven, and not in the Gehenna of fire. Long to hear: "Come, you that are blessed by my Father,"[18] and: "Well done, good and faithful servant,"[19] and so on, rather than hearing: "Depart from me, you accursed servant, wicked and lazy."[20] The Lord's is the glory to the ages. Amen.

LETTER 257

Question from the same [brother] to the same Great Old Man: "I have many sins and want to repent; yet, on account of my body's weakness, I find that I cannot maintain the ascetic life of the fathers. Therefore, I implore you to tell me how it is that I should make a beginning. Give me an order, then, and clarify this for me; what is it that you declared to me in the other response, namely: 'Do not show the treasures of your house to the Babylonians, because they will take you as a captive to Babylon'?" Response by Barsanuphius.

Brother, there are some people who are poor, whom the Lord blessed, because they have put aside all of their possessions, namely, all of the passions, having also stripped themselves of these things for his name. These are truly poor and deserve the beatitude.[21] There are others, however, who are poor,

---

15. Jas 5.16.
16. *Sayings*, Arsenius 40.
17. Cf. 1 Cor 9.24; Phil 3.12.
18. Mt 25.34.
19. Mt 25.21.
20. Cf. Mt 25.26, 41.
21. Cf. Mt 5.3.

who have acquired nothing good, whom he threatened, saying: "Depart from me, you accursed one."[22] So, one who has such possessions and is weighed down by them puts them aside and is carefree. Therefore, if you want to make a beginning for repentance, learn what the adulterous woman did: in her tears, she washed the feet of the Master.[23] Weeping washes a person from sins, but it comes about with toil, together with great effort and patience, as well as by remembering the fearful judgment and the eternal shame, and by renouncing oneself, as the Lord said: "If any want to follow me, let them deny themselves and take up their cross and follow me."[24] Denying oneself and taking up the cross signify cutting off one's will in everything and reckoning oneself as nothing.

Since you mentioned, however, that your body is weak and unable to do anything, do whatever you can, gradually abstaining from eating bread and from drinking liquid. For indeed, God accepted the two copper coins of the widow and rejoiced above all else.[25] Train yourself to practice modesty, and you will be saved. Keep the first responses, together with this one, "as the apple of your eye."[26] As for not showing your treasures to the Babylonians, I was referring to the demons, and that is how I have explained to other people what I wrote in my letter. For the demons can see clearly and are deeply embittered against you. And they wage warfare against you through vainglory, and against your naïve listeners through scandal; and you bear the judgment of both. But for those who are able to hear and keep these things, this warfare is of great joy and benefit. Strive to conceal every good deed that you perform; for this is to your benefit. May the Lord instruct you through the prayers of the saints. Amen.

LETTER 258

Question from the same person to the same Great Old Man: "Father, pray for me because I am greatly tormented by the thoughts of fornication, cowardice, and despondency. My thought tells me

---

22. Mt 25.41.
24. Mt 16.24; Lk 9.23.
26. Cf. Ps 16.8.
23. Cf. Lk 7.38.
25. Cf. Mk 12.42–43.

that, when I see the brother regarding whom I am tempted, I should converse with him, lest by not conversing with him he will receive this as cause for suspicion. Moreover, I feel also that the demons are stifling me, and I fear this greatly." Response.

Brother, since you are not trained in the warfare of the enemy, this is why he suggests to you thoughts of cowardice and despondency and fornication. Therefore, withstand them with firm heart. For even athletes are not crowned unless they exert themselves in the race;[27] and soldiers are not glorified unless they prove themselves to the king during battle. David was such a person. Do you not recite in the Psalms: "Prove me, Lord, and try me; test by fire my heart and inner self"?[28] And again: "Though an army rise up against me, yet my heart shall not fear."[29] And in regard to cowardice: "Even though I walk in the darkest shadow of death, yet I fear no evil; for you are with me."[30] And about despondency: "If the spirit of the ruler rises against you, do not leave your post."[31]

Do you not want to be tested? "For the untempted is also untested."[32] It is warfare that renders a person tested. This is the work of a monk: to endure battles and resist with brave heart. Since you are ignorant of their strategies, the devil suggests to you thoughts of cowardice and paralyzes your heart. You have to learn that God does not permit any warfare or temptation to befall you that is greater than your strength. And the Apostle teaches you, saying: "God is faithful, and he will not let you be tested beyond your strength."[33] I, too, brother, was often tempted greatly in my youth by the demon of fornication, and I would labor to battle against the thoughts and to contradict them, not consenting to them, but instead keeping eternal hell before my eyes. And after doing this each day for five years, God relieved me of these thoughts. Such a problem is abolished by unceasing prayer together with weeping.

As for the matter of stifling you, the demons do this out of envy. Indeed, if it were possible, they would even expel you from

---

27. Cf. 2 Tm 2.5.
28. Ps 25.2.
29. Ps 26.3.
30. Ps 22.4.
31. Eccl 10.4.
32. *Agraphon*, no. 90.
33. 1 Cor 10.13.

the cell; but God does not permit them to dominate you. Nor do they have the power to do so. For God could bring comfort to you quickly, but then you would not be able to withstand any other passion. You should not relax before the demons, however, by paying attention to or conversing with someone. Rather, even if you reach the point of not wanting to encounter that person, distract your glance from him with fear and firmness, and do not release your hearing toward his voice. Even if this same brother, of his own accord, unknowingly speaks to or sits beside you, remove yourself discreetly and modestly, without any sudden movement. Moreover, tell your thought to remember God's fearful judgment and the shame of those who perform inappropriate deeds. Struggle against your thought, and you will find assistance through the prayers of the saints, and God will have mercy on you. Do not be immature in your judgment, but be like an infant in evil, while in your mind be perfect. Brother, pay attention to yourself, and consider how you will encounter God. Amen.

LETTER 259

The same person implored the same Great Old Man, saying: "Father, pray for me because I am wretched in everything and I require much loving-kindness. Moreover, thoughts are sown in me, telling me to depart to a foreign place, and that I will be saved there. Pray that God will not allow these thoughts to dominate me." Response.

Brother, accursed is the one who has sown in your heart such thoughts—by suggesting that you transgress the commandments and depart for another place—and this is of course the devil. For he works these things inside you as if it were his right, so that after ridiculing you, he may render you a scandal for many people in order that you may bear their judgment. You are suffering this out of negligence and vainglory. Behold, you say: "If I leave for a foreign place, I will bear the dishonor there." But how can this be, when your heart is troubled even upon simply hearing that a brother said something against you, and when you would not want anyone to know that you erred? Nevertheless, together with negligence, the demons also work vainglory in you to destroy your soul completely.

Brother, be assured in the Lord that, if it were not for the hand of God and the prayers here of the saints, those genuine servants of God, you would not have been able to stay in the monastery even one full year. Yet, as a blind person who does not see, you, too, cannot see the beneficence that God has worked in you and that he continues to work through the prayers of the saints and of the blessed Abramios,[34] who told you and your brother that if you stay in this place, you would have me as your intercessor.

Brother, pay close attention to yourself, and struggle against your thoughts in order not to be negligent, not to have vainglory, not to uphold your own will in anything, and not to receive the thoughts sown within you by a claim to rights; otherwise, you will suffer a great fall. Moreover, be assured that wherever you may go, from one side of the earth to the other, you will not benefit as much as you will here. The prayer of the fathers here is to you as an anchor is to a boat. Acquire stringency and it will dispel from you boldness, which brings every evil to a person. And be carefree of all things; then you will have time for God. Die to all people; for this is exile. And retain the virtue of not reckoning yourself as anything; then you will find your thought to be undisturbed. Do not consider yourself as having done anything good; then your reward will be kept whole. And in addition to all these things, remember that you will not be in the body for long; and strive to say boldly at that hour: "I have prepared, and I have not been troubled."[35] Brother, without labor it is impossible to live; and without struggle, no one is crowned. Struggle to be saved by competing in battle, and God will help you. For: "He desires everyone to be saved and to come to the knowledge of the truth."[36] May he have mercy on you, child, that you may dedicate yourself to your work with long-suffering. For his is the mercy and the power and the glory to the ages. Amen.

34. This reference may also be to the patriarch Abraham, to whom Barsanuphius and John often refer in their *Letters* (62, 106, 187, 360, 382, 456, 457, 459, 469, and 607).
35. Ps 118.60.
36. 1 Tm 2.4.

LETTER 260

Question from the same [brother] to the same Great Old Man: "Father, what is it that you said in regard to my not being able to stay in the monastery for a [full] year? And for the Lord's sake pray for me, because while I am sleeping, the demon falls upon me to stifle me, and I require your loving-kindness." Response by Barsanuphius.

When I told you that, were it not for the prayers of the saints, you would not even have lasted a year in the monastery, I was referring to what monks are. For not all who live in a monastery are monks, but only those who do the work of a monk. As it is written: "Not everyone who says to me, 'Lord, Lord,' will enter into the kingdom of heaven, but only the one who does the will of my Father who is in heaven."[37] But again, you are troubling yourself; for you ask and do not persist in awaiting a response. Or then you may ask again and then report to others whatever I have told you, acting out of vainglory and seeking to please people; and so you are hindered from progressing rapidly. This is why the demon tempts you while you are sleeping and falls upon you in order to stifle you. And God allows this in order that you may be disciplined and in order that you may blame yourself as a monk; but you do not understand this, brother. Our work at this time is to examine our passions, as well as to weep and mourn. Furthermore, as you sit or pace around in your cell, blame yourself in all things, brother, and cast your weakness before God; he will help you and strengthen you in order that you may progress in him. Amen.

LETTER 261

Question from the same [brother] to the Other Old Man: "Father, for the Lord's sake, pray for me, I implore you, that I may be delivered from the passions of dishonor and vainglory. For the demon pollutes me in everything that I think I am doing well. And I also ask that you tell me the reason why we must perform memorials for the saints. Moreover, how does one vomit out the evil that one possesses?" [Response.]

37. Mt 7.21.

If you want to be redeemed from the passions of dishonor, then cut away from yourself the boldness toward all people, especially those toward whom you see your heart leaning with passionate desire; in this way, you will also be freed from vainglory. For vainglory is an associate of people-pleasing, while people-pleasing is an associate of boldness. And boldness is the mother of all passions.[38] One who performs memorials of the saints without vainglory, considering that one is doing this with [the grace of] God and not through one's own [power], becomes an associate of these saints and receives the reward from their Master. Concern for the soul's salvation and love for God cause one to vomit any evil that one possesses and sincerely to repent.

Listen, child, perceive what is unseen by means of what is seen. When something in your body is in pain, then you abstain from whatever harms you. So when your soul hurts, should you not battle to abstain likewise? There is need of great effort and toil, as the Apostle says: "I punish my body and enslave it."[39] Do your best, then, and God will help you through the prayers of your fathers. For he thirsts to see our salvation, as being the one who swore to himself "not to desire the death of a sinner but rather the return and life"[40] of that person. Much power arises from this place through the prayers of the genuine servants of God for us all. I believe that the Lord will not embarrass them. Contribute like that widow your own two copper coins, and you will make him rejoice as she did.[41] And fasten your boat to the ship of your fathers, and they will lead you toward Jesus, who alone can grant you humility, strength, prudence, and "the crown of rejoicing."[42] Amen.

LETTER 262

Question from the same [brother] to the Great Old Man: "Since I am younger and foolish, and have also assumed duties beyond me, I implore you, father, to ask that I may receive prudence from God, so that I may offer whatever is necessary, and speak or

---

38. Cf. *Sayings*, Agathon 1. The *Sayings* of Abba Agathon profoundly influenced the Gaza elders through Isaiah of Scetis, Barsanuphius and John, and Dorotheus of Gaza.

39. 1 Cor 9.27.   40. Ezek 18.23.
41. Cf. Mk 12.42.   42. Sir 1.11.

be silent whenever I should. And in anything that I doubt, pray that I may invoke God and your prayers, so that I may find the necessary support and so that I may not be deceived." Response by Barsanuphius.

It is a great joy for someone to ask something according to godly fear; for that person is assured that his request will be fulfilled. But listen, brother: if you are requesting seed for your field, then carefully cultivate it in order to receive the seed. For in regard to the beautiful and cultivated soil, it is said that it yielded one hundredfold.[43] I shall certainly not hinder my strength, but I will do my best. I shall not hinder it for the sake of God's commandment. I confess my weakness, however, that I cannot grant you this; for I am unworthy. Yet, if you believe, you will receive "according to your faith"[44] not merely this, but also anything else that you may need. For God knows what you need even before you ask him.[45] So do not hesitate, and I believe that God will respond, not for my sake but for the sake of your faith. Above all, humble yourself before God; "for he gives his grace to the humble."[46] In Christ Jesus our Lord, to whom be the glory. Amen.

LETTER 263

The same person asked the Other Old Man: "Father, how should I interpret the meaning of this response from the [Great] Old Man?" Response by John.

If you wish to learn how to interpret the meaning of the [Great] Old Man's response, this is it: Whenever you wish to speak or do something, remember the name of the [Great] Old Man, and God will sow in your heart whatever is necessary for you to do or however it is that you should speak; but always do so with humility in order that you do not lose this grace.

LETTER 264

Question from the same person to the Great Old Man: "Father, since you took mercy on my weakness and granted that, in what-

43. Cf. Mk 4.8.
45. Cf. Mt 6.8.
44. Cf. Mt 9.29.
46. Prv 3.34.

ever I say and do, I may invoke the name of God and your own prayers, then I am faring well and hastening to practice or proclaim his will in everything. On occasion, however, it happens that I become forgetful out of negligence. I implore you to ask on my behalf for vigilance from God; do not allow me to wander according to my will. Further, if I still have doubts about doing or not doing something, even after invoking God or your own prayers in some matter, can you tell me what I should do in the end? Or again, if it happens that I am asked something and, before I actually invoke God or think of what I should say, the person asking seeks a response immediately, taking me by surprise in this way, what should I do? And in regard to my eyes, I implore you to pray that I might control them; for they wander a lot." Response by Barsanuphius.

If someone should receive an order or advice or response from the fathers about anything, and that person forgets it out of oversight or negligence, knowing, however, that this is wrong, then let that person repent before God, and God will show forgiveness. So why did you write only about vigilance, brother? I pray that God grants you every good gift, and that he may stay with you to the age. If it so happens that you are doing something, while invoking God and the prayers of the saints, and you continue to have doubts, then do the task anyway; for it is God's will, since you prayed to him beforehand. As for when you are taken by surprise to respond to a question, nothing is more acute than the intellect. Address your intellect to God, and he will grant you the answer without your being disturbed. Humility protects the eyes from wandering, as well as the entire person from every evil. It is one of the great gifts, of which I have spoken to you; I shall pray that you receive it, so long as you also do your best. Pay attention to yourself, and it is not simply the saints but God himself who will give you a hand and show his mercy on you.

LETTER 265

Question from the same person to the same Great Old Man: "Compassionate father, I implore you, for you see the blindness of my soul. Again I ask that you request for me the illumination of my heart, that I may be able to discern the proper thought from that which is concealing something crooked; for I am afraid to trust it. I know—although often I do not see—that I sometimes give something to someone with passion. And I have tested my thought, to see whether it has the same pleasure when the same thing is offered through another person, without [the recipient] knowing that it actually came from me; yet it was not as pleasurable for me. And again, it happens that I do not notice that I am beginning to do or say something with passion, but afterward, while I am doing or saying this, my thought begins to take pleasure in it. What should I do, wretched as I am? Then, there is another way in which this matter afflicts me, or rather my ambitious heart is afflicted. For it happens that some people will be talking to me about something, and before they actually finish speaking, my thought gives consent and takes pleasure, believing that it is wise. I ask you, father, to pray that I may receive the strength to keep silent. For I am surprised how it is that my heart knows that these things are worth nothing but that they only empty a person of everything good, and yet it still takes pleasure in them." Response by Barsanuphius.

It is not possible for anyone to discern the thoughts without the heart laboring. Therefore, I pray that God may grant you this. Your heart will of course labor a little, but God will grant it to you. In fact, it is the same with all these things. When God grants you this gift, you will always be able to discern one thought from another through his Spirit, through the prayers of the saints, and through the labor of your heart. When you see that a particular matter gives rise to some concept within you, then be silent, just as you heard from my genuine son according to God,[47] to whom you should listen in regard to your every thought. For he is not speaking to you of his own accord, but is only saying whatever God grants him for everyone's benefit. And may God protect you, granting you the strength to keep silent in knowledge and the grace to know when it is necessary for you to speak without passion. For your heart does not fully know that these passions empty a person; otherwise, it would not allow you to take pleasure in them.

47. Barsanuphius is referring here to John the Prophet, the Other Old Man. See also *Letters* 224 and 305.

LETTER 266

Question from the same person to the same Great Old Man: "The compassion of the mercy that you are showing toward me, the sinner, once more emboldens me to bother you again. Therefore, illumine me as to how my heart can labor to receive discernment. And with regard to unceasing remembrance, if my heart is worthy of such a practice, demonstrate this for me, my lord, and strengthen me in this. For my thought fears that I may not be able to maintain this. This is why I am asking whether this matter is truly beneficial to me; so show me, master. For I believe that, even as your word leaves your mouth, it creates power in my heart." Response by Barsanuphius.

Labor of the heart implies praying to God not to allow you to be deceived or to wander in your own will; and from this, you will come to discernment. As for unceasing remembrance or conversing freely with God, make a start and do not be afraid. The Lord will both encourage and empower you; but sow in hope so that you may reap without being worn out. Blessed is the God who blesses you to make a start, who will also grant you the strength to maintain this according to your measure.

LETTER 267

Question from the same brother to the same Old Man: "In the past, a small warmth would often come to me for a few days, and then it would go away; and now, when I eagerly preserve the re-membrance for up to an hour—indeed, even that one hour I maintain with great effort—my thought makes me afraid that I might again lose it, as in the past the small warmth would desert me after a few days; and I fear that I might lose my soul entirely. So I ask you, good father, not to abandon me; but tell me what it is that causes this remembrance and warmth to flee. More-over, ask for my sake that I may receive protection of my senses; for I am held captive in many ways on their account, especial-ly when my heart desires some occasion. Indeed, of its own, it aims at springing forth passionate or foolish memories, or else other thoughts that are out of place. This is why I implore you, valiant father in the Lord, grant vigilance to your servant, that I may understand the thoughts that enter my heart and what I must do with them in order that they may not separate me from your blessing. Moreover, show me this as well: If I say or do something, and am protected by God from sinning in this—at least when this appears to me to be the case—am I then obliged to thank God when I have finished? And does such a thing lead to love of God? Or should I not accept at all the fact that I have avoided sin, but rather examine and find some fault in what was done or said, and thus seek forgiveness for it?" Response by Barsanuphius.

Labor to receive these gifts with toil of heart, and God will grant them to you continually; I am referring to the warmth and the prayer. For forgetfulness makes them flee, while this forgetfulness is caused by negligence. As for the protection of your senses, every gift is granted with toil of heart. The gift of vigilance does not allow thoughts to enter; but if they do enter, it does not allow them to cause any damage. May God grant you to be vigilant and alert. For the words "give thanks in all circumstances"[48] constitute an order, especially in the matter that you indicated to me. Furthermore, searching your faults in order to seek forgiveness is also very beneficial.

LETTER 268

Question from the same person to the same Old Man: "Holy father, I implore you to ask for me to receive strength from God because whatever I determine for myself when I am alone, I lose it when I come to be with other brothers. And I am afraid that I may become accustomed only to sinning and repenting, but not to correcting myself. In this way, I shall stay with my sins until my death. For I know that the afflictions of the passions are beneficial to me inasmuch as they swiftly crush the hardness of my soul. And let me not, the fool that I am, wish to be relieved of these from now. Father, what I am asking through your prayers, however, is whether it is beneficial for me not to be conquered continually and not to suffer affliction of the heart from this." Response.

No one ever says to another person: "I bear your concern," and then remains without concern; for in this way, one is found

---

48. 1 Thes 5.18.

to be an impostor. At the same time, however, the brother whose burden is being held must also contribute some small effort and do his best with vigilance in order to keep the commandments of his fathers. And if he should fall once, then he should rise up again. Moreover, I trust in God that, even if he is caught once and strives again to rise up, then he will not become accustomed [to falling] at all, nor will he be negligent. Instead, God will quickly bring him to the level of the zealous ones and will not take his soul until he leads him to a noble measure, namely, to maturity. So do not relax, but while you yet have time before you, work, be humble, obey, submit, and God will be at your side. For he grants grace to the humble and resists the proud.[49] Say continually: "Jesus, help me"; and he shall help you. May God liberate your soul from the passions of dishonor, child.

LETTER 269

Question from the same person to the same Old Man: "I venerate you, compassionate father and healer of my ailing soul. Woe to me! What have you recommended to me, and toward what have you attracted me? And where am I, bound up as I am by evil habit? Even if I am freed up a little, once again I return to the same routine. And if I were not ashamed before the goodness of God and your own compassion—for I know how many labors it took for him to lead me before your feet—I would actually have come to despair. Indeed, when I am protected by your prayers, I spend my time in peace. But when I have been divested of these, even a little, so that my own will begins to show, then I am immediately overcome. As I am sitting in my cell in the morning, a certain matter arises and so I leave [in order to attend to it]. Nevertheless, after dealing with it, I do not find a way to return once more [to my cell]; instead, the enemy piles up one excuse after another, which could always be resolved without me, until I am wounded and thus return late to my cell, feeling deep disgust, darkness, and despondency, and not knowing what to do. For this reason, holy father, here I am before your heart, which sees all things; treat me according to your compassion, as you wish and as you know. For of course, I do not know what to say about you; but please forgive me for God's sake." Response.

49. Cf. Prv 3.34.

Brother, it is not possible to fall into despair from these things. For the captain of a ship that is being beaten by waves does not despair about his own safety or about the safety of those who are with him. Instead, he governs the ship better, until he brings it into a harbor. In the same way, you also find that you have been captured and have been distracted in something; so bring yourself back to the start of the road, saying with the prophet: "And I said: 'I have now made a beginning,'"[50] and so forth. Test things out in order to see whether they can be done by the brothers or whether they ought to be done by you. And guard your intellect with prudence. Behold, you have not strayed from the way. For godly concern is also spiritual work, accomplished and achieved for the salvation of the soul. And do your best to see that unimportant matters do not take you out of your cell prematurely; for this is a strategy of the demons. Pay attention to yourself prudently, and God will help you through the prayers of the saints. Amen.

LETTER 270

Request from the same [brother] to the same Great Old Man to bear his sins. Response.

Brother, although you are asking of me something that is beyond me, nevertheless I shall show you the limits of love, namely, that it forces itself to move even beyond its own limits. Behold, I admire you as a person, and I assume responsibility for you and support you. But on one condition, that you also bear the keeping of my words and commandments; for these bring you salvation. In this way, you shall live without reproach.

LETTER 271

Question from the same person to the same Great Old Man in regard to the commandments that he described; and a request to be strengthened in order to keep these. Response.

50. Ps 76.11.

The one who strengthened our fathers will also strengthen your love, brother, giving you spiritual prudence to know what to do in every situation. Therefore, you should keep your tongue from idle talk and your stomach from pleasure, refrain from irritating your neighbor, stay modest, do not reckon yourself as anything, love everyone, and always have God in your intellect, remembering the time when you will appear before God's face. Keep these things, and your soil will yield one hundredfold[51] in terms of fruits for God, to whom be the glory to the ages. Amen.

LETTER 272

Question from the same person to the same Great Old Man: "Father, what does it mean not to reckon oneself as anything?"[52]

Brother, not reckoning oneself as anything means not equating oneself with anyone and not saying in regard to any good deed that you have also achieved this.

LETTER 273

Request from the same [brother] to the same Old Man in regard to transgressing the divine commandments he was given, that he might cooperate in his repentance. And a question about how one should repent, and whether when a transgression occurs the covenant is invalidated. Response.

In the name of the Lord, may it be given you according to your request. Therefore, guard yourself from feeling proud, so that you do not lose everything. And when you transgress a commandment, hasten to repentance. Do not disdain the commandments, like someone who ignores an injury because of the padding on the wound, so that you may not end up worse. Since you are holding my hand, the covenant I have given you certainly stands. Otherwise, how would God have mercy on you in order for you to hear and adhere to my commandments in Christ? Amen.

---

51. Cf. Mk 4.8.
52. Dorotheus of Gaza develops this theme in his *Spiritual Works, Letter* 2.

LETTER 274

Request for a prayer from the same [brother] to the same Great Old Man, that he might not be separated from his protection, even in the age to come. Response.

Child, if only you understood my words[53] to you, then you would know that I have given you a pledge for the salvation of your soul. Do not think that I am being unreasonable; nor do I want to separate you from my genuine children who are being saved, or from the protection of God. You, too, however, should strive not to be separated from such a life. For the Apostle did not separate anyone, but said: "If the unbelieving partner separates, let it be so."[54] May these words never be fulfilled in your case. Yet I have spoken these words to you for your protection, so that you may strive not to fall from this expectation and hope. So be strong in the Lord, who told his disciples that they would receive strength from above.[55]

LETTER 275

Question from the same [brother] to the Other Old Man: "If one considers oneself to be beneath all creatures,[56] but one's actions are not in conformity with this, then what happens?" Response by John.

So long as the deed does not match the conscience, then it is not genuine but just a mocking [illusion] of the demons.

LETTER 276

Question from the same person to the same Old Man: "Father, it is not that I consider myself to be beneath all creatures; however, when I examine my conscience, I find myself responsible and obliged to be beneath all creatures. Is this, then, also a mocking [illusion] of the demons?" Response.

53. Using the variant reading, ῥήσεις, rather than τηρήσεις. See *SC* 450, 259.

54. 1 Cor 7.15.

55. Cf. Lk 24.49.

56. See *Sayings*, Poemen 97.

Brother, now you have begun to walk in the right way; for this is the truth. May God lead you to that measure of considering yourself to be beneath all creatures. Be well in the Lord.

Question from the same person to the same Old Man: "Which is the way to salvation? Is it through labor, or through humility? And tell me about forgetfulness." Response by John.

Brother, true labor does not come without humility. For labor of itself is in vain. It is said: "Consider my humiliation and my affliction, and forgive all my sins."[57] One who has these will reach salvation quickly. Moreover, one who has humility with disregard of oneself has reached the same point, because disregard of oneself is equivalent to labor. Now, someone who has only humility itself will certainly enter, but more slowly. And if someone wants to possess genuine humility, that person should not reckon himself as being anything; for this is true humility.

One who receives the fire that the Lord came to cast upon the earth[58] does not know forgetfulness and captivity, since that person always perceives this fire. Take the example of material fire. If a person is breathing his last[59] and fire approaches, that person will immediately feel pain. In fact, no matter where a person is held captive, if a burning coal falls on him, then that person will not stay there even for a moment. Fire, brother, is not quenched; otherwise, it is not fire. Therefore, if you want to be rid of forgetfulness and captivity, there is no other way to do this except by acquiring for yourself the spiritual fire. For those things are consumed by its warmth. And one acquires this fire through desire for God. Brother, unless your heart labors in everything in search for the Lord, you cannot progress. If you spend time on these matters, then you will acquire them. For it is said: "Be still,"[60] and so on. May the Lord grant you to understand these things and labor in them.

57. Ps 24.18.
58. Cf. Lk 12.49.
59. Cf. *Sayings*, Poemen 123.
60. Ps 45.11.

Question from the same [brother] to the same [Old Man]: "Father, what is humility? And what is disregard of oneself? What is contrition of heart? And does one acquire humility by disregarding oneself in the heart? Or is it necessary also to have external injury and insolence from people? And must someone who feels humble also speak humbly and look to achieve humble things?" Response.

Humility means not reckoning oneself as anything in every situation and cutting off one's own will in everything and calmly enduring whatever occurs externally. This is true humility, in which there is no room for vainglory. The person who feels humble does not need to seek to speak humbly; rather, it is enough for that person to say: "Forgive me, and pray for me." Nor is it necessary for that person to seek after humble matters for oneself. For both of the above create vainglory and do not allow one to make progress. Nevertheless, when one receives an order and does not contradict it, then one is certainly led to progress.

There are two kinds of disregard of oneself: one derives from within the heart, and the other arises from injuries received from the outside. The second is greater, namely, the one that comes from the outside. For the one that comes from the heart requires less labor than the one that comes from other people, because the latter creates more pain in the heart. Guarding one's own heart is contrition of heart.

Question from the same [brother] to the same Old Man: "If a person receives praise from someone, should that person respond in a modest way?" Response.

Silence is of even greater benefit. For if one responds, it is as if one accepts the praise;[61] and this is vainglory. The same goes for the response, which may appear modest to that person; this,

---

61. Cf. *Sayings*, Poemen 55.

too, is vainglory. For what one seems to be saying about oneself, if it were heard from someone else, would be intolerable.

LETTER 280

Question from the same [brother] to the same [Old Man]: "It sometimes happens, however, that the other person thinks that by keeping silent, one is accepting the praise, and so that person is scandalized. What, then, should one do?" Response by John.

In regard to things unseen, the struggling monk should allow God to reassure the listener. For how does that monk even know whether the other person has not been edified rather by his silence, by the fact that he did not accept the praise, instead of being scandalized? If the other person reveals this, then one ought with humility to inform that person, saying: "Forgive me, brother; for I recognize no good in myself, and this is why I found nothing to say in response to you. Nevertheless, for the Lord's sake, pray for me."

LETTER 281

Question from the same brother to the same Old Man: "It sometimes happens that a person who is indeed a sinner will speak the truth in humility and not in vainglory. Should this person also not respond [in a similar circumstance]?" Response by John.

This person, too, should not respond. For even if this person is for a while speaking in humility, yet the one listening will regard that person as being humble, and so the former once again bears the burden. Indeed, the Lord said: "Woe to you, when all speak well of you."[62] He is referring here to sinners, who are praised but do not have corresponding deeds.

LETTER 282

Question from the same person to the same [Old Man]: "So how is it that we find some guileless people responding in modesty when they are praised?" Response.

---

62. Lk 6.26.

The fathers reached that measure of which the Lord spoke: "When you have done all these things, say, 'we are worthless slaves.'"[63] And, truly, since they consider themselves in this way, they respond according to what they are. Moreover, if they happen to hear these same things from someone else, they are not annoyed, but they even bless that person as speaking the truth.

LETTER 283

Question from the same [brother] to the same [Old Man]: "If one receives an act of kindness from another person and expresses exceeding gratitude by enumerating the kindnesses, should the benefactor not respond in this case?" Response.

Silence is good in every case. Nevertheless, in order not to appear that one is rejecting the thanks, the benefactor should say with humility: "Forgive me, Abba, and for the Lord's sake pray for me," believing in his heart that he did not do anything. For it is the Lord who is the benefactor of us all. Moreover, one should also pray to God not to be judged even for these words.

LETTER 284

Question from the same person to the same Old Man: "Father, pray for me to be delivered from the tongue and from boldness and from the stomach." Response.

In just the same way that you asked me to pray for you with regard to the tongue and boldness and the stomach, you also should do your best to abstain from these. For without labor of heart, vigilance, and mourning, these cannot be controlled. Remember that "the prayer of the righteous is powerful and effective."[64] It is humility that is able to dominate all the passions, and it is through labor that this humility is acquired. Brother, may God grant you strength with discernment and fear of God.

LETTER 285

Question from the same [brother] to the same [Old Man]: "If it is through mourning that one acquires these, as you have

63. Lk 17.10.   64. Jas 5.16.

said, then how can I guard this mourning when I go in and out among people, always attending to chores and serving others? Furthermore, does mourning of heart exist without tears?" Response by John.

It is not tears that cause mourning, but rather mourning that causes tears. If one who is among the people cuts off one's own will and does not pay attention to the faults of others, then that person can acquire mourning. For it is from this mourning that the thoughts are gathered; moreover, when they are gathered, they, too, give birth to godly sorrow, and sorrow then gives rise to tears.

LETTER 286

Question from the same [brother] to the same [Old Man]: "Since I express my words to the abbot, I feel that some other brothers are afflicted by this. What should I do then? Am I perhaps harming myself by staying here? And does this thought ridicule me, that I am supposedly paying attention to my purpose? Moreover, if my purpose, through your protection, is not according to my passion, then am I perhaps able to accomplish the entire task without harm? For I am weak and do not hate my passions. This is why I am asking, to see if you think this is correct, namely, not to seek mediation every time that I am outside the infirmary, in case their envy increases and I am crushed by this matter. Nonetheless, if I am benefiting from this, then my soul is in your hands; simply tell me what you order, father." Response.

If you are speaking with purity of heart and for your own benefit, without passion and vainglory, then ignore what other people are saying. Strive hard, with the assistance also of the prayers of the saints, until you arrive without harm at the completion of the entire matter. Mediation with your abbot without passion is a good thing, as I have already told you; for not all have the opportunity to speak with the abbot; nor is it beneficial for all to do so. If you speak according to God, then you are neither speaking nor doing any good on your own, but it is God who is in all things; and the good that comes from God does not give rise to envy. Even if it seems so for a while, yet it is swiftly quenched. The souls of us all are in the hands of God, and he is the one who protects us and strengthens us to do whatever is for our benefit.

LETTER 287

Question from the same [brother] to the same [Old Man]: "If I feel that some matter is beneficial for certain brothers, should I tell them even if I am not asked to speak? In addition, if one of these happens to be my superior or a priest, should I mention it to the abbot or should I keep silent? And then, if I happen to be asked, what should I say? Moreover, if it is indeed beneficial for me to speak of my own accord, how should I speak? For I wish to honor my monastic habit and speak neither with supposed humility nor with the authority of a teacher. For God's sake, forgive me." Response.

The fathers said that: "One who speaks for God is doing a good thing; and one who is silent for God is also doing a good thing."[65] This saying of the fathers may be interpreted in the following way. As I have told you, one who speaks without passion is doing a good thing; for that person is speaking for the sake of God. And one who sees that one is about to speak with passion and therefore keeps silent, is also doing a good thing; for that person is keeping silent for God. If you are about to say something according to God, do not be concerned about what you will say, because then you are abolishing the commandment.[66] Rather, cast the matter before God, and he will grant to your mouth what it is that you should say for the benefit of all. God knows how to gird us weak ones with strength, and he will strengthen you also, brother.

LETTER 288

Question from the same [brother] to the same [Old Man]: "Should I cut off my will and conform to the abbot only in matters which are good or even moderate, or else also in matters

65. *Sayings*, Poemen 147.
66. Cf. Mt 10.19.

where it appears that God's commandment is almost being transgressed? And if his order happens to be beyond my ability, should I decline it, so that I am not overcome by sorrow and turmoil? Moreover, what happens when someone asks me to mediate in some matter of his with the abbot, but I refrain so that it will not bring me honor, because I would be reckoning myself as being entirely something?" Response.

Brother, one who wishes to be a monk should not hold onto his own will at all in anything. Christ taught us this when he said: "I have come into the world not to do my own will."[67] For one who wants to do one thing and be relieved of another is either trying to display oneself as being more discerning than the one who gave the order, or else is being ridiculed by the demons. So then you must obey in everything, even if the matter appears to you to be sinful. Indeed, your abbot who gave you the order will bear the judgment himself, since he is responsible for giving account on your behalf.[68] If the order seems to be too heavy for you, then ask him about it and leave the matter to his discretion. If those who gave you the order are brothers, and you see that the matter will bring you harm or else is beyond your ability, again ask your abbot and do whatever he tells you. Furthermore, if you want to discern matters yourself, you will attract afflictions upon yourself. Confide everything to your abbot and do whatever he discerns. For he knows what he must do and how he must care for your soul. Then you may rest, believing that whatever he tells you is according to God and will bring you neither sorrow nor turmoil. "For every good tree bears good fruit."[69]

As for asking your abbot about some [of the other brothers], if this happens to be necessary, then do it as if fulfilling a commandment which you have heard and must carry out. For if your abbot asks you to sit at the entrance-gate and tells you: "Report to me about every movement," will you decide on your own what to do, or will you carry out the order of your abbot? So if your abbot tells you to report to him or not [about your brothers], you hold no responsibility in this regard.

67. Jn 6.38.
69. Mt 7.17.

68. Cf. Heb 13.17.

LETTER 289

Question from the same [brother] to the same [Old Man]: "If a brother asks me about some word or matter and I happen to know the answer, should I respond or not? And if I am not asked anything, but happen to notice something not being done correctly, should I mention it to the one concerned or not?" Response.

All the words of your question have one essential response alone: Guard yourself in order not to speak with vainglory but with humility and fear of God. And in regard to all that you have asked, speak and suggest when necessary—at least within your monastic community but not elsewhere—so that you may not appear to be the teacher; for those in a monastic community resemble one body.[70] If you happen to be elsewhere, do not say anything of your own accord. But if you are asked, speak with humility. God will grant you prudence, brother.

LETTER 290

Question from the same person to the same [Old Man]: "Since you have declared to me that I should speak with humility, if I am asked about something or happen to see something, what does it mean when you say 'with humility'? And if I notice my heart taking pleasure in the vainglory of speaking, or if I do not take pleasure at that time but foresee that this will come upon me later, should I be silent or not?" Response.

Saying something with humility means not speaking as a teacher, but as one who has learned from the abbot or the fathers. If it is beneficial to speak to your brother and the vainglory of pleasure tempts you, then pay attention to yourself because it may wish to prevent you from benefiting your brother; and if you listen to this vainglory, your brother will never benefit from you. Instead, reprimand this vainglory and despise it; moreover, after speaking, repent to God, saying: "Forgive me; for I have spoken in vainglory." The same applies to your second question.

70. Cf. Basil, *Longer Rules* 7, PG 31.929.

LETTER 291

Question from the same [brother] to the same [Old Man]: "Father, how is it that you have allowed me to speak, even before being asked, whenever I see something? For the fathers say that we should not speak without being asked.[71] Indeed, Abba Nisteros was admired for this, when he said in the monastery: 'The donkey and I are one.'[72] Also tell me, father, what does it mean to pay attention to the thoughts, and should one do this at a regular time, and when?" Response by John.

Brother, the old men speak according to the measure of those who listen. So there is a time and a measure when someone should serve others, and at that time one must display deeds of service. Moreover, there is also a time when the same person reaches the point of being served by others, and the measures of this are again different. Indeed, the perfect things are spoken for the perfect ones; the others apply to those who are still under the law. For they are still being tested by pedagogues.[73] But when you are dead unto the world,[74] as Abba Nisteros was, you can say: "I am a donkey." Do not feel proud, because this is harmful. The fathers assigned certain times to pay attention to the thoughts, like saying to ourselves each morning: "Give account to yourself of how you spent the night, and at night of how you spent the day."[75] And in between, whenever your thought feels heavy, be attentive.

LETTER 292

Question from the same person to the same Old Man: "If one of the elders, who is superior to me, asks me about something, should I tell him what I think is beneficial?" Response by John.

Yours is to say nothing at all; for you do not know the will of God, as to whether something is beneficial. But if any such person asks you, say: "Forgive me; for I, too, do not know."

---

71. *Sayings*, Euprepios 7 and Poemen 45. See also Nau 468.
72. *Sayings*, Nisteros the Cenobite 2.
73. Cf. Gal 3.23–24.   74. Cf. Col 2.20; Gal 6.14.
75. *Sayings*, Nisteros 5.

Question from the same [brother] to the same [Old Man]: "If a
brother does something that is not very significant, but I am afflicted by this act on account of my own will, what should I do?
Should I keep silent and not give rest to my heart, or should I
speak to him with love and not remain troubled? And if the matter afflicts others, but not me, should I speak for the sake of the
others? Or would this appear as if I have just taken on a cause?"
Response by John.

If it is a matter that is not sinful but insignificant, and you
speak simply in order to give rest to your heart, then it is to
your defeat. For you were not able to endure it as a result of
your weakness. Just blame yourself and be silent. If, however,
the matter afflicts others, then tell your abbot; and whether he
speaks or tells you to speak, you will be carefree.

Question from the same [brother] to the same [Old Man]: "If I
speak to the abbot for the sake of the others, I suspect that the
brother will be troubled; so what should I do? Moreover, if this
person afflicts both others and me, should I speak for the sake
of the others, or should I keep silent in order not to satisfy myself? If I suspect that he will not be grieved, should I also speak
for myself, or should I force myself not to do this?" Response by
John.

So far as the turmoil of the brother is concerned, if you speak
to the abbot, then you have nothing to worry about. Whenever
it is necessary to speak for the sake of others, and you are worried about it, then speak for them. As for yourself, only force
yourself not to speak.

Question from the same [brother] to the same [Old Man]: "But
my thought tells me that if my brother is troubled against me, he
will become my enemy, thinking that I have slandered him to the
abbot." Response by John.

This thought of yours is wicked; for it wants to prevent you from correcting your brother. Therefore, do not prevent yourself from speaking, but do so according to God. Indeed, the sick who are being healed will even speak against their doctors; yet the latter do not care, knowing that these will thank them afterward.

LETTER 296

Question from the same [brother] to the same [Old Man]: "If I look at my thought and notice that it is not for the brother's benefit that I wish to speak [to the abbot], but in fact with the purpose of slandering him, should I still speak or should I keep silent?" Response by John.

Advise your thought to speak only according to God and not for the sake of slander. And if your thought is conquered by criticism, even so speak to your abbot and confess to him your criticism in order that both of you may be healed—the one who was at fault and the one who was critical alike.

LETTER 297

Question from the same person to the same [Old Man]: "If my thought does not allow me to confess to the abbot that I am speaking to him with the purpose of slandering the brother, what should I do? Should I speak or not?" Response.

Do not say anything to him, and the Lord will take care of it. For it is not necessary for you to speak if it harms your soul. God will take care of the brother's correction as he wills.

LETTER 298

Question from the same [brother] to the same [Old Man]: "Since it sometimes happens that I do something which I consider to be reasonable, but someone else corrects me in this, whatever I say in my defense I end up saying with vainglory. So what should I say?" Response.

If it is not necessary to offer a defense, then be silent. If, however, the brother is concerned about the matter, then resist your vainglory and heal him.

LETTER 299

Question from the same person to the same [Old Man]: "If I do something which again is not very significant, but know that if my brother finds me doing this, he will be scandalized by me, I struggle against the temptation of vainglory to keep this concealed; for I am ashamed that he will see me. So should I not conceal it for the sake of the vainglory, or should I conceal it for the sake of the scandal? And if I do not know for certain whether he is scandalized, but only suspect this, what should I do?" Response by John.

If your heart judges you unfavorably, because your brother is scandalized, then cover it up and do not give him occasion for thought. If, however, you do not know this for certain, but only suspect it, then do not worry about it.

LETTER 300

Question from the same brother to the same Old Man: "If I say something that wounds someone, but he has not understood my words, should I ask for forgiveness from him, or should I be silent and not give him occasion for thought?" Response by John.

If your brother does not understand that you have wounded him, then be silent and you will not trouble him. Nevertheless, make every effort to seek repentance from God for his sake.

LETTER 301

Question from the same person to the same Old Man. "If someone sees a brother falling into sin and informs the abbot, how should that brother behave toward the one who informed the abbot about him?" Response by John.

If the brother is faithful and lives according to God, then if someone has spoken against him out of hatred, he should think that the one who informed the abbot did so for his benefit. Then, the saying is fulfilled in him: "The good person out of the good treasure of the heart produces good."[76] When the brother

76. Lk 6.45.

is filled with such thoughts, he should in fact love that person rather than hate him. Someone who behaves in this way is always found to make godly progress.

LETTER 302

Question from the same person to the same [Old Man]: "Since I perceive that, when I make a prostration before certain people, I blush a little out of vainglory, should I avoid making such prostrations before those people, or should I simply do whatever comes naturally?" Response by John.

Do not deliberately seek to make prostrations before certain people or privately; simply do whatever comes naturally.

LETTER 303

Question from the same [brother] to the same [Old Man]: "Should I also make prostrations before those who are younger than I? Or should I simply ask forgiveness by word, so that I may not be tempted by vainglory in doing the opposite?" Response by John.

There are certain people, who are great and honorable, yet who are indebted to others who are nothing and considered the least. Indeed, the former are obliged to pay their debt, without any sense of vainglory; for they owe it to the latter. The same applies to you. You should make a prostration before any person to whom you are indebted, whether it happens to be someone who is your inferior or superior, without any sense of vainglory, knowing that you are indebted to that person.

LETTER 304

Question from the same [brother] to the same [Old Man]: "If a passionate thought enters my heart, how should I reject it? By contradicting it? By rebuking it, in order to become angry against it? Or by hastening toward God and casting my weakness before him?" Response by John.

Brother, the passions are afflictions. And the Lord did not distinguish between them, but rather said: "Call upon me in the day of your affliction; I shall deliver you, and you shall glorify me."[77] Therefore, in the case of every passion, there is nothing more beneficial than to invoke the name of God. Contradicting a passion does not belong to everyone, but only to those who are strong according to God, who are able to subdue the demons.[78] For if someone who is not strong contradicts them, then the demons ridicule that person for being inferior to them and yet still trying to contradict them.

Similarly, rebuking the passions belongs to the great and powerful ones. Whom among the saints will you find rebuking the devil like the archangel Michael?[79] Indeed, he had the power to do so. Those of us who are weak can only take refuge in the name of Jesus. For according to Scripture, the passions are the demons, and [this is how] they are cast out.[80] What more do you want? God will strengthen you and empower you in your fear of him.

LETTER 305

Question from the same [brother] to the same [Old Man]: "Father, I ask you to give me your word that you will pray for me, just as the holy [Great] Old Man gave me his word. Furthermore, whenever I am overcome by some circumstance, my thought tells me that, since I am proud, God will not assist me to control the passion in order that I may not fall into vainglory, [supposing that] I have controlled it. Or else it tells me that if I acquire something easily, I shall also lose it easily. Or, again, it tells me that I continually hasten to receive something from God, whether for some particular reason or simply out of my own laziness. What, then, should I do?" Response by John.

If all of us are one[81]—both the [Great] Old Man in God and I with the Old Man—then I dare to say that, if he gave you his word, I, too, give you mine through him. I know that I am weak and the least; yet I cannot separate myself from the Old Man. For he is compassionate toward me so that the two of us are one. Therefore, brother, pay attention to yourself. Strive to labor in keeping the commandments. And if you are overcome

---

77. Ps 49.15.
79. Jude 9–10.
81. Cf. Jn 17.21.

78. Cf. Lk 10.20.
80. Cf. Acts 8.7 and 16.18.

by some circumstance, then neither slacken nor despair, but rise up again and God will help you. It may be that you are not able to control the passion for the reasons that you initially presented; or else, it may be that you are suffering this as a result of your laziness. In order to be liberated from both, you must cast yourself before the goodness of God, weeping in order that he might liberate you from these and from all of your passions through the prayers of the saints. Amen.

LETTER 306

Request from the same person to the same Old Man for assistance in what the Great Old Man commanded. Response by John.

Brother, in his responses to you, the [Great] Old Man left no question unanswered. Rather, he has closed your mouth on every point. For after telling you: "Keep my words and my covenant with you shall also be kept," what more do you want? Do your best in order that his covenant with you may be kept; for therein lies the inheritance of the kingdom together with the paradise of delight,[82] as well as "what no eye has seen, nor ear heard, nor the human heart conceived, what God has prepared for those who love him."[83] Therefore, you, too, ought to contribute your strength and struggle; but it is up to God to show mercy and protection and an abundance of power.[84] To him be the glory to the ages. Amen.

LETTER 307

Question from the same [brother] to the same [Old Man]: "What should I do? For I am afraid of the shame of dishonor. Moreover, if I fall into the company of certain others, I am greatly attracted and captivated by it, so that I even forget myself. When I come to myself, however, I am embarrassed to relinquish that company and to depart." Response by John.

In order for someone who is weak not to fall into such things and into vainglory, one should swiftly flee from long conversa-

---

82. Cf. Gn 2.15.
83. 1 Cor 2.9.
84. Ps 61.12.

tions and cut short such company, pretending that the abbot ordered something that must be done quickly. As for not enduring dishonor, this comes from lack of faith. Jesus became human and was dishonored; dear brother, are you perhaps superior to Jesus? This is lack of faith and demonic deceit. Anyone who wants humility, or claims that he wants it, cannot receive it unless he endures dishonor. So, then, you have heard [these words]. Do not despise them; otherwise, you shall be despised in your work.

LETTER 308

Question from the same person to the same [Old Man]: "When certain people visit the monastery, whether they happen to be secular people or spiritual fathers, my thought tells me to ask a question about the benefit of my soul or some other matter. What do you think about this?" Response by John.

Brother, one who is truly a disciple of Christ does not have any authority over oneself to do anything whatsoever of one's own accord. For even if one believes that one will benefit from the company of the visitors, one is actually transgressing the commandment that says: "Do everything with counsel."[85] What more do you want to hear than the advice of the fathers that, if some people are present and they begin speaking the word of God, then you should humbly ask your abbot: "Abba, do you want me to stay and listen, or to leave?" And calmly do whatever he tells you.[86] Even if you want to ask someone, whether it be a monk or a lay person, about something that you need, you should still inform your abbot; and if he accepts, he will personally ask whatever you want. If, on the other hand, he tells you to ask yourself, then you can ask.

LETTER 309

Question from the same person to the same [Old Man]: "If there is nothing that I wish to ask, but I simply happen to encounter

---

85. Cf. Prv 24.72, or 31.4 LXX.
86. See Abba Isaiah, *Ascetic Discourse* 3.

one of these visitors and he should ask me about something, how do you order me to behave?" Response by John.

When you encounter a visitor, your word should simply be a greeting. Afterward, say: "Pray for me; for I am leaving to fulfill some mandate." Then, leave. If he should ask you about something that you know, respond and then leave. If you do not know the answer, simply say: "I do not know," and leave.

LETTER 310

Question from the same [brother] to the same [Old Man]: "If he should find me sitting down at work and sits beside me, wishing to keep me company, what should I do then?" Response by John.

If he should find you sitting somewhere and approaches you, then receive his blessing and do the same thing. Simply tell him: "Pray for me." Even in the case where he restrains you by the arm, simply say: "Forgive me, but I have been commanded not to speak to anyone without the advice of my elder; rather, I am supposed to ask him and do whatever he tells me." If you are working and someone comes to sit beside you, find some excuse that you have been ordered to do something else, and stand up to leave.

LETTER 311

Question from the same person to the same [Old Man]: "What does Abba Isaiah mean, when he says: 'After greeting the guest, ask him how he is, and then be silent, simply sitting there beside him'?"[87] Response.

You wrote that Abba Isaiah said that one should receive a guest and, after greeting him, one should ask how he is and thereafter be silent, simply sitting there beside him. Nevertheless, this was told to an elder who was advanced both in age and in [spiritual] measure. A conscientious disciple, however, who desires to become a genuine monk will guard himself from such

87. Ibid.

conversations. For these give rise to disregard, laziness, insubordination, and terrible boldness. Some people say that John did not have time for such conversations.[88] This is what it means to be free of all cares regarding people.

Question from the same [brother] to the same [Old Man]: "My thought tells me: 'Cut off conversations immediately, and you will be free of all this.' Again it tells me: 'Cut them off a little in order not to surprise those who know you.' Tell me, then, which it is better to do." Response by John.

You ask me whether you should cut them off immediately or else little by little in order not to surprise those who know you. If you cut them off at once, you will be carefree; otherwise, you will create excuses and thoughts. By excuses, I mean: "Since he asked me first, then I should speak to him." By thoughts, I mean: "I wonder if this brother has anything against me; for he used to speak to me, and now does not." Desire this, and God will make it prosper.

Question from the same person to the same [Old Man]: "There are times when certain sick people come to the monastic community, requesting something from the hospital. The abbot has given me permission to give them what they need, and this forces me to speak with them. Could I be doing this also of my own will? Clarify this for me, father. And pray for me, that I may find rest in these matters." Response by John.

On the matter of the sick people who come and ask for something from the hospital, you are not doing anything wrong in giving[89] them what they need; for you have been ordered to do so. You should be very careful, however, not to use this as an excuse to begin a conversation with anyone or to extend the con-

---

88. *Sayings,* John the Dwarf 30. This is one of two explicit references to John the Dwarf. See also *Letter* 693.

89. Using the variant reading, δώσῃς, rather than δηλώσῃς. See *SC* 450, 307 n. 1.

versation more than is necessary, unless you need to ask him something medical or financial. Nevertheless, this, too, should be done with limits, taking care not to give any excuse to the evil will. Keep these things and you shall find rest.

LETTER 314

Question from the same person to the same [Old Man]: "My thought tells me that silence is more necessary and more beneficial to me than anything else. Is this correct?" Response by John.

Silence is nothing else than restraining one's heart from giving and taking,[90] from people-pleasing and other such actions. When the Lord rebuked the scribe by telling him about the man who fell among thieves, asking him who was his neighbor, the scribe replied: "The one who showed mercy on him."[91] Again, he said: "I desire mercy and not sacrifice."[92] Therefore, if you have heard once that mercy is greater than sacrifice, incline your heart toward mercy. For the excuse of silence brings one to arrogance before one even gains oneself, namely, before one has become blameless. Indeed, that is when one reaches stillness, when one bears the cross.[93] Therefore, if you are compassionate toward someone, you will find assistance; if you restrain yourself, supposedly to transcend such limits, then you should know that you will lose even what you have. So do not move to either one or the other extreme; but journey in the middle way, knowing what is the will of God "because the days are evil."[94]

LETTER 315

Question from the same [brother] to the same [Old Man]: "Master, make it clear to me how I can avoid the two extremes in order to journey in the middle way. Should not certain days be explicitly set aside for stillness, and other days set aside for caring for others?" Response by John.

90. Phil 4.14.
91. Lk 10.37.
92. Mt 9.13; Hos 6.6.
93. See Abba Isaiah of Scetis, *Ascetic Discourse* 13.
94. Eph 5.16.

Neither being bold in one's stillness nor despising one's stillness in times of distraction: such is truly the middle way, where
one is prevented from falling by preserving humility in stillness and vigilance in distraction, as well as by restraining one's
thought. There is no limit to the hours [of stillness that one
keeps]; how much more so is this the case with regard to the
days [of stillness]. Rather, one should bear everything that comes
one's way with thanksgiving. Moreover, one should suffer together with all those in the monastic community, thereby fulfilling
the commandment of the Apostle, namely, that if one member
is afflicted, everyone should share in the affliction[95] in order to
comfort and console that person. That is what constitutes compassion. It is a good thing to suffer with those who are ill and to
contribute to their healing. For if a doctor receives a reward in
caring for the sick, how much more so will someone who suffers
as much as possible with one's neighbor in all things? Indeed,
unless one is compassionate in all circumstances, then even that
in which one happens to be compassionate will reveal one's own
will.

LETTER 316

Question from the same [brother] to the same [Old Man]: "You
have commanded me to travel in the middle way. There are
times, however, when I find a quiet moment and have the opportunity of sitting for a while in my cell; but then I endure great
distraction from those of my friends, whether monastics or lay
persons, who are accustomed to visiting me. If I see them, I am
afflicted; if I do not wish to see them, I am obliged to remain in
my cell, and the work of the hospital becomes hindered. Would
you order me to speak with one of the brothers who are in the
hospital with me, that he might go and handle the matter when
I cannot be there? Or should I go myself? This is what I think
about on my own human authority.[96] If there is any pretense to
rights in my thought, then let God's will be done and not my
own;[97] for one's own will does not last, but only concludes with
destruction." Response by John.

95. Cf. 1 Cor 12.26.   96. Cf. 1 Cor 9.8.
97. Cf. Lk 22.42.

When a person descends to humility, that person discovers progress. Remaining in your cell only renders you useless; for you remain without affliction. When you are carefree prematurely, our enemy prepares turmoil for you rather than rest, in order to bring you to the point of saying: "I wish I had never been born!"

As for being disturbed by other people, the fathers have said: "A person may be in the throes of death and yet still be involved in the friendships of this world."[98] Therefore, you, too, should not have any give or take with such people; then they shall be estranged from you.

As for asking the brother to render some service, if you perform the service alone, you are serving yourself; if you perform the service through your brother, then it is he who receives the greater part of your work and prayer.

As for the matter of compassion, I have already told you in the previous response. So strive, if you believe the Apostle, who says: "Who is weak, and I am not weak? Who is made to stumble, and I am not indignant?"[99] With those who are tormented, we, too, should be tormented, since we, too, are one body with them.[100]

LETTER 317

Question: "Father, how can I joyfully offer something for which I am asked when I doubt whether that person needs this at all? For when I force myself to give it, my soul is found to be hard and poor."[101] Response by John.

If you learn that the person asking is doing so out of need, then give it joyfully, as if you are doing so on behalf of God. For that is what joy is about.[102] If you learn, however, that the person does not need it, then do not give it to him, but say: "I have been commanded by the abbot to give nothing to anyone who is not in need." This is not hardness. May the Lord enlighten you, brother.

---

98. *Sayings*, Poemen 123.   99. 2 Cor 11.29.
100. Cf. Heb 13.3.
101. The term ἀπίαντος has been coined by Abba John to describe the heart that is neither rich nor fat.
102. Cf. Rom 12.8.

LETTER 318

Question: "I have found, while reading the *Ascetical Works* of the holy Basil, that whatever one has and offers to another person benefits the giver rather than the receiver, according to the commandment of the Lord.[103] How, then, is it that I am unable to keep this commandment?" Response.

This passage is addressed to hermits and to those who are able to govern themselves with discernment. For one who is in a monastic community is also under a [spiritual] father and has neither the order nor the authority to do anything of one's own accord.[104]

LETTER 319

Question from the same [brother] to the same [Old Man]: "I have also found, in reading the *Ascetical Works* of the holy Basil, that it is impossible to become a disciple of the Lord if one is attached to anything of the present world or else tolerates being removed from the commandment of God[105] by anything at all, even in the slightest way. Now, my relatives owe me a small amount of money, which I wish to distribute to the poor; what should I do if they do not seem willing to give it to me?" Response by John.

Unless you cut off the fleshly mind and acquire some audacity according to God, then you shall also fall into the temptation of pleasing people. God will grant you the power to do his will in all things. Amen.

LETTER 320

Question from the same person to the same [Old Man]: "What is the non-silence of which the fathers speak? And how does one acquire this?" Response.

In my opinion, non-silence means not being silent in [manifesting] one's thoughts.[106] For anyone who is silent in regard to

---

103. Cf. Acts 20.35.
104. See *Sayings*, Nau 290.
105. Basil, *Moral Rules* 2.3, PG 31.705B.
106. *Sayings*, Poemen 101.

expressing one's thoughts remains unhealed. Non-silence is acquired by consulting one's spiritual fathers about one's thoughts. I have spoken to my brother as I think; but perhaps you understand this matter better yourself. May the Lord grant his prudence to you as well as to me, the least of his servants.

LETTER 321

Question from the same person to the same [Old Man]: "What does it mean, father, when you told me that sleep does not harm a vigilant person at all?" Response by John.

Sleep is removed from a person who guards the flock, as Jacob did.[107] Even if sleep overtakes that person a little, then such sleep resembles vigilance for another. For the fire of the burning heart[108] does not allow that person to be plunged into sleep. Rather, such a person chants Psalms and melodies with David: "Give light to my eyes, lest I sleep the sleep of death."[109] One who has reached such a measure and tasted of its sweetness understands what I mean. For such a person is not drunk with material sleep but is able to control natural sleep.

LETTER 322

Question from the same [brother]: "If someone asks me to enter his cell, or else I invite him into mine in order to pray together, and if I wish to give a hand in order to assist someone in some task, up to what point should I refuse or insist? Of course, I am referring to cases where no commandment is transgressed." Response.

If you should enter the cell of a brother, or he enter yours, and he says: "Please," then say three times: "Forgive me." If after the third time he should still persist, then do what he wants with humility. You, too, should ask of a person three times; if that person does not wish to respond, then leave the matter alone. For arguing is evil. In all cases, whether in regard to carrying something for someone or else giving a hand, entreat the

---

107. Cf. Gn 30.31–32.   108. Ps 38.4.
109. Ps 12.4.

person three times; and if he does wish to respond, then calmly stop and do not afflict him. This, too, is the genuine way of
God;[110] pay attention to yourself, so that you may labor without
hypocrisy in a pure heart.[111] God will grant you a hand of assistance through his grace. Amen.

LETTER 323

Question from the same [brother] to the same [Old Man]: "If it
is mealtime and I am offered my portion but do not need to eat
anything, do you command me to accept it in order not to appear that I am refusing it for the sake of abstinence, and then
offer it to those who are in need in the hospital? Or should I not
do this either?" Response by John.

If you need to eat anything at mealtimes, brother, then accept the food. If not, then do not accept it; otherwise, it will give
rise to vainglory within you.

LETTER 324

Question: "Sometimes, when I perform an act of charity among
the brothers, the temptation of vainglory follows me. Is it good,
then, to do things secretly through the abbot or to do things on
my own? For in this way, I am disciplining myself. Yet, father, how
can one be freed from this vainglory? Indeed, it is sown within a
person from the right as well as from the left." Response.

You must pay close attention to both ways of acting because
they provide occasion for vainglory. Nevertheless, doing something through the abbot is always a lesser wrong because then,
your heart only has to account for itself, whereas doing something alone always brings a double warfare, namely, not only
from the heart but also from other people. Being liberated
from glory and vainglory belongs to one who has left one's old
self.[112] May the Lord bestow this freedom upon you in Christ.
Amen.

110. Cf. Mt 22.16.
111. Cf. 1 Tm 1.5.
112. Cf. Col 3.9.

LETTER 325

Question: "When I close my eyes during the services, I am able to concentrate my thoughts. Is this a good thing? Or do I seem to be doing something strange before those brothers who are present and perhaps scandalizing them?" Response by John.

If indeed, when you close your eyes during the services, your thoughts are concentrated on God, then do not consider anyone, even if, as you say, you feel that you seem to be doing something strange before those brothers who are present.

LETTER 326

Question from the same person to the same Old Man: "I have some books of my own, and my thought tells me to donate these to the monastic community in order to become carefree; then they would be the common property of the monastic community, and each brother would be able to borrow and read them. Likewise, I think the same things about my clothes. Tell me, father, whether I should do this, and which garments I should keep for [the eventuality of] physical illness." Response by John.

If you want to distribute your belongings, then it would be a good thing to donate them to the monastic community, as you say. For everything that belongs to the monastic community belongs to God. As for the garments that you require, retain two warm short-sleeved garments and one long-sleeved garment for the winter, as well as two light short-sleeved garments and one long-sleeved garment for the summer. For the winter, keep a coat for times when it is extremely cold; otherwise, simply keep your cowl and two cloaks, a summer one and a winter one, as well as two blankets, a heavy one and a light one. Also keep your woolen cover and pillow; for you will need these. With regard to your woolen garment, if you require it, then keep it. If you receive any other garment, and think you may require it, keep it and give your old one instead to the abbot. If you do not require the one you receive, then give this, too, to the abbot. The Lord will strengthen you to hear and adhere. This is progress and proper conduct according to God.

Question from the same person to the Great Old Man: "Since you have tested me and found me capable of this service in the hospital, declare to me, father, whether I should read some medical books and practice them on my own, or whether I should be free of such matters and avoid them as distracting the intellect and as giving rise to vainglory in me, since I am not vigilant. I could remain content with the knowledge that I already have and perform [healing] with oil, fire, ointments, and other such simple things as are used by those who do not read medical books. What, then, should I do? For my heart trembles before this ministry, fearing that I might make mistakes in it, thereby adding more sins to my passions." Response by the Great Old Man.

Since we have not yet reached perfection, in order to be entirely rid of the captivity of the passions, it is beneficial for us to dwell on medical matters rather than the passions. We should not, however, place all our hope in these, but only in the God who grants death and life, who says: "I shall wound, and I shall heal."[113] When you read these books and ask others about these matters, do not forget that without God there can be no healing. One who applies oneself to medicine should do so in the name of God, and God will come to one's assistance. The art of medicine does not prevent one from practicing piety; you should regard the practice of medicine in the same manner as the brothers' manual labor. Do whatever you do with fear of God, and you will be protected through the prayers of the saints. Amen.

Question from the same person to the same Great Old Man: "Once, you told me that cutting off one's own will also lies in not arguing in order to impose one's own opinion. What happens, father, if I offer something to a sick person, believing it to be beneficial for him, but often it harms him and I am afflicted because I feel that I have imposed my own will in this? Then again, I notice that I am distracted all day long and have almost no time to remember God. Moreover, I am troubled by gluttony. There-

---

113. Dt 32.39.

fore, tell me what to do; for I believe that my salvation will come
through this." Response by Barsanuphius.

If you think that this will contribute to the health of the sick
person, and therefore impose your opinion even though it happens to bring harm to that person, God will pay attention to
your heart and will not condemn you; for he knows that it was
in your desire to bring benefit that you caused harm. If, however, an experienced person tells you something and you ignore
it, then this is a result of pride and your own will. Many people
always hear about a certain city; then, when they happen to enter that city, they do not even recognize it.

Brother, all day long, you are in the memory of God, and
yet you are not aware of it? For having a commandment and
spending time to keep it constitute both obedience and remembrance of God. Indeed, brother John spoke well to you: first
bring forth leaves, and at God's command you will also bring
forth fruits. Therefore, if you do not know what is beneficial,
turn to those who know. This is [true] humility, and you shall
find God's grace.

You also said: "My salvation will come through this," and you
spoke correctly. For your arrival here did not occur without
God, but it was God who led you here. Be strong in the Lord;
for you will reap no small fruit from the distraction that you describe. Struggle against gluttony as much as you can, and the
Lord will assist you to understand and to do whatever is beneficial for you. "Be strong and bold"[114] in the Lord.

LETTER 329

Question from the same person to the same Great Old Man:
"You told me that having a commandment and spending time
to keep it constitute both obedience and remembrance of God.
I also entreat you to teach me, if possible, how to keep without
ceasing the remembrance of God in this distraction of my service
according to God or when I am among people. Moreover, if possible, pray for whatever is beneficial to me, father; for all things
are possible for you and for God."[115] Response by Barsanuphius.

---

114. Dt 31.6.   115. Cf. Mk 10.27 and 14.36.

In regard to unceasing remembrance of God, each person is able to achieve according to one's own measure. You should simply be humble; for I know more than you what is beneficial to you. This is what I am asking for you from God, "for whom all things are possible."[116]

LETTER 330

Question from the same brother to the same Great Old Man: "Merciful father, I fall down before you again and shall not cease to disturb you until you strengthen me. For whenever God grants me a little sorrow for my sins through your prayers, I gradually lose it through my outward agitation. Therefore, I ask you, father, to secure this for me as well, so that everything may be from God's mercy and from you and nothing from me. I can do nothing at all on my own, unless I am strengthened through your prayers. Furthermore, in regard to the administration of the hospital, father, I am afraid that the authority might contribute to my vainglory and boldness. It is natural for me to be burdened by gluttony when I continually handle food. So, perhaps you should test me with some humbler charge; then, I might make some progress and be relieved a little before once again being charged with serving others. You know, father, that I am not declaring these things because I have despaired in the charge assigned to me. For what can I do, wretched as I am? But I am afraid, father, that by staying here in my cell I am in fact exciting my passions, whether of my own accord or from the demons, I think. I do not know, father, but you do. Reveal to me the will of God, and lift me out of the thoughts that trouble me, strengthening me through your prayers, in order to do what you say; and forgive me." Response by Barsanuphius.

Brother, listen and be assured in the Lord that, since the time that we permitted you to assume this charge, our hand and our heart are with you. Rather, the hand of God is with you; for we entreat God through prayer for the salvation of your soul and your strengthening in this charge in order that it might prosper and be protected. There is no other way for you to be saved than this. Therefore, do not become despondent. When you

116. Mk 10.27 and 14.36.

fall, arise; when you err, blame yourself until the Lord shows you the mercy you desire. Simply do not be neglectful. Take courage in the fact that the Lord, who established you in this work, will also himself direct it. We, too, bear your concern with you. Therefore, do not let the devil deceive you with the pretense to rights. For it is said: "By smooth talk and flattery, they deceive the hearts of the simple-minded."[117] The one who assigned you to this charge is the very same one who said to his disciples: "Behold, I am sending you out";[118] and again: "Behold, I am with you."[119] Do not be afraid; and do not concern yourself with anything having to do with the hospital, growing despondent about the concern of authority. If you comprehend what I have written to you, you will not be concerned. You only need to pay attention to yourself as much as you can, and God will come to your assistance. Fare well in the Lord, taking strength in him.

LETTER 331

Question from the same person to the Other Old Man: "If the brothers who are with me make some mistake, how should I correct them without causing any trouble?" Response by John.

If you engrave the will of God within your heart, then you will not be troubled; instead, you will correct them naturally, as do the other fathers. If, however, you are not careful and are beset as any other person, then say to God in repentance: "Master, forgive me and have mercy on me." To those who are with you, say: "Brothers, notice how we are condemned and lose our souls for this." And do not shout too much, but just enough for you to be heard. If you are broken in this way, then the peaceful state according to God will come to you.

LETTER 332

Question from the same [brother] to the same person: "Father, I entreat you to tell me how I should correct them, and when I ought to act stupid or make them think that I am stupid, by overlooking whatever happened. Moreover, if I am conquered by this

117. Rom 16.18.   118. Mt 10.16.
119. Mt 28.20.

matter, should I impose some punishment on myself?" Response by John.

In your relationships with people, always be consistent. If you see that your brother is prudent and will accept [correction], then tell him by way of advice: "Brother, if we are neglectful in our work for God, then it is for the destruction of our soul. Was such a matter carried out appropriately until now? Strive to correct it from now on." If, however, your brother is imprudent, tell him: "Brother, believe me, you need to be corrected; for you are neglectful. If I speak to the abbot, he will correct you appropriately." As for acting stupid, do so according to the mistake that happened. If it is a small matter, then pretend to be stupid; if it is an important matter, then do not act stupid. Do not impose any punishment on yourself because you were conquered; nevertheless, do not also overlook the matter. Each time that you are conquered, entreat God to forgive you; otherwise, you will become neglectful.

LETTER 333

Question from the same person to the same [Old Man]: "If one of the brothers or one of the patients happens to make a mistake and I wish to correct him, sometimes I speak with irritation; should I therefore make a prostration before him? And if he leaves the hospital in anger, what should I do? In general, for which mistakes should one make a prostration? For pride and the pretense to rights darken my intellect. In fact, even if I do make a prostration before that person, vainglory still follows suit." Response by John.

Never say anything with irritation; for evil does not beget good. Rather, be long-suffering until the thought ceases. Then you will be able to speak calmly. If your brother is convinced, then all is well. If he is not, then say: "If you wish, I can speak to the abbot, and we can do whatever he decides; thus we shall both find rest." If he should leave in anger, tell the abbot, and he will punish him. Do not make a prostration before him because you are offering him the suspicion that it is in fact your own fault, and he will become more hostile toward you.

In regard to other people, hasten to act with zeal in accordance with your perception of the mistake. If the error is great, then make a prostration; if it is small, speak with your lips the regret of your heart, saying: "Forgive me, brother." Guard yourself from pride and from the pretense to rights; for these hinder our repentance. It is of course possible to make a prostration out of vainglory. Therefore, despise these three temptations and only make a prostration wherever necessary with humility, fear of God, and discernment. Do your best in these things, and God will assist you through the prayers of the saints. Amen.

LETTER 334

Question from the same [brother] to the same [Old Man]: "If, during the time I am serving the sick, the hour arrives for chanting the Psalms or else for preparing for liturgy, or some other necessity arises, and if the brothers who are with me know what medication they need to offer to each patient, do you order me to leave?[120] Or will this burden me? Indeed, if I wish to sit in my cell whenever I am not needed in the hospital, do you allow me to do this, father, or not?" Response by John.

If the brothers know what to do, then it is not a burden for you either to leave [for the services] or to sit in your cell; simply visit those who are sick.

LETTER 335

Question from the same person to the same [Old Man]: "If I give to someone according to his need, I also observe that stinginess disturbs me, with the result that I cannot give a little more or that I strive only not to give less than he needs. Now, if I am embarrassed or tempted by people-pleasing or vainglory, then my thought wishes to give more. Should I give a little less for the sake of my passion, or should I fulfill the commandment and simply meet the need?" Response by John.

If stinginess afflicts you, restraining you from giving something to your neighbor in need, then act according to the situa-

---

120. That is, in order to attend the liturgical services.

tion. If you possess a lot, give a little more; if you possess a little, give exactly the needed amount. If you wish to give according to vainglory or to please people, then do not give more than necessary, but only give precisely whatever is required. May God enlighten your heart, brother.

LETTER 336

Question from the same [brother] to the same [Old Man]: "If I happen across a vessel that I require at the hospital, but observe that I am attached to it, am I conceding to passion if I even accept it?" Response by John.

If you require the vessel and your thought battles against you, then tell your thought: "I need that vessel, but why the attachment?"[121] If your passion ceases, then accept it. Otherwise, if it is possible for the task to be accomplished by means of some other vessel, then do so in order to restrain the passion. If it cannot be done otherwise, then simply take the vessel, blaming yourself and saying: "Had it not been for my need, I would not have to accept this; instead, however, I was conquered by attachment."

LETTER 337

Question from the same person: "Someone once gave me a garment, and I accepted it joyfully without saying anything. Having examined myself, I found that I received the garment not because I needed it but rather out of greed. My thought now tells me to return it. What, then, do you order me to do?" Response.

Let us praise the person who offered the garment with his soul, and let us blame the person who received it with his soul. Let us wear the garment with humility, condemning ourselves, and let us henceforth guard ourselves against greed.

LETTER 338

Question from the same [brother] to the same [Old Man]: "So if someone happens to want to offer me something that I need, but I notice my heart desiring to accept it in a passionate way,

121. On attachment, see Abba Zosimas, *Reflections* 1.

what should I do? Should I accept it for my need, or should I reject it for my attachment?" Response by John.

Consider this matter in the same way as you deal with food. You know that we require food each day; yet we are not allowed to receive it with pleasure. If, however, we thank God, who grants food,[122] and condemn ourselves as being unworthy to receive it, then God renders it to our sanctification and blessing. Therefore, when you need something and your wish prospers, give thanks to God, who made it prosper, condemning yourself as being unworthy, and God will push away from you your attachment. For everything is possible with him, and nothing is impossible with him.[123] To him be the glory to the ages. Amen.

122. Cf. 1 Tm 4.4.
123. Cf. Jb 42.2; Mk 10.27 and 14.36.

LETTERS TO VARIOUS MONKS
(339–347ᴮ)

LETTER 339

Another brother asked the same Old Man: "It is a commandment of the Lord that we love our neighbor as ourselves[1] and that we be joyful and sorrowful with him as if he were one of our own members.[2] Therefore, to regard our neighbor being in poverty and yet ignore him is a transgression of love, even if we only have what we need and are unable to cover his needs. Tell me, then, father, how love is manifested in this case." Response by John.

OVE TOWARD one's neighbor is manifested in many ways and not only by means of actually giving him something. Listen to some other ways. If you are traveling somewhere with your neighbor and find that your thought wants to be honored more than he, rather than rejoicing in the fact that he is honored in the same way as you, then in this respect you are not regarding him as yourself. For the Apostle said: "Outdo one another in showing honor."[3] If you have something to eat and notice your thought wanting to eat alone on account of desire and not out of need, again in this respect you are not regarding him as yourself. Even when you only have enough for whatever you need, if you do not give him some of this, then in this respect you are not regarding him as yourself.

Indeed, if we wish to apply the scriptural word in this manner alone, then it will not be able to stand among us. In fact, this was not written for one person alone, but every person is called our neighbor.[4] Therefore, how can you fulfill this commandment with respect to all people when you do not have enough to give everyone?

---

1. Cf. Lv 19.18; Lk 10.27. 2. Cf. 1 Cor 12.26.
3. Rom 12.10. 4. Cf. Lk 10.36–37.

Again, loving one's neighbor as oneself also resembles this. If some loss occurs and you notice your thought taking pleasure at the fact that he is being harmed more than you, then again in this respect as well you are not regarding him as yourself. Or if you see him praised and do not rejoice with him, believing that you, too, have been praised with him; if you did not actually admit that your brother's praise also extends to you—for he is your member—then you have not tried to regard him as yourself. The same applies to so many other cases. Furthermore, regarding one's neighbor as oneself means that if you have heard something from the fathers about the way of God and your brother happens to ask you about it, then you should not retain [any attachment to] this care and benefit for the sake of envy. Rather, knowing that he is your brother, you should tell him whatever you heard according to your fear of God, without regarding yourself as a teacher; for this does not benefit you.

LETTER 340

Question from the same [brother] to the same [Old Man]: "Is it a good thing to maintain friendship with someone of one's own age?" Response.

What is good is actually not having a great deal of friendship with someone of one's age. For such a disposition does not allow mourning to arise. Nor should you maintain friendship with anyone else who may deprive you of mourning. For this is not of benefit to you; rather, it brings you harm. No one can acquire something good except through hard labor. Therefore, discipline your eyes so as not to pay attention to anyone, and they shall not fill your heart with the terrible boldness that brings to destruction all of the monk's fruits.[5]

LETTER 341

Question from the same person to the same Old Man: "If I hear about someone, that he happens to be in the state of temptation or illness, and I feel sympathy for him, tell me—first—wheth-

---

5. *Sayings*, Agathon 1.

er this sympathy comes from the demons, who wish to distract me from being preoccupied with my own sins; and—second— whether I should remember this person in my prayer. How can I help him, when I am in greater danger and deeper sin? What happens if the brother himself asks me to do this? Or, what happens if he tells me to talk to one of the fathers? Perhaps the passionate person is also being trained in love when he is praying for a neighbor. What do you think, father?" Response by John.

The fathers have declared to the younger ones that no one ought to leave their own dead in order to go and weep the dead of another.[6] For being compassionate toward one's neighbor belongs only to the perfect. For a younger person to be compassionate toward another, however, is in fact ridicule by the demons. For such a person thoughtlessly judges himself and considers himself as being well, while considering the other person as being unwell and at risk. Instead, it would be beneficial for him not to care at all about the other person. If he should happen to remember him in his heart or to hear about him from someone else, then let him say: "May God have mercy on him and on me."

Do not even ask any of the elders of your own accord to pray for someone else; for this is like assuming the same authority. If you wish to avoid this, simply mention that so-and-so is dreadfully afflicted; when the elder hears this, he will certainly pray for the person who is spiritually unwell. If someone asks you to tell the elder, then tell him for the sake of the order: "Father, pray for so-and-so." If he tells you: "Pray for me," then do so for the sake of the order: "Lord, forgive us," or: "God, help us," or: "Protect us in this matter." Do not presume that you have the authority to do so; for you were simply asked and did so out of obedience. As for showing compassion toward someone for the sake of love, you have not yet reached this measure. If your thought disturbs you about anything, then you should ask and you will learn what you must do. May God have mercy on you, brother.

6. *Sayings*, Moses 18.

LETTER 342

Question from the same person to the Great Old Man: "Father, tell me how far the limit extends in one brother's love for another brother." Response by Barsanuphius.

Brother, the love of the fathers for their children differs from the love of one brother for another. The limit that characterizes the love of spiritual fathers toward their children contains nothing fleshly or harmful; for they are safeguarded by their spiritual mind,[7] always striving, either in word or in deed, to benefit their younger disciples in every way. Thus, while loving them, they do not conceal their faults. Instead, they frequently reprimand and discipline their children. For it is with respect to them that it was said: "Reprimand, rebuke, and encourage."[8] In the same way, your own abbot often does this with you, although you do not understand why it is that he is reprimanding you, rebuking you, or encouraging you. Since, then, he does not conceal your faults for the sake of love, his love for you is revealed to be spiritual.

Each person, therefore, loves his neighbor according to his own measure. The measure of perfect love is loving and regarding one's neighbor as oneself[9] after the love that one reserves for God. Nevertheless, the younger generation should be on guard in all things. For the devil trips up the younger ones very quickly. First, they begin to converse in the company of others supposedly for the benefit of the soul, but in fact this is not the case. Thereafter, they turn to other things: to excitation, boldness, laughter, slander, and many other evils, so that the words are fulfilled in them: "Having started with the Spirit, are you now ending with the flesh? Did you experience so much for nothing?"[10] Thus the younger ones come to fall, as a result of loving one another irrationally, or else by frequenting one another's company. In their case, the measure of love for one another should be such as not to slander one another, not to hate or despise one another, not to seek their own [interest],[11] not to

---

7. Cf. Rom 8.6, 27.
9. Cf. Lv 19.18.
11. Cf. 1 Cor 13.5.

8. 2 Tm 4.2.
10. Gal 3.3.

love for the sake of bodily beauty or material benefit, not to sit with one another without very good reason in order not to fall into a boldness that destroys the fruits of the monk,[12] leaving him as a dry branch.[13] The measure of love among the younger disciples reaches only up to this point; for just as they shrink from their own boldness and idle talk, they also shrink from the same passions among their brothers; and so they tremble at the possibility of sitting beside one another inopportunely, so that they might not be entangled in these traps while also entangling their brothers, fearing the one who says: "Alas for you who make your neighbors drink until their minds are drunk and dull."[14] And again: "Bad company ruins good morals."[15] Brother, pay attention to yourself.

LETTER 343

Question from the same person to the same Great Old Man: "What should I do; for I am troubled by impure thoughts; indeed, if I perceive that another person has the same thoughts, I always say that other people are also thinking evil things about me. Moreover, neither weeping nor compunction comes to me; and so my thought tells me: 'So long as I am among people, I cannot acquire these.' Be merciful toward my weakness, and tell me, father, how I may be saved from these." Response by Barsanuphius.

You tell me that you have impure thoughts, that you hear or perceive that another person also thinks the same way, and then you say: "Behold, others are also thinking evil things about me." Well, anathematize these evil thoughts; and with regard to your brother say: "He is better than I and holier." Your thought will then cease.

As for your weeping, unless you struggle against people even while you are among them, and unless you strive not to acquire boldness against anyone, weeping and compunction will not come. If, for the sake of pretense to rights, your thoughts make you avoid your brothers, then they are also causing you to avoid

12. *Sayings*, Agathon 1.
13. Cf. Is 56.3.
14. Cf. Hab 2.15.
15. 1 Cor 15.33.

the struggle and the arena. Therefore, strive to conquer boldness before people even while you are among people. For the Apostle says: "In the case of an athlete, no one is crowned without competing according to the rules."[16] Do your best, brother, and God will come to your assistance in everything. Do not forget to keep humility, obedience, and submission, and you will be saved. In Christ Jesus our Lord, to whom be the glory to the ages. Amen.

LETTER 344

Another brother asked the Other Old Man: "Abba, I want to be saved but do not know the way of salvation. Moreover, my thought tells me: 'Why are you sitting here in the monastic community and not doing anything? Go elsewhere.' What, then, should I do?" Response by John.

Brother, God gave us the way of salvation through the sacred Scriptures, and the fathers have told us: "Ask your father and he shall inform you; ask your elders and they shall tell you."[17] If you do not wish to be deceived into leaving, on the pretext of humility, the place that is of benefit to you, do not do anything without asking and without the advice of your spiritual fathers.[18] Then, by the grace of God, "who desires everyone to be saved and to come to the knowledge of the truth,"[19] you will not be deceived.

LETTER 345

The same brother said to the Old Man: "My thought tells me that if I leave and go elsewhere in order to become a hermit,[20] I shall find perfect stillness. For I am a debtor of many sins and want to be liberated from them. Therefore, what should I do, father?" Response by John.

Brother, someone who is a debtor must first repay his debt; otherwise, wherever he may go, whether to some other city or

16. 2 Tm 2.5.
17. *Sayings*, Antony 37. Cf. also Dt 32.7.
18. Cf. Abba Isaiah of Scetis, *Ascetic Discourse* 3.
19. 1 Tm 2.4.
20. Lit., "enter a life of stillness" (Greek, ἡσυχάσω).

town, and wherever he may sit, he remains a debtor, and no-where does he have the liberty either to sit or rest. If, however, he first labors to face people's insults, he feels ashamed; and this helps him to repay whatever his debt may be. When such a person is liberated from this debt, then he may appear and sit in public, wherever he may wish, with courage and much bold-ness. Therefore, if a person does his best to endure insults and abuse, as well as dishonor and loss for the sins that he has com-mitted, then he shall learn humility and labor, while his sins shall be forgiven, according to the words: "Consider my humil-ity and my labor, and forgive all my sins."[21]

Consider also how many insults and how much abuse our Master Christ endured before the cross; and it was only after these that he came to the cross. In the same way, one cannot come to perfect stillness with fruition or to the holy rest of per-fection, unless one first suffers with Christ and endures all of his sufferings, recalling the Apostle, who said: "Let us suffer with him so that we may be glorified with him."[22] Therefore, do not be deceived; for there is no other way of salvation but this.[23] May the Lord go with you according to his will so that, as it is said in the Gospel, you may establish your foundation on a solid rock, which is Christ.[24]

LETTER 346

A brother entreated the Great Old Man, saying: "Pray for me, that God may have mercy on me; for I am wretched." Response by Barsanuphius.

Whoever wants to receive mercy should keep the command-ment about not eating of the tree;[25] such a person shall not fall into disobedience. Moreover, whoever does not fall into disobe-dience receives mercy and is saved by the grace of our God. For such a person tells his thought: "God and I are alone in this

---

21. Ps 24.18.
22. Rom 8.17.
23. Abba Isaiah, *Ascetic Discourse* 8.
24. Cf. Mt 7.24; 1 Cor 10.4.
25. Cf. Gn 2.17.

world,[26] and unless I do his will, I shall not reach him but someone else!" That person will also expect his bodily death each
day and consider how he shall encounter God. In this way, he
shall quickly attain to the way of salvation.

LETTER 347

A brother fell into temptation and requested a prayer from the
same Great Old Man. Upon being relieved of the temptation, he
announced the news to him with thanks, at the same time asking
also about the headache that he was suffering and for the illumination of his heart.[27] The Old Man responded in the following
manner.

Brother, let us pay attention to ourselves with godly fear; and
if the compassionate God relieves us of the warfare according
to his loving-kindness, then let us not become neglectful. For
many of those who were relieved became neglectful of themselves and fell on their heads. If, however, we have been relieved, then let us give thanks to God for our deliverance and
let us persist in our prayer in order not to fall into the same passions or else perhaps into others.

If someone eats something that is harmful to his stomach or
liver or spleen, but then is healed through the attention and art
of the doctor, then that person is no longer neglectful of himself in order that nothing worse may happen to him, remembering the original danger, just as the Lord spoke to the person
healed by him: "Behold, you have been made well; do not sin
any more, so that nothing worse happens to you."[28]

Brother, the finest soldiers always study the art of warfare,
even in times of peace; for a soldier does not have easily the
time to study about warfare in times of war. It is also said: "I
was prepared and I was not troubled."[29] Therefore, do not assume any boldness at all before the one who tempted you with
the passion, nor again before anyone else. For the fathers said
about such boldness that it destroys the fruits of a monk.[30] So a

---

26. *Sayings*, Alonius 1.   27. Cf. Eph 1.18.
28. Jn 5.14.   29. Cf. Ps 118.60.
30. *Sayings*, Agathon 1.

person cannot be carefree in regard to warfare until one's last breath,[31] in order not to fall down and be trapped by the crafty enemy,[32] whom the Lord abolished from us through the Spirit of his mouth. Remember what one elder used to say: "Even if a person were to create a new heaven and a new earth, he would still not be able to be carefree."[33]

As for your headache, you should struggle not to grow slackened, and you will obtain assistance. For when the Lord found his disciples relaxing, he said to them: "Be watchful and pray that you may not enter into temptation."[34] Child, the one who illumined the eyes of the blind man will also illumine the eyes of your heart with understanding of what is good and beneficial. And the God of the powers will strengthen and support you in perfect faith; for he said: "Everything is possible for the one who believes."[35] May I see you in the land of those who are saved through the grace of the protector of our souls, Jesus Christ. To him be the glory with the Father.

LETTER 347B[36]

A brother who had closed his cell door for a long time, but continued to be troubled by secret thoughts and dreams, also sought to abstain from wine completely. He announced all this to the same Great Old Man. Response.

If you truly want to be saved, brother, and to avoid the spirit of pride, then endure a little dishonor; for in this way, pride is struck down. Do not seek answers from anyone in regard to yourself, but create the answers for yourself. For Jesus said: "I am gentle and humble of heart,"[37] and: "The Son of God came not to be served but to serve,"[38] and so forth. Therefore, do not close your door but only your tongue;[39] and do not abstain from wine entirely, but only refrain from anger, which renders an ir-

---

31. Cf. *Sayings*, Antony 4 and Poemen 125.
32. Cf. Gn 3.2.   33. *Sayings*, Poemen 48.
34. Mt 26.41.   35. Mk 9.23.
36. This letter is preserved in Cromwell 18 (12th century) and the Georgian manuscripts Sinai 34 and 35.
37. Mt 11.29.   38. Mt 20.28.
39. Cf. *Sayings*, Poemen 58.

rational person drunken. Do not imitate me, because I say one thing and do another; for you have in the past seen me being served and were scandalized. There are many who teach and do not practice, about whom the Lord said: "Listen to them and follow [what they say]; but do not do as they do."[40]

Only leave on rare occasion for your personal needs; and if there is no need, then do not go outside your door. Live sparingly and not wastefully; do not be sorrowful if anyone does not comfort you, but rejoice in this. Do not pay any attention to dreams; for these are demonic and deceptive. And, as you do these things, do not consider that you are doing anything good. For we have been ordered, after keeping the commandments, to say: "We are worthless slaves."[41] Nevertheless, we shall reap later whatever we have sown in your field, and then we shall exchange your seed. May the Lord make us rejoice in finding your land fruitful one hundred times and sixty times and thirty times,[42] to the glory of the Father and the Son and the Holy Spirit.

40. Mt 23.3.   41. Lk 17.10.
42. Cf. Mt 13.8; Mk 4.8.

LETTER TO THE BROTHER OF
BARSANUPHIUS (348)

LETTER 348

A secular man, in fact the [biological] brother of the same Great Old Man, who was also advanced in age, sent a letter to him, asking to meet with him. The Old Man announced the following to him: "My brother is Jesus. If you despise the world and become a monk, then you will be my brother." Having heard this, he departed, weeping greatly. After a while, however, he returned there in order to become a monk; but he fell ill physically, swollen with dropsy. So he sent a letter asking the Old Man about this suffering. The latter responded as follows.

HE ONLY REASON that this illness has come upon you is so that you may not depart fruitless toward God. Therefore, if you endure it and give thanks, it will be reckoned for you as your ascetic life, especially since you have not long been in the monastic habit. This affliction has also occurred to you partly because you counted me, who am nothing, as well as yourself as being something. You counted me as being a great man and yourself as being the brother of such a man. Do you not know that we are all children of Adam's transgression?[1] Do you not know that we are earth and ashes?[2] Therefore, give thanks to God, who brought you to such a condition. If we had the humility of Jesus, we would say: "Who is my mother, and who are my brothers?"[3] and so on.

1. Cf. Rom 5.14.   2. Cf. Gn 18.27; Jb 42.6.
3. Mt 12.48.

INDICES

INDEX OF NAMES AND PLACES

INDEX OF SUBJECTS AND KEY WORDS

INDEX OF HOLY SCRIPTURE

Numbers refer to the *Letters* of Barsanuphius
and John appearing in this volume.

Old Testament

New Testament